DB2/SQL
A Professional Programmer's Guide

DB2/SQL
A Professional Programmer's Guide

Tim Martyn
Hartford Graduate Center

Tim Hartley
Travelers Insurance Company

McGraw-Hill Book Company
Intertext Publications

New York St. Louis San Francisco Auckland Bogotá
Hamburg London Madrid Mexico Milan Montreal
New Delhi Panama Paris São Paolo
Singapore Sydney Tokyo Toronto

Library of Congress Catalog Card Number 88-83062

10 9 8 7 6 5 4 3 2 1

ISBN 0-07-040666-9

McGraw-Hill Book Company
1221 Avenue of the Americas
New York, NY 10020

Intertext Publications/Multiscience Press, Inc.
One Lincoln Plaza
New York, NY 10023

Composed in Ventura by Context, Inc.

Dedications

For Julie and Jessie

T. M.

For Jennifer, Benjamin, and Laryssa

T. H.

Contents

Acknowledgments

We gratefully acknowledge the following individuals who played various roles in helping us bring this book to press. They are Tosh Akizawa, Michael Danchak, John Merrill, Jay Ranade, Judy Rohan, Alan Rose, Anita Saldyk, and Jill Sutherland. We would like to recognize all former students, especially Patricia Scott, who read preliminary versions of this text. These students skillfully detected a number of errors and imperfections in style and content. Naturally we assume full responsibility for any remaining errors which await discovery.

Tim Hartley acknowledges his current employer, the Travelers Insurance Company, for establishing a policy and work environment which facilitated his professional development. Both authors would like to thank the Travelers for granting access to its computing facilities.

Tim Martyn expresses his gratitude to the Hartford Graduate Center for endorsing this effort by supporting his sabbatical leave and affording other considerations. He also acknowledges his colleagues on the CIS faculty. Their subtle encouragement ("How's the book coming?") was sincerely appreciated. Finally, he would like to recognize the scholars in residence at the Arch Street Institute of Cognitive Science. Provocative discussions with these individuals may have indirectly delayed publication of this text; however, they helped keep the effort in perspective.

Preface

A number of excellent books have been published on the IBM main-frame products DB2 (under MVS) and SQL/DS (under VM and DOS). Many of these texts present a comprehensive overview of one of these products. The authors of this text have elected to restrict their attention to SQL, the language common to both these products. This book is written for a specific audience with a specific objective in mind.

OBJECTIVE

SQL is a complete database language. It has statements to

1. initially create a database

2. create the underlying physical objects

3. create the logical objects (tables and views)

4. define authorization and other management controls

5. retrieve and manipulate data in the database

This text will focus on the last task, the retrieval and manipulation of data in the database. It will present a comprehensive discussion of the SELECT, INSERT, UPDATE, and DELETE statements. Other statements in the language (e.g., the CREATE TABLE and CREATE VIEW statements) are described to provide insight into the rules and behavior of the SELECT statement and other data manipulation statements.

Any SQL statement can be issued interactively from a terminal. The same SQL statement (with minor modification) can be embedded within an application program written in some traditional programming language (e.g., COBOL, FORTRAN, PL/I, C, BAL). In fact, a desirable feature of SQL is that it allows a programmer to test a statement in an interactive environment before embedding the statement within an application program. This text will restrict its attention to "interactive" SQL as implemented in DB2 (V2.1) and SQL/DS (V2.2). Professional programmers who need to learn the additional SQL statements relevant to "embedded" SQL can consult the IBM SQL reference manuals.

The text does not address the SQL Standard as defined by the ANSI Database Committee. This standard is still evolving. From a pragmatic viewpoint, the IBM version of SQL is the de facto standard that applies not only to DB2 and SQL/DS, but also to any other product where the vendor claims to be "IBM compatible."

AUDIENCE

A wide variety of people may interact with DB2 or SQL/DS. These may be database administrators, systems analysts/designers, systems programmers, application programmers, and "users" (the "customers" who hope to benefit from the system). This book is specifically written for users and professional programmers. Both groups require an in-depth knowledge of SQL's data retrieval and manipulation statements.

In general, this text can be read by any person who has attained a basic level of computer literacy. As such, it can serve as an introduction to SQL (and therefore DB2 or SQL/DS) for anyone interested in the subject. The authors have used a preliminary version of this book as the primary text in many professional training seminars. It has also been used as a supplemental independent-study tutorial in a graduate level database course where the content and primary text focused on the theory of relational databases. It has been well received in both educational environments. The positive criticism provided by students has helped the authors in preparing the current version of this text.

ORGANIZATION OF TEXT

This book adopts a tutorial format. A topic is presented by introducing a sample query and the SQL statement that satisfies the query.

Usually this is enough to give the reader a basic idea about the syntax and behavior of the SQL feature under consideration. Thereafter, a list of pertinent comments is presented. These comments present details on syntax. However, the primary intention of the comments is to highlight the more important, and sometimes subtle, logical issues relating to the behavior of a SQL statement. This will be a constant theme throughout the text. SQL's syntax is easy. But, SQL also provides the opportunity for logical errors. Where appropriate, the comments will emphasize the possible difference between (1) the query you may have intended to execute, and (2) the query actually executed by the system in response to your SQL statement.

This text is organized into an Introduction and four major parts, some of which can be skipped, depending upon your background knowledge, your status (user or programmer) or particular objectives. We briefly outline each part below.

Introduction: The Database Environment

This Introduction is written for the reader who has no previous exposure to relational database concepts. It describes the fundamental concepts of relational database systems, the evolution of the SQL language and introduces DB2 and SQL/DS. This section is strictly conceptual. There are no behavioral objectives to be mastered by doing exercises. However, these concepts are important. Anyone who has no previous exposure to relational databases should read this section. If you have worked with any other relational database product, you can skip this introduction.

Part I: Selecting Data from a Single Table

This section introduces the SELECT statement. In particular, we restrict our attention to retrieving data from a single table. You will learn how to retrieve any rows and/or columns from a table, specify the sequence of the result, utilize the Boolean operators (AND, OR, and NOT), and perform basic calculations.

Many users are allowed only to examine, but not modify the database. Also, many users will be restricted to querying a single table. Such users should find practically everything they need to know is these chapters. For this reason, the chapters in this part of the text have more of a tutorial flavor than subsequent chapters. We expect that most professional programmers will skim the sample queries and bypass the narrative comments.

Part II: Data Definition and Manipulation

This section introduces the CREATE TABLE statement to provide background information of SQL's data types and the basic concepts pertaining to referential integrity. This information is necessary for a proper understanding of the INSERT, UPDATE, and DELETE statements which are described in detail.

Part III: More About the SELECT Statement

This section covers all aspects of the SELECT statement that were omitted in Part I. In particular, it introduces queries that require access to multiple tables. This part of the text presents a comprehensive discussion of the join operation, subqueries, and the union operation.

Part IV: More About SQL

This section introduces those SQL statements that allow you to share your data with other users of the system. It covers the CREATE VIEW statement and the use of the GRANT and REVOKE statements. It concludes with a brief examination of the transaction concept.

PHILOSOPHY

Our objective has been to write a text that teaches a few important topics (hopefully) very well. We solicit your feedback in the form of positive criticism regarding errors, changes, or enhancements that might be made to future printings or editions of this text. Your comments can be addressed to the authors at The Hartford Graduate Center, 275 Windsor Street, Hartford, CT 06120.

Introduction

This section introduces the fundamental relational database concepts, the evolution of the SQL language, and the IBM relational database products, DB2 and SQL/DS. Users with some DB2 or SQL/DS experience may choose to skip this section and begin reading Chapter I.

RELATIONAL DATABASE CONCEPTS

What Is a database?

Many people use the terms "file" and "database" as though they were synonymous. However, there is an important difference. A file is a collection of records in which each record is composed of multiple data items called fields. A database usually encompasses many files and, furthermore, provides facilities to capture relationships that exist between records. Hence, a database system transcends a file system by providing the designer with facilities to represent relationships between records. We present a simple example to illustrate this point.

Consider two files, an EMPLOYEE file and a DEPARTMENT file. An EMPLOYEE record contains fields for employee number, name, address and department name. A DEPARTMENT record contains fields for department name, location and phone number. (See Figure I.1) Now consider a request to retrieve the name and address of every employee (stored in the EMPLOYEE file) and their respective departmental locations and phone numbers (stored in the DEPART-MENT file). In a traditional file system this query would involve considerable effort. Both files would first have to be sorted in department name sequence. Then an application program would follow a match-merge process to extract the desired data. The key point is that considerable work is required by application programs. This is because a file system cannot capture the "employee-works-in-department" relationship that exists between the two record types. A database system can.

DEPARTMENT file

DEPT	DLOC	DPH

EMPLOYEE file

ENO	ENAME	EADDR	EDEPT

Figure I.1   Traditional file system.

Traditional database products, which evolved during the 1970s, captured relationships by allowing the database designer to represent the data and relationships as a tree or network structure. (A tree is just a special type of network.) Figure I.2 reflects such a network structure for our simple example. The figure denotes a database consisting of two record types that are related on a one-to-many basis. A department may have many employees and an employee works for one department. The database system would usually implement this relationship by using internal pointers to link together a given department record with all its associated employee records. Then an application program would issue commands to the database system, which effectively instructs the system to follow the pointers and return the desired data. This process, whereby the application program "navigates" its way through the network, is better than the sort-match-merge process of traditional file processing. However, there are a number of negative aspects associated with network databases.

A network structure is often too rigid from the database designer's point of view. And, the navigation process is complex from a programmer's point of view. Finally, because the application programs that navigate the database are written in traditional high-level languages (COBOL, FORTRAN, etc.), it is obvious that these early database systems are not at all "user friendly." The current generation of relational database systems addresses these problems.

What Is a Relational Database?

The relational approach to database was proposed by E. F. Codd in 1970. However, commercial products did not appear in the market-

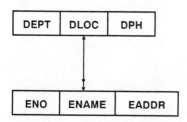

Figure I.2   Network database.

place until the early 1980s. The remainder of this section presents the basic concepts of relational database. We describe these ideas from a user viewpoint. Codd and others have developed a solid theoretical foundation of relational theory.

A relational database must fulfill at least two objectives. The first is that the system must present the data in tabular format to the user. In the simple example described above, the user would see the database as a collection of two tables. Figure I.3 illustrates an EMPLOYEE table and a DEPARTMENT table. We have two tables instead of two record types. An individual row in a table corresponds to a record occurrence; and a column in a table corresponds to a single field in a record. In fact we will often use the terms "row" and "record" interchangeably. Likewise, we will use the terms "column" and "field" interchangably.

Note that unlike the previous network design there is no explicit mapping between the tables. Instead the EMPLOYEE table contains a column to indicate which department the employee works in. This observation might lead to the mistaken conclusion that a relational

DEPARTMENT file

DEPT	DLOC	DPH

EMPLOYEE file

ENO	ENAME	EADDR	EDEPT

Figure I.3   Relational database.

database is just a friendlier presentation of the old classical file concept. However, this is definitely not the case. The second major feature of relational databases clearly distinguishes relational database systems from file systems and earlier network type database systems.

The second major feature of any relational database is its support of a "set-at-a-time" query language. This requires some explanation. With traditional systems the query language was "record-at-a-time" oriented. This meant that the query language was only capable of expressing a query to retrieve a single record. Therefore, if the programmer wanted to retrieve a set of records, the programmer would have to write code to repeatedly execute a query statement. For example, if you wanted to retrieve all the employees in the Data Processing Department, and there were 200 such employees, a query statement (to get the "next" record for an employee in the DP Department) would be executed 200 times. Each execution would retrieve one record and return it to the application program.

With a relational system the process is considerably easier because the query language is much more powerful. The language is powerful enough to request any subset of rows and columns. When the user issues a query, the system collects all the data and returns it to the user. The user issues only one query (without multiple iterations) and the system returns all the desired data.

Another important point is that relational languages for commercial database products are relatively easy to learn. One need not be a professional programmer to access the database. A computer literate user can sit at a terminal or microcomputer and enter a command in the query language. The system will extract the desired rows and show them on the display screen.

A number of query languages for relational databases have been developed. This book presents a tutorial on SQL, the most popular relational language. The user will find that SQL is indeed a simple but powerful set-at-a-time database language. Before we describe the evolution of the SQL language, we present a simple SQL statement to illustrate the aforementioned points.

Figure I.4 shows a SELECT statement that will retrieve specified rows from the EMPLOYEE table. In this case it retrieves only those rows where the EDEPT value is "DP". You would enter this statement if you wanted to find out all information about employees who

```
SELECT  *
FROM     EMPLOYEE
WHERE    EDEPT = 'DP'
```

Figure I.4   Sample SQL command.

work in the DP Department. We will discuss the details of the SE-
LECT statement in Part I of this text. For the moment we merely
note that this statement is indeed quite simple, and would retrieve
and display all the desired rows.

THE SQL LANGUAGE

SQL (Structured Query Language) was initially defined by D. D.
Chamberlin and others during the late 1970s. It was originally called
SEQUEL (Structured English Query Language) and was developed
in conjunction with IBM's relational database prototype, System R.
System R is the ancestor of the DB2 and SQL/DS commercial prod-
ucts, and SEQUEL is the ancestor of SQL.

In recent years many vendors have introduced SQL-oriented relational database products. Earlier versions of these products clearly
had a strong SQL flavor but were quite idiosyncratic. In response to
this situation, the American National Standards Institute (ANSI)
has established an "official" standard. This "official" SQL standard is
similar to SQL implemented by IBM. However, there are some differences. It appears that the data processing community will adopt
another de facto standard that we will call the "DB2" SQL standard.
Today many vendors of relational database products offer a version
of their product that is compatible with the "DB2" SQL standard.

This book will examine DB2 SQL. As you would expect, DB2 SQL
is almost identical to the SQL understood by SQL/DS. There are
some differences, but they are few in number and primarily pertain
to statements issued by database administration personnel. Those
SQL statements that retrieve and update application database tables
are practically identical. We say "practically" identical because both
of these products will continue to evolve as IBM makes new releases
available to its customers. Enhancements to the SQL language will
occur as part of this evolution. Because new releases of DB2 and
SQL/DS will occur at different times, SQL enhancements for one

product may not be present in the other product. However, given IBM's commitment to language compatibility, it is reasonable to expect that SQL enhancements for one product will soon appear in the other product. With very few exceptions (which are noted), every sample query illustrated in this text is valid for both DB2 and SQL/DS.

Both DB2 and SQL/DS support "embedded" SQL. This permits an application program written in COBOL, FORTRAN, PL/I, C, or assembler to contain SQL code. This means that a production data processing system with batch and/or transaction programs can also interface with DB2 or SQL/DS. Interactive SQL and embedded SQL are similar. However, there are some significant differences. For example, embedded SQL must identify a memory location where the data is to be placed after it is extracted from the database. Furthermore, because these traditional programming languages are record-at-a-time oriented, special SQL code is required to process a query that returns multiple rows. (This detracts from the previously mentioned set-at-a-time advantage of SQL. Note that the source of this problem is the host language, not SQL.)

EFFICIENCY CONSIDERATIONS

Ideally, in a relational database environment, application programmers and users do not have to concern themselves with machine efficiency. This task falls to the database administrator who establishes the database and specifies possible data access paths by creating indexes. (Chapter 8 will discuss this issue.) Each SQL statement is processed by a system component, called the "optimizer," to determine the most efficient way to satisfy the objective of the statement. This is an ideal scenario. To date, no vendor of any relational DBMS product has produced a perfect optimizer. In particular, this is applies to DB2 and SQL/DS. This has implications for those who write SQL statements.

We will see that a single query can have many different SQL solutions. Hence a programmer/user occasionally has some options in writing SQL statements. This might be desirable if the optimizer would always choose the most efficient data access path. However, this is not the case. Therefore, the IBM reference manuals contain documentation describing SQL efficiency techniques. This documentation will reflect changes (presumably improvements) as the systems evolve in future product releases.

Some of the comments in this text will address these SQL efficiency considerations. However, we do not elaborate on this issue because the optimizer improves with each new release of the system. Our objectine is to teach SQL per se. This text will present the various ways of expressing a query objective. After reading this text you are advised to consult the IBM documentation to become aware of the idiosyncratic behavior of the current optimizer.

USING DB2 AND SQL/DS

We conclude this introduction with a brief discussion of the process of interfacing with DB2 and SQL/DS.

Users of DB2 and SQL/DS will generally follow the same procedure when they wish to utilize the facilities of interactive SQL. Figure I.5 outlines this procedure. Users of DB2 will access the database using its SPUFI interface (see Figure I.6). Users of SQL/DS will access the database using its ISQL interface (see Figure I.7). We refer the reader to Appendix A (DB2: Using SPUFI to Issue SQL Statements) and Appendix C (SQL/DS: Using ISQL to Issue SQL Statements). These appendices present more detailed descriptions of the actual screen images encountered when working with DB2 and SQL/DS.

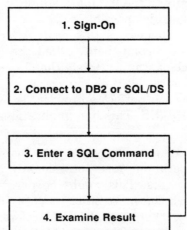

Figure I.5   Interactive SQL.

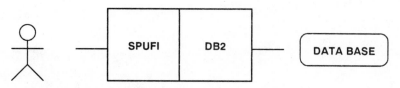

Figure I.6   Using SPUFI to access DB2 data.

We conclude our discussion of DB2 and SQL/DS with a few comments on another IBM product, QMF (Query Management Facility). QMF is not part of DB2 or SQL/DS. It is a separate product, which serves as a front end to either DB2 or SQL/DS. See Figure I.8, which illustrates the user entering SQL commands via QMF. QMF provides another, presumably more friendly, way to issue SQL statements. This permits DB2 users to bypass SPUFI and SQL/DS users to bypass ISQL. In addition, it provides report generation facilities. (SPUFI has no report generation facilities. ISQL has only primitive report generation facilities.) Finally, QMF has a number of other "housekeeping" facilities that users will find helpful. Appendix B presents a brief outline of issuing SQL statments via QMF.

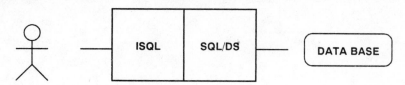

Figure I.7   Using ISQL to access SQL/DS data.

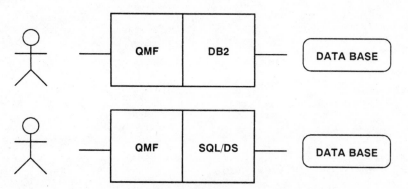

Figure I.8   QMF front-end to DB2 and SQL/DS.

I

SELECTing Data from a Single Table

Practically every user and programmer will be required to retrieve data that was previously stored in the database. For this reason, Part I of this text is devoted to introducing the SELECT statement, which is used for database retrieval. More specifically, we restrict our attention to selecting data from a single table. This is because many users will be limited to the relatively simple task of querying data located in a single table. Therefore, we have endeavored to encapsulate everything this audience needs to know in this part of the text. Discussion of queries that reference multiple tables is postponed until Part III of the text.

THE SAMPLE DATABASE

This text introduces the reader to SQL by presenting a series of sample queries against a small but realistic application database. This is an academic database designed to support the information processing requirements of a mythical college. This design consists of eight tables that will be introduced as we progress through the text. (See Appendix E for a summary of this design.) All sample queries in the first six chapters will reference the same table. This is the COURSE table, which contains one row for each course in the curriculum. It is necessary that you understand the structure and content of this table in order to avoid any confusion pertaining to the illustrated sample queries.

THE COURSE TABLE

The entire COURSE table is shown in Figure PI.1 along with a description of each column indicating the name, data type, length and content. You should simply assume that this table exists in the database and that you have been granted permission to examine its content. You are advised to scan Figure PI.1 and then note the following points.

- Any reference to a column requires that you know and correctly enter the precise column name.
- The description of data type and length is informal. A more formal presentation of SQL data types is given in Chapter 8. A proper understanding of the topics covered in Part I only requires that you comprehend the following points pertaining to SQL data types.

INTRODUCTION TO SQL DATA TYPES

In general, the database can contain three kinds of data: (1) numeric, (2) character string and (3) date/time. The COURSE table contains two numeric columns, CRED and CLABFEE. The other four columns, CNO, CNAME, CDESCP and CDEPT, contain character string data. Date/time data types will not be introduced until Chapter 7.

We will see that certain types of database operations can be applied only to certain data types. In particular, arithmetic can be performed only on numeric data and pattern matching can be applied only to character string data.

Different numeric columns can vary in length and decimal point accuracy. The CLABFEE column contains five digit numbers with two digit decimal accuracy. Hence, 999.99 is the largest value this column can contain. The CRED column contains only integer (whole number) values. Its length can be up to five digits. However, as Figure PI.1 shows, the actual values usually consist of a single digit. Chapters 5 and 6 will illustrate that differences in length and decimal accuracy can impact the result of a calculation.

COURSE Table Description

Column Name	Data Type	Length	Content
CNO	Character	3 (fixed)	Course Number: A unique "number" used to identify each course.
CNAME	Character	22 (var.)	Course Name: The name of each course will also be unique.
CDESCP	Character	25 (var.)	Course Description: Each course should have a unique description.
CRED	Integer	5	Credits: The number of credits a student earns by passing the course.
CLABFEE	Decimal	(5,2)	Course Lab Fee: A dollars and cents value that represents the lab fee paid by each student who takes the course. (Maximum value = 999.99.)
CDEPT	Character	4 (fixed)	Department Identifier: This identifies the academic department that offers the course.

COURSE Table Sample Data

CNO	CNAME	CDESCP	CRED	CLABFEE	CDEPT
T11	SCHOLASTICISM	FOR THE PIOUS	3	150.00	THEO
T12	FUNDAMENTALISM	FOR THE CAREFREE	3	90.00	THEO
T33	HEDONISM	FOR THE SANE	3	0.00	THEO
T44	COMMUNISM	FOR THE GREEDY	6	200.00	THEO
P11	EMPIRICISM	SEE IT—BELIEVE IT	3	100.00	PHIL
P22	RATIONALISM	FOR CIS MAJORS	3	50.00	PHIL
P33	EXISTENTIALISM	FOR CIS MAJORS	3	200.00	PHIL
P44	SOLIPSISM	ME MYSELF AND I	6	0.00	PHIL
C11	INTRO TO CS	FOR ROOKIES	3	100.00	CIS
C22	DATA STRUCTURES	VERY USEFUL	3	50.00	CIS
C33	DISCRETE MATHEMATICS	ABSOLUTELY NECESSARY	3	0.00	CIS
C44	DIGITAL CIRCUITS	AH HA!	3	0.00	CIS
C55	COMPUTER ARCH.	VON NEUMANN'S MACH.	3	100.00	CIS
C66	RELATIONAL DATABASE	THE ONLY WAY TO GO	3	500.00	CIS

Figure PI.1   COURSE table information.

Character string data may be fixed length (CNO and CDEPT) or variable length (CNAME and CDESCP). The difference between the fixed and variable length character strings is not immediately observable by examining Figure PI.1. However, there is a real difference in the internal representation of the data. Chapter 4 will describe these differences and their impact on the pattern matching process.

ORGANIZATION OF CHAPTERS

The first three chapters introduce the structure of the SELECT statement. You will learn the basic structure of the statement (Chapter 1), how to display the output in some desired sequence (Chapter 2), and how to specify complex retrieval conditions using the Boolean operators (Chapter 3). Professional programmers will be able to skim these chapters. The narrative comments are primarily directed to the "rookie" user who needs to learn the logical aspects of query specification in addition to the syntax of the SELECT statement.

The next three chapters cover pattern matching (Chapter 4), arithmetic expressions (Chapter 5) and built-in functions (Chapter 6). Professional programmers may also skim these chapters. However, the narrative addresses subtle points that should be read in order to obtain a comprehensive understanding of these topics.

Chapter 7 introduces a new table, the REGISTRATION table, having columns that contain date and time data types. Only professional programmers really need to read this chapter, and they can skip this chapter on the first reading. It is included at this point to be consistent with the objective of encapsulating everything pertaining to single table retrieval in Part I of the text.

1

The SELECT Statement

This chapter introduces the fundamental concepts and structure of the SELECT statement. This is by far the most frequently used SQL statement. Its purpose is to retrieve data from the database. In this chapter you will learn how to display an entire table or display just some specific rows and/or columns of a table. You will find that the sample queries are almost self-explanatory. In fact, some are so "obvious" that you will be tempted to skip reading the comments pertaining to each sample query. This may be appropriate for experienced professionals. However, users should not yield to this temptation. The commentary on each sample will highlight subtle issues which are important. Understanding these points will prove beneficial to those users who choose to master the more advanced topics covered later in this book.

DISPLAY AN ENTIRE TABLE

The goal of the first sample query is to display the entire COURSE table (i.e., display all columns of all rows). This can be achieved by coding the simplest of all possible SELECT statements.

Sample Query 1.1:   Display the entire COURSE table.

```
SELECT    *
FROM      COURSE
```

CNO	CNAME	CDESCP	CRED	CLABFEE	CDEPT
T11	SCHOLASTICISM	FOR THE PIOUS	3	50.00	THEO
T12	FUNDAMENTALISM	FOR THE CAREFREE	3	90.00	THEO
T33	HEDONISM	FOR THE SANE	3	0.00	THEO
T44	COMMUNISM	FOR THE GREEDY	6	200.00	THEO
P11	EMPIRICISM	SEE IT-BELIEVE IT	3	100.00	PHIL
P22	RATIONALISM	FOR CIS MAJORS	3	50.00	PHIL
P33	EXISTENTIALISM	FOR CIS MAJORS	3	200.00	PHIL
P44	SOLIPSISM	ME MYSELF AND I	6	0.00	PHIL
C11	INTRO TO CS	FOR ROOKIES	3	100.00	CIS
C22	DATA STRUCTURES	VERY USEFUL	3	50.00	CIS
C33	DISCRETE MATHEMATICS	ABSOLUTELY NECESSARY	3	0.00	CIS
C44	DIGITAL CIRCUITS	AH HA!	3	0.00	CIS
C55	COMPUTER ARCH.	VON NEUMANN'S MACH.	3	100.00	CIS
C66	RELATIONAL DATABASE	THE ONLY WAY TO GO	3	500.00	CIS

Comments:

1. The asterisk (*) following the SELECT is an abbreviation for "all columns." The left-to-right column sequence of the output is determined by the order in which the columns were initially specified in the CREATE TABLE statement. (The CREATE TABLE statement will be discussed in Part II of this text.)

2. The FROM COURSE clause identifies the table. Your system will undoubtedly have many tables. Each has a unique name. This name follows FROM.

3. "SELECT" and "FROM" are keywords in the SQL language. A keyword always has a specific unalterable meaning in the language. In this case, it means that these words will always imply the selection of data from a database table. Table names and column names are not keywords. They are established, according to certain rules, by the person who issued the CREATE TABLE statement. One of the rules is that a table or a column cannot be given the same name as any keyword. For this reason, keywords are also called "reserved words."

4. You could have entered this statement as a "one line" statement. Entering the following line would produce the same result.

```
SELECT * FROM COURSE
```

Throughout most of this text we usually begin the FROM clause on a new line. This will enhance readability of the SQL code. In practice, you may find it easier to type just one line. The key point is that, regardless of how you type the code, the SELECT statement is interpreted as a single statement.

5. Observe that the rows of the displayed output are not sorted. This is because:

   a. Tables do not have any predefined sort sequence.
   b. The SELECT statement does not contain an ORDER BY clause.

   In general, you can never assume the displayed result will be in sequence unless you explicitly designate some sort of sequence by using the ORDER BY clause. We will examine this clause in Chapter 2.

6. This query does not contain a WHERE clause. In the next example we will see that a WHERE clause is used to select just some of the rows from a table. The point we wish to emphasize here is that the absence of a WHERE clause means that the system will retrieve all rows from the table.

WHERE Clause

Most real world databases have tables which contain too many rows to be examined visually by the user. (It fact, many DB2 databases have tables which contain more than a million rows.) With the exception of small tables, you will rarely want to display an entire table. Instead, you will use the WHERE clause in the SELECT statement to display just those rows that you want to see. (WHERE is another SQL keyword.) The next sample query illustrates this clause.

Sample Query 1.2: Display all information about any course with a zero labfee. (More precisely, select just those rows from the COURSE table where the CLABFEE value is zero. Display every column of these rows.)

```
SELECT  *
FROM    COURSE
WHERE   CLABFEE = 0.00
```

CNO	CNAME	CDESCP	CRED	CLABFEE	CDEPT
C33	DISCRETE MATHEMATICS	ABSOLUTELY NECESSARY	3	0.00	CIS
C44	DIGITAL CIRCUITS	AH HA!	3	0.00	CIS
P44	SOLIPSISM	ME MYSELF AND I	6	0.00	PHIL
T33	HEDONISM	FOR THE SANE	3	0.00	THEO

Comments:

1. The WHERE clause follows the FROM clause. Again, we could have entered the SELECT statement in one line. The following statement is equivalent to the one shown above.

```
SELECT * FROM COURSE WHERE CLABFEE = 0.00
```

2. The syntax of the WHERE clause is

   ```
   WHERE condition
   ```

   The condition in our example is "CLABFEE = 0.00." It is the condition which specifies which rows are to be retrieved. Examine the entire COURSE table and then observe the result. Four of the rows in the COURSE table have CLABFEE values equal to zero. These rows form the displayed result. Only rows which match the WHERE condition are retrieved.

3. CLABFEE was defined as a numeric field. Hence, this is an example of a "numeric" compare. This means the system compares on mathematical value (vs. a character-by-character compare). The following WHERE conditions are all equivalent and would select the same four rows as the original example.

   ```
   WHERE  CLABFEE  =  0
   WHERE  CLABFEE  =  0.0
   WHERE  CLABFEE  =  00.00
   ```

4. Numeric values can contain a leading minus sign (–). However, no other punctuation is permitted.

5. Our example compares on an "equals" (=) condition. Other comparison operators are:
   - "less than" (<)
   - "greater than" (>)
   - "less than or equal to" (<=)
   - "greater than or equal to" (>=)
   - "not equal" (<> or ¬ =)

6. Our example illustrates a "simple" WHERE condition. It references only one column (CLABFEE) and does not contain any Boolean operators such as AND, OR and NOT. We will study the Boolean operators in Chapter 3.

7. A close examination of the output shows that it is sorted by CNO. This is a coincidental side effect. Do not rely on this happening.

The next sample query contains a WHERE clause to select rows based upon CDEPT value. This query is similar to the previous one, with one important exception. The CDEPT column contains character data. This means that the comparison value must be enclosed within apostrophes.

Sample Query 1.3:   Display all information about any course which is offered by the Philosophy Department. (More precisely, select just those rows from the COURSE table where the CDEPT value is "PHIL". Display all columns.)

```
SELECT  *
FROM    COURSE
WHERE   CDEPT = 'PHIL'
```

CNO	CNAME	CDESCP	CRED	CLABFEE	CDEPT
P11	EMPIRICISM	SEE IT-BELIEVE IT	3	100.00	PHIL
P22	RATIONALISM	FOR CIS MAJORS	3	50.00	PHIL
P33	EXISTENTIALISM	FOR CIS MAJORS	3	200.00	PHIL
P44	SOLIPSISM	ME MYSELF AND I	6	0.00	PHIL

Comments:

1.   Syntax: The character string must be contained within apostrophes. Our example illustrates WHERE CDEPT = 'PHIL'. (Note, this is not the case with numeric data. The previous example referenced CLABFEE. That WHERE clause did not contain apostrophes.)

2. Character string data is compared on a character-by-character basis. Two strings are equal only if all corresponding characters match. You should note whether the two strings being compared are of the same length. In the above example, because we are comparing CDEPT, a four character column, to "PHIL", we have a simple case of comparing two strings of the same length. Each character of CDEPT must exactly match "PHIL" for a row to be selected.

A special case occurs where the strings being compared do not have the same length. When this occurs, the same character-by-character comparison applies; however, the system assumes that the shorter string has blanks appended to its right side. This system action means that you do not have to type trailing blanks at the end of character constants placed in WHERE clauses. For example, if you wanted to display information about courses offered by the CIS Department, you could use either of the following WHERE clauses.

```
WHERE  CDEPT  =  'CIS'
WHERE  CDEPT  =  'CIS '
```

It should be emphasized that two strings are considered to be equal only if all corresponding characters match. This means that you have to be careful about leading and embedded blanks. Note that the following WHERE clauses would not match with a left-justified four-character CDEPT value of "CIS".

```
WHERE  CDEPT  =  ' CIS'
WHERE  CDEPT  =  'C I S'
```

3. CDEPT is a fixed length column. (This is why the system stores trailing blanks in CDEPT when a terminal operator enters a string which is shorter than four characters. See Chapter 9.) The same comparison rules apply to columns which contain variable length character data. See the next sample query.

The next sample query references CNAME, a column which contains variable length character data. Observe that the character string comparison process is the same as described for fixed length character strings.

Sample Query 1.4:   Display all information about the course with the CNAME value of "COMMUNISM".

```
SELECT  *
FROM    COURSE
WHERE   CNAME = 'COMMUNISM'
```

CNO	CNAME	CDESCP	CRED	CLABFEE	CDEPT
T44	COMMUNISM	FOR THE GREEDY	6	200.00	THEO

Comments:

1. Because CNAME contains variable length character data, the system will not attach trailing blanks to any data value which is smaller than the maximum column length.

2. Although there is no good reason for doing so, you can still attach trailing blanks to a character string. The following WHERE clause is valid.

   ```
   WHERE CNAME = 'COMMUNISM
   ```

3. The previous examples illustrate "full" character string comparisons. This means that a row is selected only if each pair of corresponding characters match. In Chapter 4 we will discuss "partial" character string comparisons. This will help you search for any character string pattern regardless of its position within the column.

4. Reminder: Very often something called "number" is defined as a character string. Such is the case with the "course number" (CNO) column. Real-world systems contain part numbers, policy numbers, social security numbers, etc., stored as character data simply because no calculations are to be performed with these values. Also, they sometimes contain alphabetic characters. When these "numbers" are stored as character strings, you must use apostrophes in the WHERE clause.

Exercises:

1A. Display all rows where the labfee is less than $150.

1B. Display all rows where the number of credits exceeds 3.

1C. Display all information about courses offered by the Theology Department.

1D. Display all information about the Relational Database course.

1E. Display all information about course number P44.

Usually we compare character data using the equals (=) condition. Occasionally we need to compare character data using the other comparison operators (<, >, <=, >=, <>). Consider the following sample query, which requires such a comparison.

Sample Query 1.5: Display all information about courses having CNAME values which follow "HEDONISM" in alphabetical sequence.

```
SELECT  *
FROM    COURSE
WHERE   CNAME > 'HEDONISM'
```

CNO	CNAME	CDESCP	CRED	CLABFEE	CDEPT
T11	SCHOLASTICISM	FOR THE PIOUS	3	150.00	THEO
P22	RATIONALISM	FOR CIS MAJORS	3	50.00	PHIL
P44	SOLIPSISM	ME MYSELF AND I	6	0.00	PHIL
C11	INTRO TO CS	FOR ROOKIES	3	100.00	CIS
C66	RELATIONAL DATABASE	THE ONLY WAY TO GO	3	500.00	CIS

Comments:

1. The system will compare each CNAME value with the character string "HEDONISM." All CNAME values contain just the standard alphabetic characters (A–Z). This means that the evaluation will be based upon the conventional alphabetic sequence.

2. A special case exists when the character strings being compared contain digits, special symbols and both uppercase and lowercase letters. DB2 and SQL/DS will evaluate a character sequence according to the sequence specified by the EBCDIC code. This code specifies the collating sequence for all characters found within the system. Figure 1.1 illustrates the EBCDIC sequence.

Within the EBCDIC code you will note that special characters (e.g., &, ?, +) will sort before lowercase letters which, in turn, sort before uppercase letters which, in turn, sort before the digits. Whenever you compare character data, the system will first pad fill the right side of the shorter character string with blanks, and then compare the strings based upon the EBCDIC sequence. Listed below are some character strings which have been sorted according to the EBCDIC sequence.

```
???FIDO???
jessie
julie
Jessie
JEssie
JULIe
JULIE
Zeek
3M
77aaaaaaaAAAAAAAA
```

Exercises:

1F. Display every row where the course number is less than "C01".

1G. Display every row where the course name is greater than or equal to "RATIONALISM".

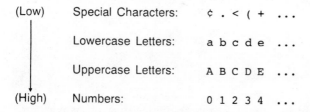

Figure 1-1   Hierarchy of EBCDIC characters.

DISPLAYING SPECIFIED COLUMNS

All of the previous examples selected every column. This was be-cause the statement began with "SELECT *". In practice we usually want to examine just some specified columns. The current example illustrates how to achieve this objective. We simply specify the col-umn names after "SELECT". Only those specified columns are dis-played.

Sample Query 1.6:   Display the CNO, CNAME, and CDEPT values (in that order) for every row in the COURSE table.

```
SELECT CNO, CNAME, CDEPT
FROM    COURSE
```

```
-----------------------------------------------------
CNO      CNAME                           CDEPT
-----------------------------------------------------
C11      INTRO TO CS                     CIS
C22      DATA STRUCTURES                 CIS
C33      DISCRETE MATHEMATICS            CIS
C44      DIGITAL CIRCUITS                CIS
C55      COMPUTER ARCH.                  CIS
C66      RELATIONAL DATABASE             CIS
P11      EMPIRICISM                      PHIL
P22      RATIONALISM                     PHIL
P33      EXISTENTIALISM                  PHIL
P44      SOLIPSISM                       PHIL
T11      SCHOLASTICISM                   THEO
T12      FUNDAMENTALISM                  THEO
T33      HEDONISM                        THEO
T44      COMMUNISM                       THEO
```

Comments:

1. Syntax: Each column name must be separated by a comma. You may optionally include one or more spaces before or after the comma.

2. You must know the names of the columns. Usually you are working with a familiar database and, therefore, this will not be a problem. Otherwise you must do one of the following.

    a. Ask somebody who knows. ("Poor show.")

    b. Issue a statement beginning with "SELECT *". The output will display all the names of the columns. (Again, "Poor Show." You are wasting computer resources, especially if this statement selects many rows.)

    c. Examine the documentation that the database administrator should have produced and made available to you. This should contain the names of the columns that you can access.

    d. Let's assume that documentation is not available, and you correctly reject the first two approaches. Then you must examine the system's Catalog. Information about tables and columns is stored in the Catalog. (A comprehensive discussion of the DB2 and SQL/DS Catalogs is beyond the scope of this text. However, certain catalog features will be presented at appropriate points in our examination on the SQL Language.)

3. This example happens to select the three columns in the same left-to-right order as was established by the database administrator; this is the same order which is displayed when you issue a query beginning with "SELECT *". This is not required. Columns can be displayed in any left-to-right order. See the next sample query.

4. Note that the current query did not have a WHERE clause. Hence, all rows of the COURSE table are retrieved. But only the three specified columns are displayed.

This next example produces essentially the same result as the previous example. The content is the same. The only difference is the specification of the left-to-right column sequence.

Sample Query 1.7:   Display the CDEPT, CNAME, and CNO values (in that order) for every row in the COURSE table.

```
SELECT CDEPT, CNAME, CNO
FROM    COURSE
```

CDEPT	CNAME	CNO
CIS	INTRO TO CS	C11
CIS	DATA STRUCTURES	C22
CIS	DISCRETE MATHEMATICS	C33
CIS	DIGITAL CIRCUITS	C44
CIS	COMPUTER ARCH.	C55
CIS	RELATIONAL DATABASE	C66
PHIL	EMPIRICISM	P11
PHIL	RATIONALISM	P22
PHIL	EXISTENTIALISM	P33
PHIL	SOLIPSISM	P44
THEO	SCHOLASTICISM	T11
THEO	FUNDAMENTALISM	T12
THEO	HEDONISM	T33
THEO	COMMUNISM	T44

Comments:

1. The SELECT clause specifies the left-to-right ordering of the displayed columns. The example shows that CDEPT is the leftmost column, followed by CNAME and then CNO.

2. Again, we have no WHERE clause. Hence, all rows are retrieved.

3. You can specify any valid COURSE column name after "SELECT" as long as the COURSE table is referenced in the FROM clause. You can even enter the same column name more than once. This means that the following query is valid.

```
SELECT CDEPT, CNAME, CLABFEE, CLABFEE, CLABFEE
FROM COURSE
```

This is obviously redundant. But, it is valid and will produce three identical CLABFEE columns. (There is a situation where this does make sense. In some systems the result of the query may be passed onto an external program for further processing. This external program may then perform different calculations on the same data. Users of QMF may utilize this technique.)

Exercises:

1H. Select course name and description, in that order, for every course.

1I. Select department, course number, labfee and credits, in that order, for every course.

DISPLAY SOME SUBSET OF ROWS AND COLUMNS

This next example combines the previously described techniques to select some subset of rows (using the WHERE clause) and some subset of columns (by explicitly specifying column names after "SELECT"). The example does not introduce any new SQL reserved words.

Sample Query 1.8:   Select the CNO, CDEPT, and CLABFEE values for every course with a CLABFEE value less than $100.

```
SELECT  CNO, CDEPT, CLABFEE
FROM    COURSE
WHERE   CLABFEE <   100.00
```

CNO	CDEPT	CLABFEE
C22	CIS	50.00
C33	CIS	.00
C44	CIS	.00
P22	PHIL	50.00
P44	PHIL	.00
T12	THEO	90.00
T33	THEO	.00

Comments:

1. This example illustrates the general format of a typical SELECT statement. This is

    ```
    SELECT  col1,col2,...,coln
    FROM    table-name
    WHERE   condition
    ```

2. In the current example the **WHERE** condition referenced CLABFEE, and we happened to select CLABFEE to be displayed in the output. It is not necessary to display a column used in a retrieval condition. The following example, which retrieves all three credit courses, only displays the course name and description. It may not be reasonable to display the CRED column because it will be the same for all displayed rows.

    ```
    SELECT  CNAME, CDESCP
    FROM    COURSE
    WHERE   CRED = 3
    ```

3. Remember that no punctuation is allowed in numeric constants. Therefore, even though we are comparing on 100 dollars, the example does not show a "$" before the "100."

Exercises:

1J. Select course number and labfee for all courses where the labfee exceeds $100.

1K. Select the course names of all CIS courses.

Observe that the displayed output for all previous sample queries did not contain any duplicate rows. This can occur. Consider the next sample query.

Sample Query 1.9: Display every academic department which offers courses. (Select every row of the COURSE table. Display just the CDEPT column.)

```
SELECT  CDEPT
FROM    COURSE
```

```
-------
CDEPT
-------
CIS
CIS
CIS
CIS
CIS
CIS
PHIL
PHIL
PHIL
PHIL
THEO
THEO
THEO
THEO
```

Comments:

1. This sample query does realize the objective of displaying every department which offers courses. However, because a department offers many courses, there are many duplicate rows in the displayed output. The system does not automatically remove duplicate rows from the output display. You must use the reserved word "DISTINCT" to prevent duplicate rows from being displayed. This will be described in the next sample query.

2. You should recognize when duplicate rows can possibly occur. This implies that you know some facts about the content of the COURSE table. Let us assume that our mythical college has established a reasonable policy that course numbers, course names and course descriptions must be unique. (Chapters 8 and 9 will describe how the system can enforce this policy.) Assuming that our COURSE table reflects this policy, you can be certain that duplicate rows will not be displayed under the following circumstances.

   a. The SELECT clause contains CNO, CNAME, or CDESCP. (Or, a "SELECT *" implicitly references these columns.)

   b. The WHERE clause compares the CNO, CNAME, or CDESCP columns using an equals (=) comparison operator. This implies that only one row can be selected.

All of our previous sample queries and exercises met one of these conditions. Hence, duplicate rows never appeared in any of the previous output displays. The current example only references CDEPT. No reference is made to CNO, CNAME, or CDESCP. Hence, duplicates can and do occur in the result.

3. General Advice: Examine each SELECT statement (prior to execution) to see if it references a "unique" column which will inhibit duplicate rows from being displayed. If this is not the case, you should anticipate duplicate rows in the output display.

Exercise:

   1L. Select every row. Display just the course labfees. (Do not attempt to remove possible duplicate rows.)

DISTINCT Keyword

The next sample query is identical to the previous one with the additional stipulation that the displayed output does not contain any duplicate rows. We use the keyword "DISTINCT" to achieve this objective.

Sample Query 1.10:   Display every academic department which offers courses. Do not display duplicate values.

```
SELECT DISTINCT CDEPT
FROM    COURSE
```

```
-------
CDEPT
-------
CIS
PHIL
THEO
```

Comments:

1. Syntax: The reserved word "DISTINCT" must directly follow "SELECT".

2. Only duplicate rows will be removed. In this example the row consists of a single column. The next sample query will display multiple columns. We will see that a row is considered to be a duplicate of another row only if every column value in the first row matches every corresponding column value in the second row.

3. You are not required to remove duplicate rows. The previous sample query, by displaying the duplicate rows, indicated how many courses were offered by various academic departments. (Chapter 3 will introduce the COUNT function which would better serve this purpose.) The use of DISTINCT is entirely contingent upon the preference of the user.

The next sample query selects just some rows and displays multiple columns. Such queries are less likey to produce duplicate rows. However, as the example illustrates, duplicate rows can occur.

Sample Query 1.11:   For each course with a labfee less than $100, display the academic department which offers the course and the number of awarded credits.

```
SELECT  CDEPT, CRED
FROM    COURSE
WHERE   CLABFEE < 100.00
```

```
-------------------
CDEPT       CRED
-------------------
CIS            3
CIS            3
CIS            3
PHIL           3
PHIL           6
THEO           3
THEO           3
```

Comments:

1. The SELECT command did not reference any of the "unique" columns (CNO, CNAME, CDESCP). Hence, duplicate rows can be present in the displayed result.

2. You could simply decide whether or not you want to see duplicate rows and then include or exclude DISTINCT according to your decision. This is an acceptable approach. However, the use of DISTINCT asks the system to do some extra work to remove the duplicate rows. Therefore, if the result is large, and you determine that it will not contain duplicate rows, it is better to avoid asking the system to do the unnecessary work of removing nonexistent duplicate rows.

Sample Query 1.12:   Same as previous sample query. However, do not display duplicate rows.

```
SELECT  DISTINCT CDEPT, CRED
FROM    COURSE
WHERE   CLABFEE <  100.00
```

CDEPT	CRED
CIS	3
PHIL	3
PHIL	6
THEO	3

Comment:

Only rows which were complete duplicates of other rows were not displayed. (The reader should closely examine the results of this query as compared to the previous.) The key concept is that DISTINCT does not refer to any individual column. It refers to the entire row.

Exercises:

1M. Display the set of all course labfees. Do not display any duplicate values.

1N. Display the credits and labfees for all CIS courses. Allow duplicate rows to be displayed.

1O. Display the credits and labfees for all CIS courses. Do not display any duplicate rows.

DISPLAYING CONSTANT DATA

It is possible to incorporate constant data into a column of the result table. The next sample query shows the inclusion of a character string which serves to describe the result table.

Sample Query 1.13: Display the course number and name of every course which as a labfee over $100. Include a third column in the result table which shows "EXPENSIVE COURSE" in each row.

```
SELECT  CNO, CNAME, 'EXPENSIVE COURSE'
FROM    COURSE
WHERE   CLABFEE > 100
```

CNO	CNAME	COL1
T11	SCOLASTICISM	EXPENSIVE COURSE
T44	COMMUNISM	EXPENSIVE COURSE
P33	EXISTENTIALISM	EXPENSIVE COURSE
C66	RELATIONAL DATABASE	EXPENSIVE COURSE

Comments:

1. The constant to be displayed in the result table is specified in the SELECT clause. Any constant, numeric or character, can be specified.

2. The constant is shown redundantly in each row. This is the only option SQL provides. It would probably be desirable to include the "EXPENSIVE COURSE" phrase just once as a title to the result table. However, you would have to use the host system report generator facilities to achieve this objective.

3. The system will generate a column header for the constant data. (In this case QMF generated "COL1".) If a second column of constant data were present, it would have "COL2" as its column header, etc.

SUMMARY

This chapter has introduced the basic structure of the SQL SELECT statement. We showed three clauses of this statement.

```
SELECT  column names
FROM    table name
WHERE   condition
```

The query is formulated by:

1. Identifying the table which contains the desired data. The table name is placed in the FROM clause.

2. Identifying the columns to be displayed. The column names are placed in the SELECT clause. ("SELECT *" will display all columns.)

3. Coding a condition in the WHERE clause which specifies the row selection criteria. The absence of a WHERE clause means that every row will be selected.

SUMMARY EXERCISES

The following exercises all pertain to the STAFF table, which has four columns. These are ENAME, ETITLE, ESALARY, and DEPT.

1P. Display the entire STAFF table.

1Q. Display all information about any employee whose yearly salary is less than $1000.

1R. Display all information about any employee who is employed by the Theology Department.

1S. Display the names and titles of all staff members.

1T. Display the department id of any department employing a staff member whose salary is less than $900. Remove possible duplicate rows.

2

Sorting the "Result Table"

Whenever you display more than a few rows, it is usually desirable to have the result displayed in some specific row sequence. This objective can be realized by including an ORDER BY clause in the SELECT statement. This chapter will present five sample queries which demonstrate the simplicity and flexibility of the ORDER BY clause.

Before presenting the sample queries a simple but very important point needs to be emphasized. The process of executing a SELECT statement effectively identifies a table which constitutes the displayed output. We call this table the "result table." Very often this result table consists of just a single column and/or a single row. Nevertheless, it is still a table. The content of the result table happens to be derived from the table specified in the FROM clause. But it is a different table. We emphasize this rather obvious point because sorting applies to the result table only. The result table is a temporary table and cannot be saved with any SQL command. It disappears when the next SQL command is executed. (However, users of QMF can save the result table.) The key point is that you can make no assumptions about the sequence of the underlying table referenced in the FROM clause. As stated in Chapter 1, this "permanent" table has no inherent row sequence. This is not changed by the query which contains an ORDER BY clause.

ORDER BY Clause

The first sample query illustrates the ORDER BY clause to sort the result table by a single column. Note this clause is merely appended to a standard SELECT statement as described in the previous chapter.

Sample Query 2.1:   Display the entire COURSE table. Sort the output display by the CLABFEE values.

```
SELECT  *
FROM    COURSE
ORDER   BY CLABFEE
```

CNC	CNAME	CDESCP	CRED	CLABFEE	CDEPT
T33	HEDONISM	FOR THE SANE	3	0.00	THEO
P44	SOLIPSISM	ME MYSELF AND I	6	0.00	PHIL
C33	DISCRETE MATHEMATICS	ABSOLUTELY NECESSARY	3	0.00	CIS
C44	DIGITAL CIRCUITS	AH HA!	3	0.00	CIS
P22	RATIONALISM	FOR CIS MAJORS	3	50.00	PHIL
C22	DATA STRUCTURES	VERY USEFUL	3	50.00	CIS
T12	FUNDAMENTALISM	FOR THE CAREFREE	3	90.00	THEO
P11	EMPIRICISM	SEE IT-BELIEVE IT	3	100.00	PHIL
C11	INTRO TO CS	FOR ROOKIES	3	100.00	CIS
C55	COMPUTER ARCH.	VON NEUMANN'S MACH	3	100.00	CIS
T11	SCHOLASTICISM	FOR THE PIOUS	3	150.00	THEO
T44	COMMUNISM	FOR THE GREEDY	6	200.00	THEO
P33	EXISTENTIALISM	FOR CIS MAJORS	3	200.00	PHIL
C66	RELATIONAL DATABASE	THE ONLY WAY TO GO	3	500.00	CIS

Comments:

1. Syntax: When used, the ORDER BY clause is always the last clause in any SELECT statement.

2. The sort occurs in ascending sequence. This is the default unless otherwise specified. We could have explicitly requested an ascending sort sequence by including the ASC parameter in the ORDER BY clause. The following ORDER BY clause is equivalent to the one shown in the example.

```
ORDER BY CLABFEE ASC
```

The ASC parameter is rarely used in practice. Its only purpose is to enhance readability of a query by explicitly indicating an ascending sort sequence.

It is possible to display output in a descending row sequence. The next sample query will illustrate the DESC parameter to achieve this objective.

3. The sort field, CLABFEE, is numeric. Hence, the sort reflected a sequence based on mathematical value. If there were negative values in the CLABFEE column, they would have appeared before the zero and positive values. We can also sort on character string columns. The next sample query will illustrate sorting on a character column.

4. There are duplicate values in the CLABFEE column. We can make no assumptions about the sort sequence within matching values. Sample Query 2.3 will illustrate sorting on multiple columns to establish a second level sort field within matching values.

5. Note that the sort column of this query is not the leftmost column. Most users typically establish the sort column as the leftmost column. This example illustrates that you can sort on any column.

6. Finally, we emphasize that sorting applies to the displayed result only. The data within the stored table remains unchanged.

Exercise:

2A. Display the entire course table. Sort the result by the CDEPT column in ascending sequence.

DESCENDING SORT

The next sample query demonstrates the use of the DESC parameter to produce a result which is sorted in descending sequence.

Sample Query 2.2:   Select the course number, name, and credit of any course which is offered by the Computer and Information Science Department. Sort the result by course number in descending sequence.

```
SELECT  CNO, CNAME, CRED
FROM    COURSE
WHERE   CDEPT = 'CIS'
ORDER   BY CNO DESC
```

```
----------------------------------------------------
CNO     CNAME                            CRED
----------------------------------------------------
C66     RELATIONAL DATABASE                3
C55     COMPUTER ARCH.                     3
C44     DIGITAL CIRCUITS                   3
C33     DISCRETE MATHEMATICS               3
C22     DATA STRUCTURES                    3
C11     INTRO TO CS                        3
```

Comments:

1. Syntax: DESC follows the column name in the ORDER BY clause. One or more spaces must separate the column name and the DESC parameter. (A comma cannot be used as a separator.)

2. The sort column (CNO) contains character data. Recall that the EBCDIC code specifies the sequence for character data. Review the comments for Sample Query 1.5 which describe the EBCDIC sequence.

3. Within the COURSE table every CNO value is unique. Hence, the row sequence was completely determined.

4. Unlike the preceding sample query, this query selects just some columns. An ORDER BY clause can be placed at the end of any valid SELECT statement. However, there is one restriction. The ORDER BY clause must specify columns which are referenced in the SELECT clause. For example, the current example could not sort by CLABFEE because CLABFEE is not selected for display. (See the Summary comments at the conclusion of this chapter.)

Exercise:

2B. Display the course name and labfee for all courses offered by the Philosophy Department. Sort the result by course name in descending sequence.

SORTING ON MULTIPLE COLUMNS

Recall that in Sample Query 2.1 the sort column (CLABFEE) contained nonunique values. For this reason, the row sequence was not completely determined. The next sample query illustrates that the ORDER BY clause may reference multiple columns. We will see that proper specification of multiple columns in the ORDER BY clause permits complete determination of the row sequence in any desired order.

Sample Query 2.3:   Display the department id and name of every course. Sort the result by department id. Within each department, sort by course name.

```
SELECT  CDEPT, CNAME
FROM    COURSE
ORDER   BY CDEPT, CNAME
```

```
---------------------------------------
CDEPT   CNAME
---------------------------------------
CIS     COMPUTER ARCH.
CIS     DATA STRUCTURES
CIS     DIGITAL CIRCUITS
CIS     DISCRETE MATHEMATICS
CIS     INTRO TO CS
CIS     RELATIONAL DATABASE
PHIL    EXISTENTIALISM
PHIL    EMPIRICISM
PHIL    RATIONALISM
PHIL    SOLIPSISM
THEO    COMMUNISM
THEO    FUNDAMENTALISM
THEO    HEDONISM
THEO    SCHOLASTICISM
```

Comments:

1. Terminology: This example has two sort columns (fields). There are different ways of expressing the sort relationship between the two columns. The following statements are equivalent.

    a. CDEPT is the major sort field, and CNAME is the minor sort field.

    b. CDEPT is the primary sort field, and CNAME is the secondary sort field.

    c. CDEPT is the first level sort field, and CNAME is the second level sort field.

    d. The sort sequence is CNAME within CDEPT.

2. Syntax: The "ORDER BY" is followed by the major sort field, which is followed by the minor sort field. The sort field column names must be separated by a comma.

3. Both the major and minor sorts default to ascending sequence. We can mix ascending and descending sequences within the different sort fields. (See Sample Query 2.5.)

4. Both the major and minor sort fields contain numeric data. This is not necessary. (See Sample Query 2.5.)

5. There is no practical limit on the number of sort fields. The following ORDER BY clause is valid and would establish a four-level sort sequence.

```
ORDER BY CRED, CLABFEE, CDEPT, CNAME
```

Exercise:

2C. Display the CLABFEE, CNO, and CRED columns (in that order) for every row in the COURSE table. Sort the displayed rows by CNO within CLABFEE. (CLABFEE is the major sort field, and CNO is the minor sort field.)

ORDER BY Column-number

The ORDER BY clause can also reference a column by its relative position in the output display. This is a convenience which can save you keystroke effort. The next sample query produces an output display which is sorted by the second column.

Sample Query 2.4:   Display the CNO, CLABFEE, and CRED values, in that order, for all courses. Sort the result by the second column (i.e., CLABFEE).

```
SELECT  CNO, CLABFEE, CRED
FROM    COURSE
ORDER   BY 2
```

CNO	CLABFEE	CRED
T33	0.00	3
P44	0.00	6
C33	0.00	3
C44	0.00	3
P22	50.00	3
C22	50.00	3
T12	90.00	3
P11	100.00	3
C11	100.00	3
C55	100.00	3
T11	150.00	3
T44	200.00	6
P33	200.00	3
C66	500.00	3

Comments:

1. The use of a relative column number is not necessary in this example. The following equivalent clause will achieve the same objective.

   ```
   ORDER BY CLABFEE
   ```

   The use of relative column numbers is an acceptable convenience for use with one-time ad hoc queries. For statements which will be saved for future execution, it is better to explicitly name the column in the ORDER BY clause. This enhances readability and is not affected by a reordering of column names in the SELECT clause. (This is especially true for statements to be embedded in application programs.)

2. There are situations which require use of the relative column number for sorting. Chapters 5 and 6 will present built-in functions and calculated columns. Display columns generated by these techniques do not have predefined names. Such columns must be referenced by their relative column position. Future sample queries will illustrate this point.

3. The DESC parameter can be used with relative column numbers. The following clause is valid.

   ```
   ORDER BY 2 DESC
   ```

Exercise:

2D. Display the entire COURSE table sorted in descending sequence by the third column.

The final sample query in this chapter illustrates that all of the previously described variations of the ORDER BY clause can be incorporated within a single clause. This clause references both column numbers and names. This example is not very realistic. However, it does demonstrate the flexibility of the ORDER BY clause.

Sample Query 2.5: Display the CDEPT, CLABFEE, and CRED values, in that order, for all courses. CDEPT is the first-level sort field (ascending); CRED is the second-level sort field (descending); and CLABFEE is the third-level sort field (descending).

```
SELECT  CDEPT, CLABFEE, CRED
FROM    COURSE
ORDER   BY CDEPT, 3 DESC, CLABFEE DESC
```

CDEPT	CLABFEE	CRED
CIS	500.00	3
CIS	100.00	3
CIS	100.00	3
CIS	50.00	3
CIS	0.00	3
CIS	0.00	3
PHIL	0.00	6
PHIL	200.00	3
PHIL	100.00	3
PHIL	50.00	3
THEO	200.00	6
THEO	150.00	3
THEO	90.00	3
THEO	0.00	3

Comments:

1. This sample query sorts on three columns. The ORDER BY clause:
   - References some columns by name (CDEPT and CLABFEE) and another by relative column number (CRED is identified as the third column).
   - Sorts one column (CDEPT) in ascending sequence and two columns (CRED and CLABFEE) in descending sequence.

2. Note that none of the displayed columns contain unique values. Hence, duplicate rows can (and do) appear in the output display. Observe that because this result is sequenced, it is easier to detect duplicate rows. Recall that duplicate rows can be removed from the displayed output by use of DISTINCT.

Exercise:

2E. Display the CDEPT, CLABFEE, and CNAME values of all three credit courses. Sort the output result. CDEPT is the first-level sort field (ascending); CLABFEE is the second-level sort field (descending); CNAME is the third-level sort field (ascending).

SUMMARY

This chapter has expanded on the fundamental structure of the SQL SELECT statement. This statement structure now incorporates the ORDER BY clause.

```
SELECT column names
FROM    table name
WHERE   condition
ORDER   BY sort columns
```

The result table can be sorted on any displayed column which can be referenced by column name or relative column number. The default sort sequence is ascending (ASC). A descending sequence can be established by using the DESC parameter.

There is one limitation which can be a nuisance. We must select any column we choose to sort by. Assume that CLABFEE is very confidental data, and therefore we do not want it to appear on a printed report to be produced from the query results. Yet we might like to print out the CNAME fields in ascending sequence according to the CLABFEE value, from the least to the most expensive. The following SELECT command seems to be a reasonable solution, but it will *not* work.

```
SELECT CNAME
FROM    COURSE
ORDER BY CLABFEE
```

The sort field (CLABFEE) is not selected for display. Hence, this statement produces a syntax error. Fortunately, most systems have a report generator facility which permits certain columns that appear in the results table to be omitted from the report. (Note that such reporting facilities are not part of the SQL language.) Therefore, to produce a list of just course names in sequence by labfee, the user must follow two separate steps.

Step 1. (SQL)   SELECT CNAME, CLABFEE
                  FROM   COURSE
                  ORDER BY CLABFEE

Step 2. Use the facilities of the host system report generator to prevent the CLABFEE column from being printed.

We conclude with some final comments regarding the terms "sort" and "sequence." We have casually used these terms as though they were synonymous. However, to be precise, the objective of all previous sample queries was to display the result table in some specified row sequence. The system may have to execute a sort utility to achieve this objective. In Part II of this text we will discuss indexes. There we will note that the system can sometimes utilize an index to avoid execution of a sort utility. At this point you should not focus on the internal processes which the system follows to produce the output in row sequence. However, you should be aware that the ORDER BY clause usually requires the system to do more work. This could be significant if the number of rows is large. Therefore, you are advised to exercise judgment in use of the ORDER BY clause.

SUMMARY EXERCISES

The following exercises all refer to the same STAFF table described at the end of Chapter 1. The column names are ENAME, ETITLE, ESALARY, and DEPT.

2F. Display the entire STAFF table. Sort it by employee name.

2G. Display the name and salary of any employee whose salary is less than $1000. Sort the result by salary in descending sequence.

2H. Display all information about employees who work in the Theology Department. Sort the result by employee title.

2I. Display the department id, employee name, and salary for all employees. Sort the result by salary within department.

2J. Display the department id, employee title, and salary for all staff members. Let department be the major sort field (in ascending sequence) and salary be the minor sort field (in descending sequence).

3

Boolean Connectors:
AND-OR-NOT

Row selection in the previous chapters was based on a single condition. In this chapter we present the use of Boolean connectors to facilitate row selection based upon multiple conditions. The first twelve sample queries illustrate the classical Boolean connectors of AND, OR and NOT. The remaining sample queries introduce the keywords IN and BETWEEN. You will learn that you can do without IN and BETWEEN because the classical operators provide the expressive power to formulate any row selection criteria. However, you will also find that IN and BETWEEN are very useful because they provide a more compact way of expressing certain row selection conditions.

AND Connector

The first sample query illustrates the AND connector. The AND is placed between two row selection conditions within the WHERE clause. The intent is to request the system to select an individual row only if both of the conditions are satisfied.

Sample Query 3.1:   Display all information about any CIS course which has a zero labfee.

```
SELECT  *
FROM    COURSE
WHERE   CLABFEE = 0
AND     CDEPT = 'CIS'
```

CNO	CNAME	CDESCP	CRED	CLABFEE	CDEPT
C33	DISCRETE MATHEMATICS	ABSOLUTELY NECESSARY	3	0.00	CIS
C44	DIGITAL CIRCUITS	AH HA!	3	0.00	CIS

Comments:

1. Logic: The example shows two conditions that are connected by the AND Boolean connector. These two conditions are

   a.   CLABFEE = 0

   b.   CDEPT = 'CIS'

   We emphasize that an individual row must match both conditions in order to be selected. Note that both of the output rows match the selection criteria. Observe that the COURSE table contains additional rows that match just one or the other, but not both, of these conditions. There are philosophy and theology courses which have zero labfees. Likewise, there are computer and information science courses with nonzero labfees. These rows were not selected because they met only one of the two specified conditions.

2. Syntax: The primary requirement is that individual conditions be syntactically correct. The sample query shows the conditions written on separate lines. This is not required but it enhances readability. Recall that a SELECT statement is free form and can be written on any number of lines. Therefore, each of the following statements is equivalent to the current example.

```
SELECT  *
FROM    COURSE
WHERE   CLABFEE = 0 AND CDEPT = 'CIS'

SELECT  *
FROM    COURSE
WHERE   CLABFEE = 0 AND
        CDEPT = 'CIS'

SELECT  * FROM COURSE
WHERE   CLABFEE = 0 AND CDEPT = 'CIS'

SELECT  * FROM COURSE
WHERE   CLABFEE = 0
        AND
        CDEPT = 'CIS
```

3. The order in which the conditions are specified should have no effect upon performance. The following compound WHERE conditions should execute with the same efficiency and will produce the same result.

```
WHERE CLABFEE = 0 AND CDEPT = 'CIS'

WHERE CDEPT = 'CIS' AND CLABFEE = 0
```

Exercise:

3A. Select all information about three credit courses offered by the Philosophy Department.

Like the previous sample query, the following example connects multiple conditions using AND. This time both of the conditions reference the same column (CLABFEE). The intention is to select rows where the CLABFEE value falls within a certain range.

Sample Query 3.2:   Display all information about any course having a lab fee which is strictly between zero and one hundred dollars.

```
SELECT  *
FROM    COURSE
WHERE   CLABFEE > 0
AND     CLABFEE < 100
```

CNO	CNAME	CDESCP	CRED	CLABFEE	CDEPT
T12	FUNDAMENTALISM	FOR THE CAREFREE	3	90.00	THEO
P22	RATIONALISM	FOR CIS MAJORS	3	50.00	PHIL
C22	DATA STRUCTURES	VERY USEFUL	3	50.00	CIS

Comments:

1. Logic: The example selected rows where the CLABFEE value was strictly greater than zero and strictly less than one hundred. Note that rows with CLABFEE values of 0 and 100 were not selected.

2. Syntax: The column name must be specified in both conditions. The following WHERE clause is invalid and will cause an *error*.

```
WHERE CLABFEE > 0 AND < 100
```

Exercise:

3B. Display all information about any course which has a labfee between and including $100 and $500.

MULTIPLE ANDS

It is possible to connect multiple conditions using many AND connectors. The next example illustrates four conditions which are AND connected. In this case a given row will be selected only if it matches all four of the specified conditions.

Sample Query 3.3:   Display all information about any three credit philosophy course which has a labfee strictly between zero and one hundred dollars.

```
SELECT  *
FROM    COURSE
WHERE   CLABFEE > 0
AND     CLABFEE < 100
AND     CDEPT = 'PHIL'
AND     CRED = 3
```

CNO	CNAME	CDESCP	CRED	CLABFEE	CDEPT
P22	RATIONALISM	FOR CIS MAJORS	3	50.00	PHIL

Comment:

For all practical purposes there is no limit on the number of conditions which can be used in a **WHERE** clause.

Exercise:

3C.   Select all information about any three-credit theology course with a labfee between and including $100 and $400.

OR Connector

Like the AND connector, the OR connector will connect multiple conditions within a WHERE clause. However, OR connectors have a different impact on the logic of the row selection process. Assuming that just two conditions are OR connected, a given row will be selected if it matches either or both of the specified conditions. The next sample query illustrates this point.

Sample Query 3.4: Display all information about any course offered by the CIS or PHIL Departments.

```
SELECT  *
FROM    COURSE
WHERE   CDEPT = 'CIS'
OR      CDEPT = 'PHIL'
```

CNO	CNAME	CDESCP	CRED	CLABFEE	CDEPT
P11	EMPIRICISM	SEE IT - BELIEVE IT	3	100.00	PHIL
P22	RATIONALISM	FOR CIS MAJORS	3	50.00	PHIL
P33	EXISTENTIALISM	FOR CIS MAJORS	3	200.00	PHIL
P44	SOLIPSISM	ME MYSELF AND I	6	0.00	PHIL
C11	INTRO TO CS	FOR ROOKIES	3	100.00	CIS
C22	DATA STRUCTURES	VERY USEFUL	3	50.00	CIS
C33	DISCRETE MATHEMATICS	ABSOLUTELY NECESSARY	3	0.00	CIS
C44	DIGITAL CIRCUITS	AH HA!	3	0.00	CIS
C55	COMPUTER ARCH.	VON NEUMANN'S MACH.	3	100.00	CIS
C66	RELATIONAL DATABASE	THE ONLY WAY TO GO	3	500.00	CIS

Comments:

1. Logic: The OR is an "inclusive" OR. This means a row will be selected in the special case where it matches both of the specified conditions. This cannot happen in the current example because both conditions specify a different "equals" compare on the same CDEPT field. The next sample query will illustrate a situation where some rows will match on both conditions.

2. Syntax: As with previous examples, SQL's free form allows flexibility. The following statements are equivalent to the current sample example.

```
SELECT *
FROM    COURSE
WHERE   CDEPT = 'CIS' OR CDEPT = 'PHIL'

SELECT *
FROM    COURSE
WHERE   CDEPT = 'CIS' OR
        CDEPT = 'PHIL'

SELECT * FROM COURSE
WHERE   CDEPT = 'CIS' OR CDEPT = 'PHIL'

SELECT *
FROM    COURSE
WHERE   CDEPT = 'CIS'
        OR
        CDEPT = 'PHIL'
```

3. Syntax: Both conditions refer to the same CDEPT column. However, as with the AND connector, this column must be explicitly specified in each condition. This means that the following WHERE clause is invalid.

```
WHERE CDEPT = 'CIS' OR 'PHIL'
```

4. The order in which the column names are specified should not affect performance. The following compound WHERE clauses should execute with the same efficiency and produce the same result.

```
WHERE CDEPT = 'PHIL' OR CDEPT = 'CIS'
WHERE CDEPT = 'CIS'  OR CDEPT = 'PHIL'
```

Exercise:

3D. Display all information about every course offered by the Philosophy or Theology Departments.

The next sample query illustrates a situation where it is possible for a given row to match on both conditions. This demonstrates the "inclusive" behavior of the OR connector.

Sample Query 3.5:   Display all information about any CIS course or any course with a zero labfee.

```
SELECT  *
FROM    COURSE
WHERE   CLABFEE = 0.00
OR      CDEPT = 'CIS'
```

```
---------------------------------------------------------------------------------
CNO      CNAME              CDESCP                 CRED    CLABFEE    CDEPT
---------------------------------------------------------------------------------
T33      HEDONISM           FOR THE SANE            3       0.00      THEO
P44      SOLIPSISM          ME MYSELF AND I         6       0.00      PHIL
C11      INTRO TO CS        FOR ROOKIES             3     100.00      CIS
C22      DATA STRUCTURES    VERY USEFUL             3      50.00      CIS
C33      DISCRETE MATHEMATICS  ABSOLUTELY NECESSARY  3      0.00      CIS
C44      DIGITAL CIRCUITS   AH HA!                  3       0.00      CIS
C55      COMPUTER ARCH.     VON NEUMANN'S MACH.     3     100.00      CIS
C66      RELATIONAL DATABASE  THE ONLY WAY TO GO    3     500.00      CIS
```

Comment:

This SELECT statement will display any row which has a CLABFEE value of zero or a CDEPT value of "CIS". Observe that all courses having a labfee of zero are selected, regardless of their department id. And, all CIS courses are selected, regardless of their labfee. Also, rows which match both conditions will be selected. Note that a row which matches both conditions, like the rows with CNO values of "C33" and "C44", will only occur once in the output display.

Exercise:

3E.   Select all information about any course which is offered by the Theology Department or is worth six credits.

Multiple ORs

As with the AND connector, it is possible to connect any number of conditions using multiple OR connectors. The next example illustrates four conditions which are OR connected. In this case a row will be selected if it matches any of the four specified conditions.

Sample Query 3.6:   Display all information about any course which has a labfee equal to 50, 100, 150 or 200 dollars.

```
SELECT  *
FROM    COURSE
WHERE   CLABFEE = 50
OR      CLABFEE = 100
OR      CLABFEE = 150
OR      CLABFEE = 200
```

CNO	CNAME	CDESCP	CRED	CLABFEE	CDEPT
T11	SCHOLASTICISM	FOR THE PIOUS	3	150.00	THEO
T44	COMMUNISM	FOR THE GREEDY	6	200.00	THEO
P11	EMPIRICISM	SEE IT - BELIEVE IT	3	100.00	PHIL
P22	RATIONALISM	FOR CIS MAJORS	3	50.00	PHIL
P33	EXISTENTIALISM	FOR CIS MAJORS	3	200.00	PHIL
C11	INTRO TO CS	FOR ROOKIES	3	100.00	CIS
C22	DATA STRUCTURES	VERY USEFUL	3	50.00	CIS
C55	COMPUTER ARCH.	VON NEUMANN'S MACH.	3	100.00	CIS

Comments:

1. For all practical purposes, there is no limit on the number of conditions which can be OR connected.

2. Note that the CLABFEE column must be explicitly referenced in each of the four conditions. Sample Query 3.13 will introduce the IN operator, which offers a more compact way of expressing this query.

Exercise:

3F.   Display all information about any course which has a labfee in the set {0.00, 90.00, 150.00}.

NOT Keyword

All previous examples specified conditions which explicitly identified, in a positive sense, the rows to be selected for display. The next sample query introduces the use of the NOT keyword, which allows you to indicate those rows which you do not want selected for display.

Sample Query 3.7: Display the course name and department id of any course which is not offered by the CIS department.

```
SELECT CNAME, CDEPT
FROM    COURSE
WHERE   NOT CDEPT = 'CIS'
```

```
-----------------------------------------
CNAME                      CDEPT
-----------------------------------------
SCHOLASTICISM              THEO
FUNDAMENTALISM             THEO
HEDONISM                   THEO
COMMUNISM                  THEO
EMPIRICISM                 PHIL
RATIONALISM                PHIL
EXISTENTIALISM             PHIL
SOLIPSISM                  PHIL
```

Comments:

1. Syntax: The NOT operator can be placed before any legitimate conditional expression. The current example has a single condition which is negated by use of NOT. The format of the WHERE condition is

   ```
   WHERE NOT (conditional expression)
   ```

   Later in this chapter we will see more complex examples where NOT is used in conjunction with WHERE clauses which contain multiple conditions.

2. The following statement is equivalent to the current example. It uses the special "not equals" comparison operator ($\neg=$).

   ```
   SELECT *
   FROM    COURSE
   WHERE   CDEPT ¬= 'CIS'
   ```

3. Avoid making the common mistake of placing the NOT before a comparison operator. The following WHERE clause is *invalid* because the NOT immediately precedes the equal sign.

   ```
   WHERE CDEPT NOT = 'CIS'
   ```

   In general, "NOT" cannot be interchanged with "$\neg$".

4. If you are familiar with the basics of set theory, it may be helpful to think of the NOT as a keyword which identifies the complement of a subset of rows from a table. The condition (CDEPT = 'CIS') effectively identifies a subset of rows from the COURSE table. By placing a NOT before this condition, you are requesting the system to select the complement of this subset.

Exercise:

3G. Select the course number, name and labfee of any course with a labfee other than 100.

The next sample query shows a WHERE clause with two conditions, each of which is negated by use of NOT, and subsequently AND connected. We will classify this WHERE clause as "complex," because, unlike all the previous WHERE clauses, it contains two different Boolean operators (NOT and AND). Our comments on the logic of this sample query serve as a prelude to the following detail discussion on the hierarchy of Boolean operators.

Sample Query 3.8:   Display the name and department id of all courses with the exception of those courses offered by the CIS and PHIL Departments.

```
SELECT  CNAME, CDEPT
FROM    COURSE
WHERE   NOT CDEPT = 'CIS'
AND     NOT CDEPT = 'PHIL'
```

```
-----------------------------------------
CNAME                      CDEPT
-----------------------------------------
SCHOLASTICISM              THEO
FUNDAMENTALISM             THEO
HEDONISM                   THEO
COMMUNISM                  THEO
```

Comments:

1. This is the first sample query where we have utilized two different Boolean operators (NOT and AND). This raises the question of hierarchy of execution which will be described shortly. With respect to the current example, we merely note that the system evaluates the NOT before the AND. This means that the WHERE clause is the AND of two negated conditions. Therefore, the system will select any row which meets both of the negated conditions. If a row has a CDEPT value not equal to "CIS" and it is also not equal to "PHIL," it will be selected.

2. You must always be careful when composing queries which use different Boolean operators. For example, many people would articulate the current sample query as

> "Select course names and departments for courses which are not offered by the CIS or PHIL Department"

This statement may be grammatically correct. However, note that using "or" in the above English language statement may entice the careless user to place an OR into the WHERE clause. The resulting SELECT statement (shown below) appears innocuous upon initial inspection. But, when we consider its precise meaning we observe that it is a rather silly way of selecting every row from the COURSE table.

```
SELECT  CNAME, CDEPT
FROM    COURSE
WHERE   NOT CDEPT = 'CIS'
OR      NOT CDEPT = 'PHIL'
```

Any CIS course would be selected by the second expression (NOT CDEPT = 'PHIL') and any PHIL course would be selected by the first expression (NOT CDEPT = 'CIS').

3. Observe that the problem identified above and subsequent logical problems described on the following pages are only indirectly related to the SQL language. The primary source of such problems is the ambiguous use of natural language and a careless approach toward the semantics of the Boolean operators. This transcends not only SQL but any other computer programming language.

Exercise:

3H. Select the course number and labfee for any course which has a labfee other than $100 and $200.

HIERARCHY OF BOOLEAN OPERATORS

Whenever a WHERE clause contains more than two conditions which are connected by different Boolean operators, the system must decide upon the order of execution. If the WHERE clause does not contain any parentheses, the system will follow a specific sequence. This sequence is defined by a hierarchy which dictates that:

- NOTs are evaluated first
- ANDs are evaluated next
- ORs are evaluated last

If you have programmed in any other language, you will recognize that this is the same hierarchy that you most likely encountered in that language. If SQL is your first computer language, then you should pay close attention to the next four sample queries which illustrate the hierarchy of Boolean operators.

Sample Query 3.9: Display all information about any theology course which has a zero labfee, or any course (regardless of its department and labfee) which is worth six credits.

```
SELECT  *
FROM    COURSE
WHERE   CDEPT = 'THEO' AND CLABFEE = 0
OR      CRED = 6
```

CNO	CNAME	CDESCP	CRED	CLABFEE	CDEPT
T33	HEDONISM	FOR THE SANE	3	0.00	THEO
T44	COMMUNISM	FOR THE GREEDY	6	200.00	THEO
P44	SOLIPSISM	ME MYSELF AND I	6	0.00	PHIL

Comments:

1. Logic: Observe the effect of the AND being evaluated before the OR. A given row will be selected if it meets either or both of the following conditions.

   a.   CDEPT = 'THEO' AND CLABFEE = 0
   b.   CRED = 6

The system will examine each row of the COURSE table. If a given row has both a CDEPT value of "THEO" and a CLABFEE value of zero, it will be selected. The first row (Course number of "T33") was the only row which met this condition. Furthermore, if a given row has a CRED value of 6, it will also be selected. The last two rows (Course numbers "T44" and "P44") met this condition. The COURSE table does not contain any rows which match both of the above conditions. If it did, such rows would have been selected.

2. Syntax: We cannot arbitrarily change the order of the conditions. Consider the following statement, which is *not* equivalent to the sample query.

```
SELECT  * FROM COURSE
WHERE   CDEPT = 'THEO'
AND     CRED = 6
OR      CLABFEE = 0
```

This query would select any six-credit theology course or any course with a zero labfee (regardless of its department and credits).

3. The following two statements are equivalent to the current example. The first reorders the conditions without affecting the logic. The second makes use of parentheses which will be explained on the next page. The parentheses are superfluous, but they help readability.

```
SELECT  * FROM COURSE
WHERE   CRED = 6
OR      CDEPT = 'THEO' AND CLABFEE = 0

SELECT  * FROM COURSE
WHERE   (CDEPT = 'THEO' AND CLABFEE = 0)
OR      CRED = 6
```

USE OF PARENTHESES

SQL permits the use of parentheses to override the Boolean operator hierarchy. Parentheses make explicit the order of evaluation and enhance readability. The next sample query incorporates the same three conditions as the preceding sample query. This time we illustrate the use of parentheses to change the order of system evaluation. The two conditions adjacent to the OR are enclosed within parentheses. This means they will be evaluated first. Note that the semantic meaning of this sample query is very different from the preceding one. The only syntax change, the parentheses, effectively changes the semantic meaning of the WHERE clause.

Sample Query 3.10: Display all information about theology courses which have a zero labfee or are worth six credits.

```
SELECT  *
FROM    COURSE
WHERE   CDEPT = 'THEO'
AND     (CLABFEE = 0 OR CRED = 6)
```

CNO	CNAME	CDESCP	CRED	CLABFEE	CDEPT
T33	HEDONISM	FOR THE SANE	3	0.00	THEO
T44	COMMUNISM	FOR THE GREEDY	6	200.00	THEO

Comments:

1. Logic: Observe that the parentheses cause the OR to be evaluated before the AND. The effect is that a given row will be selected if it meets both of the following conditions.

    a. CDEPT = 'THEO'

    b. CLABFEE = 0 OR CRED = 6

Therefore, this example, unlike the previous, will only select theology courses. Furthermore, these theology courses must meet at least one of the conditions, CLABFEE = 0 or CRED = 6. Observe the displayed result. Note that the row for course number P44, which was present in the previous example, is absent. This is because it is not a theology course.

2. Syntax: The two conditions which are OR connected within the parentheses are written on one line. This enhances readability, but it is not necessary. The following query is equivalent to the current example.

```
SELECT  *  FROM COURSE
WHERE   CDEPT = 'THEO'
AND     (CLABFEE = 0
OR      CRED = 6)
```

3. If we observe that we want six-credit theology courses or zero labfee theology courses, we might have written the following equivalent statement.

```
SELECT  *  FROM COURSE
WHERE   (CDEPT = 'THEO' AND CRED = 6)
OR      (CDEPT = 'THEO' AND CLABFEE = 0)
```

Some individuals would find this statement to be a more explicit representation of the query objective. Note that the parentheses are not required in this statement. The default hierarchy will produce the same result.

4. General Recommendation: Always utilize parentheses to make explicit the logic of your WHERE clause.

Exercises:

3I. Select all information about any six-credit philosophy course, or any course with a labfee which exceeds $200 (regardless of its department id or credits).

3J. Select all information about any three-credit course with a labfee which is less than $100 or greater than $300.

Hierachy Involving NOT

The next sample query involves all three of the Boolean operators. Recall the hierarchy is NOT, followed by AND, followed by OR. Note that this example does not adhere to the recommendation specified on the previous page; parentheses are absent. This will force you to think about the hierarchy. Again, this is a tutorial example. In practice, you should use parentheses.

Sample Query 3.11:   Display all information about all non-CIS courses or any course (regardless of department) which has a zero labfee and is worth three credits.

```
SELECT  *
FROM    COURSE
WHERE   NOT CDEPT = 'CIS'
OR      CLABFEE = 0
AND     CRED = 3
```

CNO	CNAME	CDESCP	CRED	CLABFEE	CDEPT
T11	SCHOLASTICSM	FOR THE PIOUS	3	150.00	THEO
T12	FUNDAMENTALISM	FOR THE CAREFREE	3	90.00	THEO
T33	HEDONISM	FOR THE SANE	3	0.00	THEO
T44	COMMUNISM	FOR THE GREEDY	6	200.00	THEO
P11	EMPIRICISM	SEE IT - BELIEVE IT	3	100.00	PHIL
P22	RATIONALISM	FOR CIS MAJORS	3	50.00	PHIL
P33	EXISTENTIALISM	FOR CIS MAJORS	3	200.00	PHIL
P44	SOLIPSISM	ME MYSELF AND I	6	0.00	PHIL
C33	DISCRETE MATHEMATICS	ABSOLUTELY NECESSARY	3	0.00	CIS
C44	DIGITAL CIRCUITS	AH HA!	3	0.00	CIS

Comment:

In this example, the hierarchy of operations happens to fit the objective of the sample query. However, it is better to make the logic explicit by using parentheses. The following equivalent statement does so.

```
SELECT  * FROM COURSE
WHERE   NOT CDEPT = 'CIS'
OR      (CLABFEE = 0 AND CRED = 3)
```

The above parentheses are superfluous. However, they emphasize that any given row (even a CIS row) will be selected if it has a zero labfee and is worth three credits. To perhaps overdo the use of parentheses, we rewrite the statement with parentheses enclosing the first condition to emphasize that we want the system to evaluate the NOT condition first.

```
SELECT  * FROM COURSE
WHERE   (NOT CDEPT = 'CIS')
OR      (CLABFEE = 0 AND CRED = 3)
```

Exercise:

3K. Select all information about any course with a labfee which is not greater than $100 or any other course, regardless of its labfee, which is offered by the Theology Department and is worth six credits.

The next example illustrates the use of parentheses to override the default hierarchy. In this example, the NOT is evaluated last.

Sample Query 3.12: Display all information about every row in the COURSE table except any CIS course which has a zero labfee.

```
SELECT  *
FROM    COURSE
WHERE   NOT (CDEPT = 'CIS' AND CLABFEE = 0)
```

CNO	CNAME	CDESCP	CRED	CLABFEE	CDEPT
T11	SCHOLASTICISM	FOR THE PIUS	3	150.00	THEO
T12	FUNDAMENTALISM	FOR THE CAREFREE	3	90.00	THEO
T33	HEDONISM	FOR THE SANE	3	0.00	THEO
T44	COMMUNISM	FOR THE GREEDY	6	200.00	THEO
P11	EMPIRICISM	SEE IT - BELIEVE IT	3	100.00	PHIL
P22	RATIONALISM	FOR CIS MAJORS	3	50.00	PHIL
P33	EXISTENTIALISM	FOR CIS MAJORS	3	200.00	PHIL
P44	SOLIPSISM	ME MYSELF AND I	6	0.00	PHIL
C11	INTRO TO CS	FOR ROOKIES	3	100.00	CIS
C22	DATA STRUCTURES	VERY USEFUL	3	50.00	CIS
C55	COMPUTER ARCH.	VON NEUMANN'S MACH.	3	100.00	CIS
C66	RELATIONAL DATABASE	THE ONLY WAY TO GO	3	500.00	CIS

Comments:

1. The logic expressed in this example is staightforward. We simply write a condition to identify the rows we do not want. This is

```
CDEPT = 'CIS' AND CLABFEE = 0
```

Then we negate this condition by placing a NOT in front of the entire condition, which must be enclosed by parentheses.

```
NOT (CDEPT = 'CIS' AND CLABFEE = 0)
```

2. Consider the reason the following condition without parentheses will not achieve the desired objective.

```
NOT CDEPT = 'CIS' AND CLABFEE = 0
```

The absence of parentheses means the NOT will be evaluated first, but it only applies to the first condition. This is equivalent to the following condition.

```
(NOT CDEPT = 'CIS') AND CLABFEE = 0
```

Only non-CIS rows with zero labfees would be selected by this condition. Observe that the current sample query selected some rows for CIS courses and some rows with nonzero labfees.

3. The sample query could have been expressed a number of other ways. The following conditions are logically equivalent to the current example.

- `(NOT CDEPT = 'CIS') OR (NOT CLABFEE = 0)`
- `CDEPT <> 'CIS' OR CLABFEE <> 0`

These clauses are no better than the original. We are merely illustrating logical equivalencies. To restate a point we made earlier, the issue of logic per se transcends SQL. You must be careful whenever you are writing complex queries.

Exercise:

3L. Select all information about any course except three-credit philosophy courses.

IN Keyword

The next sample query introduces the use of IN. This provides a convenient way of asking the system to select a row if a given column contains any value in a specified set of values.

Sample Query 3.13: Display the course number, description, and credits for any course which is worth 2, 6, or 9 credits.

```
SELECT  CNO,CDESCP,CRED
FROM    COURSE
WHERE   CRED IN (2, 6, 9)
```

CNO	CNAME	CDESCP	CRED
T44	COMMUNISM	FOR THE GREEDY	6
P44	SOLIPSISM	ME MYSELF AND I	6

Comments:

1. Syntax: The set of values must be enclosed within parentheses with commas separating each value. These values can be numeric (the current example) or character. Character values must be enclosed in quotes. (See next sample query.) The values in the current example happen to be written in sequence. This helps readability, but it is not required. For all practical purposes, there is no upper limit on the number of values that comprise the comparison set. (However, in SQL/DS, at least two values must be specified within the comparison set.)

2. While the IN keyword is useful, it is also superfluous. This is because any condition using IN can be replaced with an equivalent sequence of OR conditions. The following statement is equivalent to the current example.

```
SELECT  CNO,CDESCP,CRED
FROM    COURSE
WHERE   CRED=2
OR      CRED=6
OR      CRED=9
```

Exercise:

3M. Display all information about any course which has a labfee equal to any value in the following set of values: {12.12, 50.00, 75.00, 90.00, 100.00, 500.00}.

NOT IN

The next example illustrates use of the NOT IN phrase which, as you would expect, is the converse of IN. It will instruct the system to select a row if a given column value contains any value other than a value in a specified set of values.

Sample Query 3.14: Display the course name, description, and department id of any course which is not offered by the Theology or Computer and Information Science Departments.

```
SELECT  CNAME,CDESCP,CDEPT
FROM    COURSE
WHERE   CDEPT NOT IN ('THEO', 'CIS')
```

CNAME	CDESCP	CDEPT
EMPIRICISM	SEE IT - BELIEVE IT	PHIL
RATIONALISM	FOR CIS MAJORS	PHIL
EXISTENTIALISM	FOR CIS MAJORS	PHIL
SOLIPSISM	ME MYSELF AND I	PHIL

Comments:

1. Logic: The NOT IN phrase, like IN, is useful but superfluous. The current example could have contained any of the following equivalent WHERE clauses.

   ```
   WHERE NOT CDEPT = 'THEO'
   AND   NOT CDEPT = 'CIS'

   WHERE CDEPT <> 'THEO'
   AND   CDEPT <> 'CIS'

   WHERE NOT (CDEPT = 'THEO' OR CDEPT = 'CIS')
   ```

   It is permissable to place a NOT before a condition containing IN. The following WHERE clause is also equivalent to the current example. Notice that NOT appears before "CDEPT" instead of "IN."

   ```
   WHERE NOT CDEPT IN ('THEO', 'CIS')
   ```

   Using NOT IN appears to be more compact and comprehensible.

2. Syntax: Because CDEPT contains character data, the specified values ('THEO', 'CIS') must be enclosed within apostrophes and the system will perform a character-by-character compare.

3. Again, a reminder; the "¬" symbol cannot be substituted for the NOT keyword.

Exercise:

3N. Display all information about every course where the labfee is not one of the following: {12.12, 50.00, 75.00, 90.00, 100.00, 500.00}.

BETWEEN Keyword

The next sample query illustrates the use of BETWEEN to identify a range of values. A row will be selected if a given column has a value within the specified range.

Sample Query 3.15:   Display the course name and labfee of any course with a labfee between, and including, 100 and 200 dollars.

```
SELECT  CNAME,  CLABFEE
FROM    COURSE
WHERE   CLABFEE BETWEEN 100.00 AND 200.00
```

```
----------------------------------------------
CNAME                          CLABFEE
----------------------------------------------
SCHOLASTICISM                   150.00
COMMUNISM                       200.00
EMPIRICISM                      100.00
EXISTENTIALISM                  200.00
INTRO  TO  CS                   100.00
COMPUTER  ARCH.                 100.00
```

Comments:

1. Note that BETWEEN really means "between and including." The system will select rows which match the extreme values.

2. The BETWEEN keyword is also superfluous. An equivalent WHERE clause can always be written using an AND connector. The current WHERE clause could have been rewritten as

   ```
   WHERE    CLABFEE >= 100.00
   AND      CLABFEE <= 200.00
   ```

   Observe the above approach required that the column name (CLABFEE) be specified in both conditional expressions. The use of the "BETWEEN____AND____" phrase provides another approach which some users might find more attractive.

3. Although it may be grammatically correct to say "where labfee is between 200 and 100," it would be silly to code the following WHERE clause.

   ```
   WHERE CLABFEE BETWEEN 200.00 AND 100.00
   ```

   The system would interpret this clause as the following AND-connected clause which would always produce a "No Hit" situation.

   ```
   WHERE    CLABFEE >= 200.00
   AND      CLABFEE <= 100.00
   ```

   There is no number which is greater than 200 and less than 100. Hence, when using BETWEEN, always reference the smaller value first as the example illustrates.

Exercise:

30. Display the course number and labfee for any course with a labfee between and including 50.00 and 400.00 dollars.

NOT BETWEEN

The NOT BETWEEN is used to select rows where a given column value falls outside of a specified range. The next sample query is the converse of the previous. It will select every COURSE table row which was omitted from the previous result.

Sample Query 3.16:   Display the course name and labfee of any course with a labfee less than $100 or greater than $200.

```
SELECT  CNAME,  CLABFEE
FROM    COURSE
WHERE   CLABFEE  NOT  BETWEEN  100  AND  200
```

```
-----------------------------------------------
CNAME                          CLABFEE
-----------------------------------------------
FUNDAMENTALISM                  90.00
HEDONISM                         0.00
RATIONALISM                     50.00
SOLIPSISM                        0.00
DATA STRUCTURES                 50.00
DISCRETE MATHEMATICS             0.00
DIGITAL CIRCUITS                 0.00
RELATIONAL DATABASE            500.00
```

Comments:

1. Note that NOT BETWEEN will exclude extreme values from the result. This is because it is the negation of the result which would have been produced by BETWEEN. (More formally, it yields the complement of the set identified by the BETWEEN condition.)

2. The following WHERE clause is equivalent to that of the current example.

```
WHERE   CLABFEE < 100
OR      CLABFEE > 200
```

Note the comparison operators are "strictly greater than" and "strictly less than." This is because the NOT BETWEEN clause excludes extreme values from being selected.

As with any conditional expression, a NOT can precede the condition. Therefore, we could place the NOT before the column name instead of coding the NOT BETWEEN phrase. Hence, the following WHERE clause is also equivalent to that of the current example.

```
WHERE NOT CLABFEE BETWEEN 100 and 200
```

3. Again, the BETWEEN phrase must always reference the smaller value first. If we were to enter the following WHERE clause:

```
WHERE CLABFEE NOT BETWEEN 200 AND 100
```

the system would interpret this as

```
WHERE   CLABFEE < 200
OR      CLABFEE > 100
```

Every value must match this condition, which means that all rows would be retrieved. This is not the query objective.

Exercise:

3P. Display the course number and labfee of any course with a labfee which is less than $50 or greater than $400.

The next sample query shows that BETWEEN can also be used to identify a range for character string data.

Sample Query 3.17:   Display the name and labfee of any course with a course name beginning with the letter "D".

```
SELECT  CNAME, CLABFEE
FROM    COURSE
WHERE   CNAME BETWEEN 'D' AND 'DZZZ'
```

```
-----------------------------------------------
CNAME                         CLABFEE
-----------------------------------------------
DATA STRUCTURES                 50.00
DISCRETE MATHEMATICS             0.00
DIGITAL CIRCUITS                 0.00
```

Comments:

1. Recall that the EBCDIC code defines the character sequence for DB2 and SQL/DS. This was described earlier in the comments for Sample Query 1.5. Under the realistic assumption that no course name which begins with "D" will be greater than "DZZZ," this example effectively retrieves every course with a course name beginning with the letter "D".

   It is important that you understand the idea of a character sequence. Note that if "DZZZ XXX" was a legitimate course name, it would not be selected by the SELECT statement because it is greater than "DZZZ".

2. The intent of this query is to have the system search for a character string pattern in the CNAME field. This pattern is a "D" followed by any string. We will see in the next chapter that the LIKE keyword provides a far more convenient way of searching for character string patterns.

Exercise:

3Q. Display the course name and description for any course with a description which begins with the word "FOR".

The last example in this chapter does not introduce any new concepts or techniques. The sole purpose is to illustrate that any of the aforementioned techniques can be used within a single SELECT statement. The only reason that this statement is longer than previous statements is because of the relative complexity of the query objective. Examine each line of code within the statement and observe that each implements one of the SQL language constructs presented earlier in this text.

Sample Query 3.18: Display the department id, course name and labfee of any three credit CIS, THEO, or MGT course with a labfee between, and including, $50 and $300. Display the result by course name within department id sequence (ascending).

```
SELECT  CDEPT, CNAME, CLABFEE
FROM    COURSE
WHERE   CDEPT IN ('CIS', 'THEO', 'MGT')
AND     CLABFEE BETWEEN 50 AND 300
AND     CRED = 3
ORDER   BY CDEPT, CNAME
```

```
--------------------------------------------------
CDEPT   CNAME                    CLABFEE
--------------------------------------------------
CIS     COMPUTER ARCH.            100.00
CIS     DATA STRUCTURES            50.00
CIS     INTRO TO CS               100.00
THEO    FUNDAMENTALISM             90.00
THEO    SCHOLASTICISM             150.00
```

Exercise:

3R. Select the department id, course number, and description for any computer science or theology course with a labfee which is less than $100 or greater than $400. Display the result by course number within department.

SUMMARY

This chapter presented the formulation of more complex WHERE clauses by use of the traditional Boolean operators. We described the syntax and behavior of AND, OR and NOT.

```
WHERE cond1 AND cond2
        A given row is selected only if both cond1 and cond2
        are true.
WHERE cond1 OR cond2
        A given row is selected if either cond1 or cond2 or both
        are true.
WHERE NOT cond
        A given row is selected if cond is not true (is false).
```

When a complex WHERE clause contains more than two individual conditions you are encouraged to use parentheses to make explicit the order of evaluation. Otherwise the traditional hierarchy of evaluation applies. This means that NOTs are evaluated first, followed by ANDs, followed by ORs.

Two other useful keywords were presented which can help in the formulation of more compact and readable code. These are BETWEEN and IN, both of which can be prefaced by NOT. These are summarized below.

```
WHERE col BETWEEN val1 AND val2
        A given row is selected if its col value is within the
        range specified by val1 and val2.
WHERE col NOT BETWEEN val1 AND val2
        A given row is selected if its col value falls outside the
        range specified by val1 and val2.
WHERE col IN (val1,val2,...,valn)
        A given row is selected if its col value equals any of the
        specified values.
WHERE col NOT IN (val1,val2,...,valn)
        A given row is selected if its col value does not equal
        any of the specified values.
```

SUMMARY EXERCISES

The following exercises all refer to the STAFF table. The column names are ENAME, ETITLE, ESALARY, and DEPT.

3S. Display all information about any member of the Philosophy or Theology Departments.

3T. Display all information about any member of the Theology Department whose salary exceeds $52.

3U. Display the name of any staff member whose salary is greater than or equal to $52, but less than or equal to $1000.

3V. Display the name and title of any staff member assigned to the Theology Department who earns $51 or $54.

3W. Display the name and salary of any staff member whose salary equals one of the following values: 51, 53, 100, 200, 25,000.

3X. Display the names and salaries of staff members who earn less than $100 or more than $1000. Display the result in ascending sequence by name.

3Y. Display the department id of every department which employs a staff member whose salary exceeds $5000. Do not show duplicate department ids.

4

Pattern Matching

There are times when you may wish to retrieve information from rows having similar, but not necessarily equal, values in a given column. As an example, suppose you wished to display information about all introductory courses. One approach is to examine the CNAME column in the COURSE table for course names with the words "INTRODUCTION" or "INTRODUCTORY" or perhaps even "INTRO." In this case we want to select rows based upon some pattern. SQL provides a method for identifying patterns. It is not necessary to provide or even know a complete column value in order to identify a row for selection.

SQL allows us to provide partial information by using the keyword LIKE. The LIKE keyword is used in the WHERE clause in place of the comparison operator. The format is:

```
WHERE column-name LIKE pattern
```

Column-name identifies the column to be searched for the pattern. The pattern is a character string (enclosed within apostrophes). Pattern matching applies only to character string columns.

We will see that SQL must be given some idea of where the partial string of characters is located. This will be done by use of two special wildcard characters which are part of the pattern. These characters are the percent sign (%) and the underscore character (_).

USE OF PERCENT (%) SYMBOL

The first sample query in this chapter illustrates the use of the percent sign (%) in the pattern string. This symbol is interpreted as a wildcard which can represent any character string of any length. In particular, it also represents the empty string of length zero.

The following example will search the CNAME column for character strings which have "INTRO" as the five leftmost characters. The percent sign is used to represent any remaining characters.

Note that CNAME is a variable-length character column. Pattern string recognition can be used with both fixed and variable-length character columns. However, it is important to be aware of the difference. This point will be discussed later in this chapter. The first three sample queries all illustrate pattern recognition using the same variable-length character column, CNAME.

Sample Query 4.1:   Display the course number and name of all introductory courses. (More precisely, display the CNO and CNAME values of any row which has a CNAME value beginning with "INTRO".)

```
SELECT  CNO, CNAME
FROM    COURSE
WHERE   CNAME LIKE 'INTRO%'
```

```
-----------------------------------------------------
CNO     CNAME
-----------------------------------------------------
C11     INTRO TO CS
```

Comments:

1. The pattern string "INTRO%" contains one percent sign at the end. This means that any number of characters following "INTRO" will be considered to be a match. However, the characters "INTRO" must be found in the column as the leftmost characters. After these five characters SQL will consider anything found in the column to meet the selection criteria.

    If the following character strings were present in the CNAME column, they would all match the pattern used in the current example.

    ```
    "INTRODUCTION TO COMPUTERS"
    "INTRO TO COMPUTERS"
    "INTRO. TO COMPUTERS"
    "INTRODUCTORY COMPUTER SCIENCE"
    "INTRODUCTION TO COMPUTERS"
    "INTRO TO INTRODUCING"
    "INTRO"
    ```

2. Note that a CNAME value of "INTRO" matches the pattern. This is because the percent symbol also represents the empty string.

3. The following CNAME values would not match the "INTRO%" pattern.

    ```
    "AN INTRODUCTION TO CIS"
    " INTRO TO COMPUTERS"
    ```

    Both of these character strings have "INTRO", but not as the leftmost five characters. The pattern for the current example requires such.

Exercise:

4A.   Display all information about any course which has a description beginning with the string "FOR THE".

The next sample query is similar to the preceding. This time we are examining the rightmost part of a character string.

Sample Query 4.2:   Display all CNAME values which end with the letters 'CISM'.

```
SELECT  CNAME
FROM    COURSE
WHERE   CNAME LIKE '%CISM'
```

```
------------------------------------
CNAME
------------------------------------
SCHOLASTICISM
EMPIRICISM
```

Comments:

1. The placement of the percent sign at the beginning of the pattern informed the system that the desired characters would be found in the rightmost positions of the column. Zero or more characters preceding "CISM" is considered to be a match. Again, note that because the percent symbol matches the empty string, a CNAME value of "CISM" would match the current pattern.

2. It is unlikely that a variable-length character column will ever have blank characters in the rightmost position. (A designer often defines a column to be variable length just to avoid this situation.) However, it is not impossible. This can occur if the terminal operator explicitly enters trailing blanks in the column. Therefore, it is possible for the CNAME column to contain "SCHOLASTICISM ". The pattern '%CISM' would not match on this value because the last four characters "ISM " do not match "CISM."

Exercise:

4B. Display the course name and description of any course having a description which ends with the letter "E".

The next sample query illustrates the use of multiple percent symbols.

Sample Query 4.3: What are the names of courses which have the letter sequence "SC" appearing anywhere in the course name?

```
SELECT  CNAME
FROM    COURSE
WHERE   CNAME LIKE '%SC%'
```

```
-----------------------------------
CNAME
-----------------------------------
SCHOLASTICISM
DISCRETE MATHEMATICS
```

Comments:

1. The pattern "%SC%" will match on the string "SC" anywhere within the CNAME column. In particular, it will match these characters if they occur in the middle of the string. "DISCRETE MATHEMATICS" was such a match. Because the percent symbol matches on the empty string, the pattern also matches on strings which begin or end with "SC". Hence "SCHOLASTICISM" was a match.

2. Any number of percent symbols can occur within a pattern string. The following will match on any CNAME value which begins with "F", has an embedded blank, followed by "OO", and ends with a period.

```
WHERE CNAME LIKE 'F% %OO%.'
```

Exercise:

4C. Display the course number and description of any course with a period, hyphen, or exclamation mark anywhere in its description. (*Hint*: Use OR connector with multiple patterns.)

The next sample query involves pattern matching with a fixed-length character column (CDEPT). There is only one situation where fixed length character strings need special consideration. This is when you want to match on the rightmost characters of the string. This is because, unlike variable-length strings, fixed-length strings often have one or more trailing blanks. Usually this occurs because the system will attach trailing blanks to any string which is smaller than the column length. Therefore, you have to construct the pattern string to account for possible trailing blanks. This is the case with the CDEPT column, which is four characters long, but can contain department ids which are shorter.

Sample Query 4.4: Display the department id of any course where the department id ends with "S". Do not display duplicate values.

```
SELECT  DISTINCT CDEPT
FROM    COURSE
WHERE   CDEPT LIKE '%S'
OR      CDEPT LIKE '%S '
OR      CDEPT LIKE '%S  '
OR      CDEPT LIKE 'S   '
```

```
------
CDEPT
------
CIS
```

Comments:

1. It is important to understand the semantics of the sample query. We assume that stored trailing blanks are not really part of the department id. This means we would like a match on the CIS department even though the CDEPT column contains "CIS ".

    The WHERE clause has four conditions which are connected with OR operators. Each condition tests for "S" in one of the four character positions of a CDEPT value.

    -   CDEPT LIKE '%S' tests for "S" in the fourth position.
    -   CDEPT LIKE '%S ' tests for "S" in the third position followed by a space.
    -   CDEPT LIKE '%S ' tests for "S" in the second position followed by two spaces.
    -   CDEPT LIKE 'S   ' tests for "S" in the first position followed by three spaces.

2. Note that the pattern "%S%" is an inadequate solution. It will account for trailing blanks; and it will match with "CIS ". However, it will also select any row with an "S" anywhere in its course name, not necessarily the last significant (non-blank) character. This is not consistent with the query objective.

3. Note that the pattern "%S" will not work because it fails to account for the trailing blanks. The current solution is far from ideal. (Imagine if CDEPT were 50 characters long.) However, it is the best that can be realized.

Exercise:

4D. Display the department id of any course where the department id ends with "IL". Do not display duplicate values.

USE OF UNDERSCORE (_) SYMBOL

Previous examples illustrated the percent sign as a wildcard symbol which could represent a substring of any length. The next sample query introduces another wildcard symbol, the underscore (_), which will always represent exactly one character position.

Sample Query 4.5:   Display course name and department id of any course which has the letter "H" present in the second position of its department id.

```
SELECT  CNAME, CDEPT
FROM    COURSE
WHERE   CDEPT LIKE '_H_ _'
```

```
-----------------------------------
CNAME                    CDEPT
-----------------------------------
SCHOLASTICISM            THEO
FUNDAMENTALISM           THEO
HEDONISM                 THEO
COMMUNISM                THEO
EMPIRICISM               PHIL
RATIONALISM              PHIL
EXISTENTIALISM           PHIL
SOLIPSISM                PHIL
```

Comments:

1. The difference between the percent sign and the underscore is twofold. First, the percent sign allows any number of characters to match while the underscore allows only one. Second, the percent sign is considered a match if zero characters are found. The underscore always requires exactly one character to be present.

2. The CDEPT column is defined as a four-character fixed length field. The positions of the underscore characters in the pattern permit three of the characters to be of any value, including blanks. The one character present in the pattern, the letter "H," must be found precisely in the second position of the column for a match to occur.

3. An alternative solution to this sample query is presented in the second comment about the next sample query.

Exercise:

4E. Display the course name and department id of any course with a three-character department id (i.e., the fourth position is a blank).

The next sample query references a variable length column (CNAME) and uses both of the wildcard symbols.

Sample Query 4.6:   Display the names of courses which have a vowel as the second letter of their name.

```
SELECT  CNAME
FROM    COURSE
WHERE   CNAME LIKE '_A%'
OR      CNAME LIKE '_E%'
OR      CNAME LIKE '_I%'
OR      CNAME LIKE '_O%'
OR      CNAME LIKE '_U%'
```

```
-----------------------------------
CNAME
-----------------------------------
FUNDAMENTALISM
HEDONISM
COMMUNISM
RATIONALISM
SOLIPSISM
DATA STRUCTURES
DISCRETE MATHEMATICS
DIGITAL CIRCUITS
COMPUTER ARCH.
RELATIONAL DATABASE
```

Comments:

1. This example demonstrates a combination of the wildcard characters. The underscore implies that any character can appear in the first position. Each pattern is defined with a vowel in the second position, thereby identifying specific values acceptable for a match. The remaining positions of the column may be any value of any length as shown by the use of the percent sign.

2. The technique of combining wildcard characters could have been used to solve the previous sample query. The following WHERE clause would work.

   ```
   WHERE CDEPT LIKE '_H%'
   ```

   This technique is helpful with long fixed length strings because it is not necessary to type the precise number of trailing underscore symbols to match the exact column length.

3. The example showed a series of patterns, all to be tested against the same column. It might seem that there should be some shorthand method of specifying this request. Unfortunately, there is no abbreviated method available.

4. A pattern string may contain any number of wildcard symbols. For example the following WHERE clause will match on any course name with an "E" in to second position, an "I" in the sixth position and is at least ten characters long.

   ```
   WHERE CNAME LIKE '_ E _ _ _ I _ _ _ _ %'
   ```

Exercise:

4F. Display the name and description of any course where the description has "THE" in the fifth, sixth, and seventh positions, and an "A" in the tenth position.

NOT LIKE

The last sample query of this chapter illustrates the NOT LIKE phrase. As you would expect, this is used to select rows which do not conform to a specified pattern.

Sample Query 4.7:   Display the names of all courses which do not have a vowel as the second letter.

```
SELECT   CNAME
FROM     COURSE
WHERE    CNAME NOT LIKE '_A%'
AND      CNAME NOT LIKE '_E%'
AND      CNAME NOT LIKE '_I%'
AND      CNAME NOT LIKE '_O%'
AND      CNAME NOT LIKE '_U%'
```

```
------------------------------------
CNAME
------------------------------------
SCHOLASTICISM
EMPIRICISM
EXISTENTIALISM
INTRO TO CS
```

Comments:

1. The NOT LIKE phrase is similar in spirit to the NOT IN and NOT BETWEEN described in the previous chapter. NOT has the effect of selecting every row which does not match the pattern string.

2. This query could have been expressed in other ways. The example shows the NOT keyword placed immediately before the LIKE keyword. However, that is not a requirement. The WHERE clause could have been formed with the NOT before the column name.

```
WHERE    NOT CNAME LIKE '_A%'
AND      NOT CNAME LIKE '_E%'
AND      NOT CNAME LIKE '_I%'
AND      NOT CNAME LIKE '_O%'
AND      NOT CNAME LIKE '_U%'
```

Another equivalent WHERE clause is

```
WHERE NOT
         (CNAME LIKE '_A%'
OR        CNAME LIKE '_E%'
OR        CNAME LIKE '_I%'
OR        CNAME LIKE '_O%'
OR        CNAME LIKE '_U%')
```

This approach simply negates the entire WHERE clause shown in Sample Query 4.6 by enclosing the conditions in parentheses and placing a NOT in front of the entire compound condition.

Exercise:

4G. Display the course name and description of any course where the course name does not end with an "E" or an "S".

SUMMARY

The WHERE clause can contain the keyword LIKE to test for a pattern in a character string. The general format is

```
WHERE column-name LIKE pattern
```

The pattern is enclosed in quotes and may contain two special wildcard characters. The percent sign (%) represents any string of any length. The underscore (_) represents exactly one character.

SUMMARY EXERCISES

The following exercises all refer to the STAFF table. The column names are ENAME, ETITLE, ESALARY and DEPT. Note the ENAME and ETITLE are variable length fields and DEPT is a fixed length field.

4H. Display all information about any staff member whose name begins with the letters "MA".

4I. Display all information about any staff member whose title ends with the digit 1, 2, or 3.

4J. Display the name and title of any staff member who has the letter "S" occurring anywhere in both his name and title.

4K. Display the department id of any department which has the letter "E" in the third character position. Do not display duplicate values.

4L. Display the name of any staff member who has the letter "I" in the fifth character position. Display the result in ascending alphabetical sequence.

4M. Display any DEPT value which ends with the letter "G" followed by one or more trailing blanks.

5

Arithmetic Expressions

This chapter introduces some of the computational facilities supported by SQL. You will discover that it is easy to perform basic calculations with data retrieved via a SELECT statement. However, it should be noted that SQL has restrictions which prevent it from performing complex mathematical processing. This is because SQL is a database language. It is not a general purpose programming language. (Any complex mathematical processing can be done by using embedded SQL within a more powerful programming language like COBOL. The embedded SQL is used to extract the necessary data from the database, and the programming language facilities are used to perform the complex mathematical processing.) This chapter will present the use of arithmetic expressions which can be used to perform basic arithmetic in an interactive SQL environemnt.

The following sample queries illustrate simple calculations using data from the COURSE table. The results of the calculations are displayed in column format. The calculations are specified by arithmetic expressions which usually have a simple formulation. There are, however, some potentially dangerous circumstances pertaining to SQL's numeric data types, decimal accuracy, and overflow conditions which require attention to details. Some of these details are not at all "user friendly," but we believe they can be understood by anyone who works through the sample queries.

ARITHMETIC EXPRESSIONS

The ability to perform calculations on the data and derive values from existing information is useful in formulating and answering "what-if" type questions. This would prove beneficial to a college administrator involved with budgetary forecasting. We present a variety of "what-if" sample queries which require calculations involving the CLABFEE column.

Sample Query 5.1: Suppose that we are interested in the impact of increasing the labfee charges for all CIS courses. What would be the labfee for each CIS course if its current labfee is increased by $25.00? Display each CIS course name followed by the current labfee and the adjusted labfee.

```
SELECT CNAME, CLABFEE, CLABFEE + 25.00
FROM    COURSE
WHERE   CDEPT = 'CIS'
```

CNAME	CLABFEE	COL1
INTRO TO CS	100.00	125.00
DATA STRUCTURES	50.00	75.00
DISCRETE MATHEMATICS	0.00	25.00
DIGITAL CIRCUITS	0.00	25.00
COMPUTER ARCH.	100.00	125.00
RELATIONAL DATABASE	500.00	525.00

Comments:

1. Syntax: Arithmetic Expressions

   The SELECT clause begins "SELECT CNAME, CLABFEE" (which produces the first two columns of the output display) followed by "CLABFEE + 25.00" which is an arithmetic expression. This arithmetic expression caused the system to calculate and display the third column with the desired adjusted labfee values. There are many details to be addressed regarding writing correct arithmetic expressions. However, for the moment, we will simply describe an arithmetic expression as a meaningful combination of column names, constants and arithmetic operators. Usually, but not always, the formation of a "meaningful" arithmetic expression is quite simple.

   Below is a list of valid SELECT clauses which, in addition to containing column names, contain one or more arithmetic expressions. They illustrate the standard arithmetic operators of addition (+), subtraction (-), multiplication (*), and division (/).

   a.   SELECT CNAME, 25.00 + CLABFEE

   b.   SELECT CNAME, CRED * 2

   c.   SELECT CLABFEE + 25.00, CLABFEE * 2

   d.   SELECT CLABFEE + 100.00, CRED - 1, CNAME

   e.   SELECT CLABFEE * CRED / 10

   The above clauses show spaces between the arithmetic operator and the operands. This improves readability but it is not necessary.

2. Logic:

    The calcuation involved adding a constant value (25.00) to the CLABFEE value for each row in the COURSE table. It is important to realize that the system performs the calculation in a temporary storage area and has no effect on the data stored in the COURSE table. The SELECT statement only displays data or data derived by some calculations. It never changes the data stored in a table.

3. Column Headings for Calculated Columns:

    A column which contains values produced by an expression has no predefined column name. The current example shows that the system produced "COL1" as the column heading for the third column containing the results of the calculation. However, this heading will vary according to your host system. (Recall, it is possible to enter SQL commands to DB2 via SPUFI or QMF. SQL commands can be entered to SQL/DS via ISQL and QMF.)

    This "COL1" heading was assigned by QMF operating in a DB2 environment. If there were multiple expressions in the SELECT clause, QMF would have generated "COL2", "COL3", etc., as the column headings. If the query had been run against DB2 using SPUFI no column headings would be given to the result. Had the query been executed through QMF or ISQL in a SQL/DS environment, the column headings would be "EXPRESSION1", "EXPRESSION2", etc.

Exercise:

5A. What would be the credit value for each philosophy course if its current credit value was doubled? Display each course number, current credit, and adjusted credit values.

Sample Query 5.2: What would be the labfee for CIS courses if labfee charges were reduced by $25.00.

```
SELECT  CNAME, CLABFEE, CLABFEE - 25.00
FROM    COURSE
WHERE   CDEPT = 'CIS'
```

CNAME	CLABFEE	COL1
INTRO TO CS	100.00	75.00
DATA STRUCTURES	50.00	25.00
DISCRETE MATHEMATICS	0.00	-25.00
DIGITAL CIRCUITS	0.00	-25.00
COMPUTER ARCH.	100.00	75.00
RELATIONAL DATABASE	500.00	475.00

Comments:

1. This example demonstrates the subtraction operation. There are two CIS courses which have zero labfees. Subtracting $25.00 from these labfees produced negative values which were accurately presented in the result. The system automatically displays any negative value with a minus sign.

2. The column involved in the expression may be used in the WHERE clause either directly by column name or as part of an expression. (Sample Query 5.11 will illustrate an example of an expression in a WHERE clause.) It might have been a good idea to avoid any negative labfees derived in this example by eliminating any course with a labfee of less than $25 from consideration. The following statement would do so.

```
SELECT  CNAME, CLABFEE, CLABFEE - 25.00
FROM    COURSE
WHERE   CDEPT = 'CIS'
AND     CLABFEE >= 25.00
```

DATA TYPE CONSIDERATIONS

The arithmetic expressions illustrated in the first two examples did not mix data types. By this we mean that all the constants and columns referenced in the expressions were of the same data type (decimal). The CLABFEE column contains decimal values and the constant (25.00) was expressed as a decimal. The result of the calculation, as you would expect, is a decimal.

You are allowed to mix data types in arithmetic expressions. For example, the expressions in the previous examples could have been written as "CLABFEE + 25" and "CLABFEE - 25." (In fact, most people probably would write them this way.) In these expressions the CLABFEE values are still decimal values, but the constant (25) is expressed as an integer. No problems would occur in this situation. The output display of the calculated result would still be a decimal value. However, there are a number of circumstances where the mixing of data types in expressions is potentially dangerous. For this reason, we must present some introductory concepts on the different kinds on numeric data types found within SQL. (Chapter 8 will present a more comprehensive discussion of the SQL data types.) Then we describe the behavior of the system when it encounters arithmetic expressions with operators of different data types. The following sample queries describe these problems and techniques to resolve them.

SQL NUMERIC DATA TYPES

So far we have only distinguished integer values from decimal values. In the COURSE table, CRED is the only column containing integers and CLABFEE is the only column containing decimal values. Chapter 8 will present the CREATE TABLE statement which is used to establish the specific SQL data type for each column. However, it is helpful to preview some details about the numeric data types. A column which is to contain numeric values may be specified as one of four distinct data types. These are described below with comments.

1. SMALLINT: An integer whose range is -32,768 to +32,767

2. INTEGER: An integer whose range is -2,147,483,648 to +2,147,483,647

3. DECIMAL: (P,S) A decimal number where:
   - P = precision: The total number of digits (not to exceed 15)
   - S = scale: The number of digits in the fractional part of the number (i.e., after the decimal point)

4. FLOAT: A number expressed in exponential notation, sometimes called scientific notation. We will describe this notation in Sample Query 5.8.

Note that any column defined as SMALLINT or INTEGER will never be capable of storing decimal values. The CRED column was defined as SMALLINT. A column defined as DECIMAL or FLOAT can contain decimal values. The CLABFEE column was defined as DECIMAL (5,2). It can contain decimal values. Its range is −999.99 to +999.99 and its decimal accuracy is limited to two decimal position.

MIXING DATA TYPES

Whenever the system encounters an arithmetic expression with operands of different data types, it must determine the data type of the result of the calculation. It does so by following the rules specified in Figure 5.1. (We postpone discussion of FLOAT data type.) We make the following observations about the mixing of data types as shown in this figure 5.1.

1. The result of a calculation never has the SMALLINT data type. Whenever two integers are involved in a calculation, the result has an INTEGER data type.

2. Whenever we mix integer (SMALLINT or INTEGER) values with DECIMAL values, the result has a DECIMAL data type. Its accuracy is limited to 15 digits.

The next sample queries illustrate the mixing of different numeric data types in an arithmetic expression. These examples will show that the mixing of different numeric data types usually helps you express the desired calculation. However, there are some potential pitfalls which you need to be sensitive to.

	SMALLINT	INTEGER	DECIMAL
SMALLINT	INTEGER	INTEGER	DECIMAL
INTEGER	INTEGER	INTEGER	DECIMAL
DECIMAL	DECIMAL	DECIMAL	DECIMAL

Figure 5.1　Data type result of mixed mode calculation (FLOAT not shown).

The following example illustrates an arithmetic expression which contains a decimal operand (CLABFEE) and an integer operand (2).

Sample Query 5.3:   What would be the labfee for each CIS course if the labfee charges were doubled?

```
SELECT  CNAME, CLABFEE, CLABFEE * 2
FROM    COURSE
WHERE   CDEPT = 'CIS'
```

```
-----------------------------------------------------------------------
CNAME                        CLABFEE                        COL1
-----------------------------------------------------------------------
INTRO TO CS                   100.00                       200.00
DATA STRUCTURES                50.00                       100.00
DISCRETE MATHEMATICS            0.00                         0.00
DIGITAL CIRCUITS                0.00                         0.00
COMPUTER ARCH.                100.00                       200.00
RELATIONAL DATABASE           500.00                      1000.00
```

Comment:

The CLABFEE column is defined as a decimal number with two positions to the right of the decimal point. In our present query we multiplied this value by 2 (an integer). Observe that the result of the query is shown as a decimal value, not an integer. When the system processes one value of integer and another value of decimal, the result is decimal. Also note that the result has two positions to the right of the decimal point. The decimal accuracy of the result is specified to be the same as that of the decimal operand (CLABFEE).

Exercise:

1B.   What would be the labfee of a theology course if each such course was charged $10.50 per credit? Display the course number and the adjusted labfee.

DECIMAL ACCURACY CONSIDERATIONS

Arithmetic expressions can be problematic even when you do not mix data types. This is because the decimal accuracy of the calculation result may not be what is desired. Sometimes it may be too precise (Sample Query 5.4) and sometimes it is not precise enough (Sample Query 5.5).

When both operands are decimal, conventional rules of everyday arithmetic are used to determine the scale. The system produces as accurate an answer as possible. However, this accuracy may be more than is necessary.

Sample Query 5.4: What would be the labfee for each CIS course if its current labfee was multiplied by 2.375?

```
SELECT  CNAME, CLABFEE, CLABFEE * 2.375
FROM    COURSE
WHERE   CDEPT = 'CIS'
```

```
-------------------------------------------------------------------
CNAME                     CLABFEE                    COL1
-------------------------------------------------------------------
INTRO TO CS                100.00                237.50000
DATA STRUCTURES             50.00                118.75000
DISCRETE MATHEMATICS         0.00                  0.00000
DIGITAL CIRCUITS             0.00                  0.00000
COMPUTER ARCH.             100.00                237.50000
RELATIONAL DATABASE        500.00               1187.50000
```

Comments:

1. Mutiplying a value with three decimal positions (2.375) by a value with two decimal positions (CLABFEE) produces a result with a decimal accuracy of five (3 + 2) positions.

2. You would probably like to truncate the calculated result to two decimal positions. You must use the the data conversion built-in functions (to be presented in the next chapter) or you can use the reporting facilities of your host system.

The next example illustrates a special situation where the decimal accuracy is not precise enough. In fact, *decimal accuracy is totally lost.* Recall that the result of a computation with two integers produces an integer result. This is not a problem with addition, subtraction, and multiplication. But there is a potential problem with division. Consider the next sample query where the solution is wrong if you want the calculated result to contain decimal accuracy.

Sample Query 5.5:   For each philosophy course, divide the credits in half. Display the course name, credits, and the result of dividing the credits in half.

```
SELECT CNAME, CRED, CRED/2
FROM    COURSE
WHERE   CDEPT = 'PHIL'
```

CNAME	CRED	COL1
EMPIRICISM	3	1
RATIONALISM	3	1
EXISTENTIALISM	3	1
SOLIPSISM	6	3

Comments:

1. Division with integers yields an integer result. You can get lucky as with the last row where the division worked out evenly. The other three rows show that 3/2 yields 1. This is probably an unacceptable answer.

2. How do we fix this? By intentionally mixing data types and using a decimal constant as in the following correct solution.

```
SELECT CNAME, CRED, CRED/2.0
FROM    COURSE
WHERE   CDEPT = 'PHIL'
```

The next example mixes data types with the division operation. Note that because the divisor is 3, it is possible to get a repeating decimal as a result. In this case the system will display the decimal result to its maximum 15-digit precision.

Sample Query 5.6:   What would be the labfee for each CIS course if the labfee charges were cut to one-third of their present value?

```
SELECT  CNAME,  CLABFEE,  CLABFEE / 3
FROM    COURSE
WHERE   CDEPT = 'CIS'
```

```
---------------------------------------------------------------------
CNAME                       CLABFEE                        COL1
---------------------------------------------------------------------
INTRO TO CS                 100.00         33.333333333333
DATA STRUCTURES              50.00         16.666666666666
DISCRETE MATHEMATICS          0.00          0.000000000000
DIGITAL CIRCUITS              0.00          0.000000000000
COMPUTER ARCH.              100.00         33.333333333333
RELATIONAL DATABASE         500.00        166.666666666666
```

Comment:

The expression contains a decimal and an integer value. Therefore, the result is decimal. We also see that our decimal result was extended several positions to the right of the decimal point. Because the result is decimal, the system displays the result with the greatest precision possible for a decimal value. This is 15 digits. Again, note that SQL did not automatically round the result. Host system facilities can be used to round such results.

Exercise:

5C. Assume that any course with a nonzero labfee will have its labfee increased by 50%. Display the course number, current and adjusted labfees for such courses.

All previous arithmetic expressions contained a constant. This is not always the case. Consider the next example.

Sample Query 5.7: What is the labfee to credit hour ratio for courses offered by the CIS department?

```
SELECT  CNAME, CLABFEE / CRED
FROM    COURSE
WHERE   CDEPT = 'CIS'
```

```
-----------------------------------------------------------------
CNAME                                              COL1
-----------------------------------------------------------------
INTRO TO CS                              33.333333333333
DATA STRUCTURES                          16.666666666666
DISCRETE MATHEMATICS                       .000000000000
DIGITAL CIRCUITS                           .000000000000
COMPUTER ARCH.                           33.333333333333
RELATIONAL DATABASE                     166.666666666666
```

Comments:

1. In this example we derived information using two different values stored in the database. (There are no constants in the expression.) The labfee for each course was divided by the number of credits for that course to produce the calculated value we requested — the average labfee per credit. The system operates on a row-by-row basis. For each row selected, the CLABFEE value is divided by the CRED value. The result is displayed together with the corresponding CNAME value.

2. Again note that the calculation involves an integer (CRED) and a decimal (CLABFEE) and so the result is decimal. The division operation resulted in some repeating decimals which the system displayed to the maximum 15-digit accuracy.

FLOATING-POINT NUMBERS

In our previous discussion of SQL data types we bypassed examination of the FLOAT data type. This is sometimes called scientific notation or exponential notation, which is a numeric representation used by the system to store exceptionally large or small numbers. In particular, you would use this data type to represent values which are either too big or too small to be stored as a DECIMAL data type (maximum of 15 digits). Numeric values of this type are used by astronomers and nuclear physicists. A business application may occasionally require such values, but usually the DECIMAL data type satisfies its requirements. Below we present a brief description of the FLOAT data type to complete our introduction to the SQL data types.

The FLOAT data type represents numeric values using exponential notation with ten as the base value. The following examples illustrate floating-point constants which can be used in SQL arithmetic expressions.

	FLOAT Notation	Decimal Equivalent
a.	123E+06	123,000,000
b.	1.234E+10	12,340,000,000
c.	1.2E+20	120,000,000,000,000,000,000
d.	123E-06	.000123
e.	1E+00	1

With the exception of (c) all the above could have been expressed using conventional integer or decimal constants. Because 1.2E20 exceeds 15 digits we need floating-point notation to express its value. It is not necessary to explicitly enter plus signs or nonsignificant leading zeros when typing floating-point constants. For example, 123E+06 could have been written as 123E6.

Arithmetic expressions which mix data types can include floating-point values. Figure 5.2 is an extension of Figure 5.1 describing the data type of a calculated result. Note that whenever a floating-point value is part of a calculation the result is represented as a floating-point value. The next sample query demonstrates the fact.

Sample Query 5.8: What would be the labfee for each CIS course if the labfee charges were doubled (same as Sample Query 5.3)? This time display the adjusted labfee as a floating-point number.

```
SELECT CNAME, CLABFEE, CLABFEE * 2E0
FROM    COURSE
WHERE   CDEPT = 'CIS'
```

```
-----------------------------------------------------------------
CNAME                         CLABFEE                      COL1
-----------------------------------------------------------------
INTRO TO CS                    100.00                  2.000E+02
DATA STRUCTURES                 50.00                  1.000E+02
DISCRETE MATHEMATICS             0.00                  0.000E+00
DIGITAL CIRCUITS                 0.00                  0.000E+00
COMPUTER ARCH.                 100.00                  2.000E+02
RELATIONAL DATABASE            500.00                  1.000E+03
```

Comment:

This example illustrates the precedence of floating point over decimal in an arithmetic operation. CLABFEE is multiplied by a floating-point number with a value of 2. The result is displayed as a floating-point number.

	SMALLINT	INTEGER	DECIMAL	FLOAT
SMALLINT	INTEGER	INTEGER	DECIMAL	FLOAT
INTEGER	INTEGER	INTEGER	DECIMAL	FLOAT
DECIMAL	DECIMAL	DECIMAL	DECIMAL	FLOAT
FLOAT	FLOAT	FLOAT	FLOAT	FLOAT

Figure 5.2   Data type result of mixed mode calculation.

HIERARCHY OF ARITHMETIC OPERATORS

All previous arithmetic expressions contained just one arithmetic operator. It is common practice to formulate an expression which has multiple arithmetic operators. Consider the following examples where COLA, COLB, and COLC represent numeric columns in some table.

    a.   COLA + COLB + COLC + 100

    b.   COLA * COLB * 2

    c.   COLA + COLB - COLC

When an expression contains multiple arithmetic operators, the system must determine the sequence of operations. For the above examples it does not make any difference. For example, in (c) the system could add COLA and COLB to produce an intermediate result which it then subtracts COLC from. Or, it could subtract COLC from COLB and then add this result to COLA. Either way, the result is the same. Using parentheses notation, we are noting that

$$(COLA + COLB) - COLC = COLA + (COLB - COLC).$$

This equivalency does not always occur. Consider the following examples.

    d.   COLA + COLB * COLC

    e.   COLA / COLB * COLC

The order of execution for these expressions is significant. Assume COLA = 10, COLB = 5 and COLC = 2. Then (d) evaluates to 30 if you do the addition first and then multiply; it evaluates to 20 if you multiply first and then add. Expression (e) evaluates to 4 if you divide first and then multiply; it evaluates to 1 if you multiply first and then divide. You can specify the desired sequence by using parentheses. However, if the expression does not contain parentheses, the system will follow a standard hierarchy of arithmetic operations.

The hierarchy of arithmetic operators is defined as:
- Multiplication and division operations are evaluated first in a left to right scan of the expression.
- Then addition and subtraction operations are evaluated in a left to right scan of the expression.
- The order of evaluation can be changed by enclosing an expression, or part of an expression, in parentheses. Expressions within parentheses are evaluated first according to the order of the operators just mentioned. After evaluating within the parentheses, the operators outside are then evaluated.

This is the same hierarchy that applies to high school algebra and many other computer programming languages. This means that expressions (d) and (e) above would be interpreted as

COLA + (COLB * COLC)

(COLA / COLB) * COLC

It is strongly recommended that you use parentheses to make explicit the desired order of execution. We rewrite expressions (a) through (e) after substituting the aforementioned values.

a. 10 + 5 + 2 + 100 evaluates to 117
b. 10 * 5 * 2 evaluates to 100
c. 10 + 5 - 2 evaluates to 13
d. 10 + 5 * 2 evaluates to 20
e. 10 / 5 * 2 evaluates to 4

You are advised to examine to following expressions to verify your understanding of the order of execution as specified by the hierarchy.

(10 + 5) * 2 evaluates to 30
10 / (5 * 2) evaluates to 1
10 + 5 * 10 + 2 evaluates to 62
(10 + 5) * (10 + 2) evaluates to 180
(10 + 5 * 10) + 2 evaluates to 62
(10 + 5) * 10 + 2 evaluates to 152

The next sample query requires writing an arithmetic expression with multiple arithmetic operators. The order of execution is significant. Parentheses are used to make this explicit.

Sample Query 5.9.1: What would be the average labfee per credit hour for CIS courses if each labfee were increased by $25.00?

```
SELECT  CNAME,  CLABFEE,  CRED,
        (CLABFEE + 25.00) / CRED
FROM    COURSE
WHERE   CDEPT = 'CIS'
```

CNAME	CLABFEE	CRED	COL1
INTRO TO CS	100.00	3	41.666666666
DATA STRUCTURES	50.00	3	25.000000000
DISCRETE MATHEMATICS	0.00	3	8.333333333
DIGITAL CIRCUITS	0.00	3	8.333333333
COMPUTER ARCH.	100.00	3	41.666666666
RELATIONAL DATABASE	500.00	3	175.000000000

Comment:

This query required that the addition of 25.00 to each labfee be performed before the division by the number of credits. We enclosed this addition operation in parentheses to ensure that it was performed first. Had we not done this the result would have been different. (See the next sample query.)

Sample Query 5.9.2:   Erroneous attempt at previous sample query. See what happens when the necessary parentheses are omitted.

```
SELECT  CNAME, CLABFEE, CRED,
        CLABFEE + 25 / CRED
FROM    COURSE
WHERE   CDEPT = 'CIS'
```

CNAME	CLABFEE	CRED	COL1
INTRO TO CS	100.00	3	108.00
DATA STRUCTURES	50.00	3	58.00
DISCRETE MATHEMATICS	0.00	3	8.00
DIGITAL CIRCUITS	0.00	3	8.00
COMPUTER ARCH.	100.00	3	108.00
RELATIONAL DATABASE	500.00	3	508.00

Comments:

1. The absence of parentheses means that the division is performed first. This is inconsistent with the objective of the query.

2. There is another lesson to be learned from this erroneous solution. Consider the first row of the output table. The calculated result was calculated as (100.00 + 25/3) which, from a strictly mathematical viewpoint, evaluates to 108.33. Yet the output shows 108.00. What happened? Why did the system lose decimal accuracy? The reason is that division was done first using two integer values. Hence the result is an integer. The division 25/3 yields exactly 8 (not 8.33). Then this integer (8) is added to the decimal (100.00) to produce a decimal result (108.00). Again, be careful with integer division.

Exercise:

5D. For any course with a labfee less than $200, display its course number and its adjusted labfee which is $35 more than 150% of the current labfee.

Overflow Conditions

When performing arithmetic there is the possibility that the result of the operation will exceed the range of values that can be represented in a given data type. Such a case is possible if, for example, the largest allowable integer value was multiplied by another large integer. The result would be a value too large to be represented within the defined limits of integers in the system. (See the previous discussion on "Data Type Considerations" for maximum values for each data type.) When such a situation arises it is called an "overflow condition." The system responds with a warning message informing you of this event. Note, because the result could not be represented, it is lost. This requires a reformulation of the expression.

Overflow can usually be avoided by causing the system to change the data type of internal representation of the result. For example, if two large integers are to be manipulated in such a way as to produce a result beyond the range of values for an integer value (–2,147,483,648 to 2,147,483,647), then we can convert the result to a decimal number. The result is determined based on the data types of the operands. In order to influence the result it is necessary to simply include a decimal operand in the arithmetic expression in such a way as not to affect the value of the result. This could be accomplished by multiplying by 1.0 or adding 0.0. The important point is that the values of one and zero must be expressed as decimal values. The following examples illustrate the aforementioned points.

The next example does not result in an overflow condition. The calculated value is within the range of the data type of the result and so the output is accurate.

Sample Query 5.10.1: Multiply the CIS credit values by 100,000. Display the credits followed by the result of the calculation.

```
SELECT  CRED, CRED * 100000
FROM    COURSE
WHERE   CDEPT = 'CIS'
```

```
----------------------------------
   CRED                    COL1
----------------------------------
      3                  300000
      3                  300000
      3                  300000
      3                  300000
      3                  300000
      3                  300000
```

Comment:

Although CRED is defined as a SMALLINT and has a maximum value of 32767, the internal result is an INTEGER with a maximum value of 2147483647. Whenever two integer values are used in arithmetic the result is always an INTEGER, even if both operands have a data type SMALLINT. The calculated value (300,000) is within the integer range as the output illustrates.

The next example deliberately forces an overflow condition.

Sample Query 5.10.2:   Multiply the CIS credit values by 1 billion. Display the credits followed by the result of the calculation.

```
SELECT  CRED,  CRED * 1000000000
FROM    COURSE
WHERE   CDEPT = 'CIS'
```

```
-----------------------------------
  CRED              COL1
-----------------------------------
     3        ???????????
     3        ???????????
     3        ???????????
     3        ???????????
     3        ???????????
     3        ???????????
```

Comment:

The result of executing this example reveals an overflow. The CRED column is defined as SMALLINT and the constant value in the expression is an INTEGER. Therefore, the result of the operation is an INTEGER. Because the value of the result is beyond what can be represented in the system as an INTEGER an overflow results.

The column producing the overflow contains question marks in the result to reflect that the result has been lost. This indicator value is repeated for every row in which the overflow occurs. The next sample query illustrates techniques to avoid this problem

Sample Query 5.10.3:   Same as before, but avoid overflow.

```
SELECT CRED, 1.0 * CRED * 1000000000,
       (0.0 + CRED) * 1000000000
FROM   COURSE
WHERE  CDEPT = 'CIS'
```

CRED	COL1	COL2
3	3000000000.0	3000000000.0
3	3000000000.0	3000000000.0
3	3000000000.0	3000000000.0
3	3000000000.0	3000000000.0
3	3000000000.0	3000000000.0
3	3000000000.0	3000000000.0

Comment:

An overflow is prevented in the current sample query in two different ways. The COL1 result is converted to decimal by multiplying by 1.0. This has no effect on the value of the result. A decimal number can have a maximum value of 999,999,999,999,999 which is more than adequate to contain the result produced by this query.

The COL2 result is converted to a decimal value by adding 0.0 to CRED before performing the multiplication. This also has no effect on the value of the result. It is important to note that the addition of 0.0, causing the conversion to decimal, is performed before the multiplication. If the expression had been entered without parentheses as 0.0 + CRED * 1000000000, the multiplication would have been performed before the conversion to decimal had been accomplished and an overflow would have resulted.

What if the result of the calculation exceeded the 15-digit limit of decimal values? Then you would have to use floating-point constants to convert the result to floating-point notation. You would use the same technique as shown in the example, except you would use 0E0 instead of 0.0 and 1E0 instead of 1.0.

CALCULATED CONDITIONS

All previous examples have shown arithmetic expressions placed within a SELECT clause. Arithmetic expressions can also occur in a WHERE clause. The intent is to have the system display a given row only if it meets criteria determined by some calculation. Such a condition is called a calculated condition.

Sample Query 5.11:   Which CIS courses have a labfee per credit hour which is greater than $30?

```
SELECT  CNAME, CLABFEE / CRED
FROM    COURSE
WHERE   CDEPT = 'CIS'
AND     CLABFEE / CRED > 30
```

```
---------------------------------------------------------------
CNAME                                                       COL1
---------------------------------------------------------------
INTRO TO CS                              33.333333333333
COMPUTER ARCH.                           33.333333333333
RELATIONAL DATABASE                     166.666666666666
```

Comments:

1. The condition "CLABFEE / CRED > 30" contains an arithmetic expression (CLABFEE / CRED) which is evaluated for each row. If the result is greater than 30 the row is selected.

2. The example also displays the evaluation of "CLABFEE / CRED". This is not necessary, but it does help to verify the result.

3. An expression may appear on either side of the operator in a WHERE clause. In the present query the condition could have been expressed as:

```
WHERE CDEPT = 'CIS'
AND 30 < CLABFEE / CRED
```

SORTING BY A CALCULATED COLUMN

It is possible to display a result which is sorted by a column generated by an arithmetic expression. The technique is exactly the same as described in Chapter 2. However, we cannot reference a column name in the ORDER BY clause because a calculated column does not have any predefined column name. Recall that a sort column may be specified for sequencing based upon its relative position in the SELECT clause. (Review Sample Query 2.4.) The benefit of this facility now surfaces. To sort a result by a calculated column simply specify its column position in the ORDER BY clause.

Sample Query 5.12: What would be the labfee for each CIS course if its current labfee is increased by $25.00. Sort the result by the adjusted labfee value.

```
SELECT  CNAME, CLABFEE, CLABFEE + 25.00
FROM    COURSE
WHERE   CDEPT = 'CIS'
ORDER   BY 3
```

CNAME	CLABFEE	COL1
DISCRETE MATHEMATICS	0.00	25.00
DIGITAL CIRCUITS	0.00	25.00
DATA STRUCTURES	50.00	75.00
INTRO TO CS	100.00	125.00
COMPUTER ARCH.	100.00	125.00
RELATIONAL DATABASE	500.00	525.00

Comment:

It would be incorrect to specify "ORDER BY COL1". You cannot specify a column header generated by the host system in the ORDER BY clause. The only way to sort on a calculated column is to reference it by its relative position.

The final example of this chapter incorporates many of the aforementioned techniques pertaining to arithmetic expressions.

Sample Query 5.13:   We want to evaluate the impact of increasing the labfee of CIS courses by 10%. We are only concerned about those CIS courses with labfees that will exceed $100 after the increase. For these courses display the course number, the current and adjusted labfee followed by the current cost per credit and the adjusted cost per credit. Finally, display the output in ascending sequence by the adjusted labfee which should be located in the third column.

```
SELECT  CNO, CLABFEE, CLABFEE * 1.10,
        CLABFEE/CRED, (CLABFEE * 1.10)/CRED
FROM    COURSE
WHERE   CDEPT = 'CIS'
AND     CLABFEE * 1.10 > 100
ORDER   BY 3
```

CNO	CLABFEE	COL1	COL2	COL3
C11	100.00	110.0000	33.333333333333	36.66666666666
C55	100.00	110.0000	33.333333333333	36.66666666666
C66	500.00	550.0000	166.666666666666	183.33333333333

Exercise:

5E.   Assume the standard labfee should be equal to 50 times the credit value of a course. (For example, the standard labfee for a two-credit course is $100.) Display the course number and name of any course which has a labfee less than this standard. For these courses, also display the difference between the current labfee and the standard amount. Display the result in descending sequence by this difference.

SUMMARY

This chapter has introduced the use of arithmetic expressions to perform basic computations with data selected from a table. These expressions have a syntax similar to algebraic expressions described in a typical high school algebra textbook. However, in SQL you need to be careful about the data types of the columns as they can impact the decimal accuracy of the result and possibly cause an overflow condition.

The presence of an arithmetic expression in a SELECT clause will generate a column in the output display. We emphasize *column* because the next chapter introduces built-in functions, some of which perform calculations on the selected data to produce a *row* which summarizes the selected data. Figure 5.3 below outlines the conceptual difference between generating a new column in the output display using an arithmetic expression (Figure 5.3a) and generating a summary row using an arithmetic built-in function (Figure 5.3b). Chapter 6 will present the details of arithmetic built-in functions.

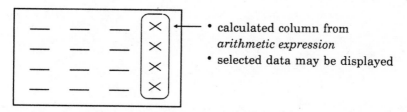

Figure 5.3a   Arithmetic expressions.

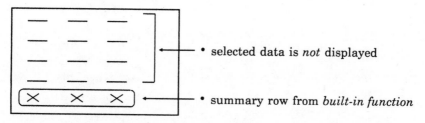

Figure 5.3b   Column built-in functions.

SUMMARY EXERCISES

The following exercises refer to the STAFF table. Recall that the column names are ENAME, ETITLE, ESALARY, and DEPT.

5F. Assume all staff members are given a $100 raise. Display the name and adjusted salary of every staff member.

5G. Assume all staff members are given a 15% raise. Display the name, old and new salary amounts for every staff member.

5H. Assume all salaries are decreased by $100. Display the name and adjusted salary of every staff member whose adjusted salary is less than $25,000.

5I. Consider only staff members whose current salary is less than $25,000. Assume this group of staff members is given a $1000 raise. Display their name and adjusted salary in descending salary sequence.

6

Built-in Functions

The previous chapter presented arithmetic expressions that allow you to perform computations with selected data. This chapter continues the same theme. We introduce SQL's built-in functions, which provide further computational facilities and also permit additional types of processing of selected data.

SQL has two categories of built-in functions. The first is column functions, which operate on a group of rows and produce a single value descriptive of a designated column for all rows in the group. Second, there are scalar functions which operate on individual rows by modifing the displayed values from a specified column. The scalar category is further subdivided into data type conversion functions, string manipulation functions, and date/time functions. This chapter will examine all of the column functions and most, but not all, of the scalar functions. Some of the scalar functions will be presented later in this book. Figure 6.1 presents an overview of SQL's built-in functions.

COLUMN FUNCTIONS

A column function is used to scan a column of selected values and perform a computation based on those values. The column functions are: AVG, SUM, MAX, MIN, and COUNT.

Column functions operate on groups of rows and generate a single row for each group. At the outset we will simply consider the entire COURSE table as a single group. Sample Queries 6.1 through 6.8 will select rows from this group and then apply column functions to produce a result consisting of a single row. Thereafter, we introduce the GROUP BY clause, which decomposes selected rows into multiple groups and applies the function to each separate group.

Column Functions	Scalar Functions		
	Data Type Conversions	String Manipulation	Date/Time
SUM	DECIMAL	LENGTH	DATE
AVG	INTEGER	SUBSTR	DAY
MIN	FLOAT	VALUE	DAYS
MAX	DIGITS		MONTH
COUNT	HEX		YEAR
	VARGRAPHIC		TIME
			TIMESTAMP
			MICROSECOND
			SECOND
			MINUTE
			HOUR
			CHAR

Figure 6.1   SQL built-in functions.

AVG Function

The first sample query applies the AVG function to the entire COURSE table which is treated as a single group.

Sample Query 6.1: What is the average labfee for all courses described in the COURSE table?

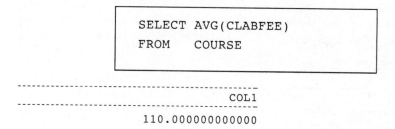

```
SELECT  AVG(CLABFEE)
FROM    COURSE
```

```
----------------------------------------------------
                                            COL1
----------------------------------------------------
            110.000000000000
```

Comments:

1. A column function returns a result of the same data type as the column to which it is applied. CLABFEE is defined as a decimal value. Therefore, the result produced by the AVG function is also decimal.

2. The AVG function is applied to all the CLABFEE values in the COURSE table. Because this function must perform a division, the result is displayed to the maximum decimal accuracy of 15 digits.

3. The result is a calculated value, not a value actually stored in the table. Therefore, the same rules apply regarding column headings as did with the calculated columns discussed in Chapter 5. (See Sample Query 5.1.)

4. Note the value returned by the AVG function is a single row. For this reason, it makes no sense to include an ORDER BY clause to sort the result. However, it would not cause an error.

5. In this example the group processed was the entire table. This does not have to be the case. A column function could be applied to a subset of rows by using a WHERE clause to form a smaller group. See the next sample query.

MIN and MAX Functions

The next sample query applies multiple column functions to a group which is a subset of rows from the COURSE table.

Sample Query 6.2:   What are the lowest and highest labfees for courses offered by the Philosophy Department?

```
SELECT MIN(CLABFEE), MAX(CLABFEE)
FROM   COURSE
WHERE  CDEPT = 'PHIL'
```

```
-------------------------------------
      COL1              COL2
-------------------------------------
      .00             200.00
```

Comments:

1. The present query demonstrates that column functions can be applied to a subset of the table by specifying selection criteria in a WHERE clause.

2. The SELECT clause contains multiple built-in functions, MIN and MAX, both of which are applied to the same CLABFEE column. It is also possible to use the same function with different columns. It is even possible to apply the same function to the same column more than once in a single SELECT clause.

3. Again, we note that a column function returns a result of the same data type as the column to which it is applied. The labfee column is defined as a decimal value. Therefore, the result of the MIN and MAX functions is also decimal.

It is reasonable to ask about the largest and smallest values of character string data. Therefore, the system will allow the MAX and MIN functions to be applied to columns containing character data.

Sample Query 6.3: What are the course numbers of the courses with the largest and smallest values in the CNO column? In other words, if the values in the CNO column were arranged in alphabetical order, what would be the first and last values?

```
SELECT  MIN(CNO), MAX(CNO)
FROM    COURSE
```

COL1	COL2
C11	T44

Comments:

1. When MAX and MIN are used with character data the EBCDIC coding scheme is used to determine the largest and smallest values. Review Sample Query 1.5 for an overview of the EBCDIC sequence.

2. It is unreasonable to apply the SUM and AVG functions to character data. Hence, the system will reject any attempt to do so.

Exercises:

6A. Display the average, maximum, and minimum course labfees for those CIS courses which have non-zero labfees.

6B. Display the first course name which appears in alphabetical sequence.

COUNT(*) Function

The next two sample queries illustrate variations on the COUNT function. The first variation, COUNT(*), determines the number of rows selected by a SELECT statement.

Sample Query 6.4:   How many theology courses are recorded in the COURSE table?

```
SELECT  COUNT ( * )
FROM    COURSE
WHERE   CDEPT = 'THEO'
```

```
--------------------
          COL1
--------------------
           4
```

Comments:

1. COUNT(*) simply counts the number of rows which match the selection criteria. The result is always an integer.

2. COUNT(*) is different from the other column functions in that it does not consider any values within the selected rows. It merely notes the presence of a row which matches the selection criteria.

COUNT (DISTINCT) Function

The second variation of the COUNT function allows us to examine the values in a specified column to determine how many unique values are present in that column.

Sample Query 6.5: How many different academic departments offer courses?

```
SELECT  COUNT(DISTINCT CDEPT)
FROM    COURSE
```

```
--------------------
          COL1
--------------------
            3
```

Comments:

1. The COUNT (DISTINCT) built-in function is used to determine the number of unique values that exist for a particular column. Unlike COUNT(*), this form of the COUNT function must examine column values.

2. The result informs us that there are three different departments which offer courses. (We do not learn the names of the departments or how many courses each department offers.) If a department offers more than one course, it is only counted once because of the DISTINCT keyword. This is similar to the way the DISTINCT keyword eliminated duplicate rows from the result of queries discussed earlier. It now serves to ignore duplicate values in the count performed by the COUNT function.

SUM Function

Sample Query 6.6:   What is the sum of all the labfee values for CIS courses?

```
SELECT  SUM(CLABFEE)
FROM    COURSE
WHERE   CDEPT = 'CIS'
```

```
--------------------
          COL1
--------------------
      750.00
```

Comment:

This query demonstrates the SUM column function, which allows the values of a numeric column to be totaled. In this query all six rows identifying the computer science department courses were selected. Their labfee values were added together and the total presented as the result of the query.

Exercise:

6C. How many courses are offered by the Philosophy Department and what is the total labfee for these courses?

Use of DISTINCT

Each of the column functions allows the DISTINCT keyword to be used as part of the statement, thus allowing only unique values to be considered. Any value which appears in more than one row in the identified column will be used only once to produce the function result. Sample Query 6.5 has already demonstrated DISTINCT used with the COUNT function. The next sample query demonstrates DISTINCT used with the SUM function.

Sample Query 6.7:   What is the total of the unique labfee values for computer science courses?

```
SELECT  SUM(DISTINCT CLABFEE)
FROM    COURSE
WHERE   CDEPT = 'CIS'
```

```
--------------------
          COL1
--------------------
     650.00
```

Comments:

1. The output value (650.00) is the result of applying the SUM function to all distinct CLABFEE values for rows corresponding to the CIS Department. Examination of the CIS rows shows that two CIS courses have the same labfee value of 100.00. The effect of specifying DISTINCT before CLABFEE in the function argument is to use only one occurrence of this value in the computation. This accounts for the difference between the 650.00 result shown above and the 750.00 result shown for the previous sample query.

2. DISTINCT can be used with any column function. With the AVG function only distinct values are considered. When used with the MIN and MAX functions, it serves no real purpose because the smallest and largest values will be the same even if duplicate values exist in more than one row.

USING BUILT-IN FUNCTIONS WITH ARITHMETIC EXPRESSIONS

Built-in functions can be used with arithmetic expressions to have the system perform more complex calculations. A function may be applied to an expression or an expression can contain a function.

Sample Query 6.8: Display two values. The first is the sum of all labfees, assuming each has been increased by $25. The second is the result of adding $25 to the sum of all the labfees.

```
SELECT  SUM(CLABFEE+25),
        SUM(CLABFEE)+25
FROM    COURSE
```

```
-------------------------------------
           COL1        COL2
-------------------------------------
         1890.00     1565.00
```

Comments:

1. COL1: SUM(CLABFEE+25)

    This sample query further demonstrates the capabilities of using calculated values. The expression, CLABFEE+25, constitutes the argument of the function. The system will increment each CLABFEE by 25 and then apply SUM to these values to determine the result.

2. COL2: SUM(CLABFEE)+25

    Note the difference between this computation and the previous. Here the SUM was first evaluated using just CLABFEE as its argument. This intermediate result (1540.00) was then increased by 25 to produce the displayed result.

3. Complex Arithmetic Expressions

We are not limited to expressions with just one column value and constant. Built-in functions can be applied to any arithmetic expression with one important exception. A column function cannot use an expression as an argument if that expression already contains a column function. In other words, we cannot nest column functions within each other.

Exercise:

6D. Assume new labfees are to be calculated at $50 for each credit. What would be the average labfee for courses offered by the Theology Department? Display the result as a decimal value.

A COMMON ERROR

The SELECT clauses in all the previous examples in this chapter have contained built-in functions and only built-in functions. It seems reasonable that you might like the output to contain both raw values from a table along with some calculated values produced by a built-in function. For example, you might like to calculate average labfees for each academic department and display each value along with the corresponding department name. You might be inclined to code the following statement to achieve this objective.

```
SELECT  CDEPT, AVG(CLABFEE)
FROM    COURSE
```

This statement causes an error. Notice that the SELECT clause contains both a column name and a column built-in function. This is illegal unless the column name is referenced by a GROUP BY clause. The next section will present the GROUP BY clause.

GROUP BY Clause

SQL provides the capability of forming smaller groups from all of the rows in the entire table and then having the column functions applied to each group. In the same way that we might manually separate each group through the WHERE clause and operate on that group, the system does this for us in the context of a single query. The column that the rows are to be grouped by is identified in the GROUP BY clause. When a GROUP BY clause is included in a query, all the selected rows are further arranged or grouped by a common value within the named column. This process is performed automatically without the need to specify actual values that may be present in the grouping column. Then the column function is applied to each group.

Sample Query 6.9:   For each department which offers courses, determine the average labfee for courses offered by the department.

```
SELECT  CDEPT, AVG(CLABFEE)
FROM    COURSE
GROUP   BY CDEPT
```

```
-------------------------------------------------
CDEPT                            COL1
-------------------------------------------------
CIS            125.000000000000
PHIL            87.500000000000
THEO           110.000000000000
```

Comments:

1. The GROUP BY clause resulted in all COURSE rows being effectively reorganized in an intermediate result where the rows are grouped by the CDEPT column. This intermediate result has all rows with the same value in the CDEPT column placed in separate groups.

   In the present example all rows were arranged by common CDEPT values. After the groups were formed, the AVG function was applied to the CLABFEE values in each group. Because there are three distinct CDEPT values (CIS, PHIL, THEO), three groups were formed and three averages returned, each in a separate row.

2. Note the SELECT clause contains a column name, CDEPT, along with a column function. The CDEPT value can be displayed with the function results because of the presence of the GROUP BY CDEPT clause. This column value is a characteristic of the group. (It is the same for every value in the group.) Therefore, it may be displayed with the summary information produced by the function.

3. The database is not at all changed by the use of the GROUP BY clause. The rows of the table being selected from are not actually rearranged in the table.

4. Because multiple rows are displayed, it makes sense to consider sorting the result. Note, however, that the output is already sorted by the CDEPT column. This occurred because the system will establish an internal sequence to establish the groups. Hence, the displayed sequence is somewhat of an accidental side effect of the grouping. Future enhancements to the system could mean that grouping is done by some other technique. Therefore, it is best to include an ORDER BY clause to explicitly indicate the desired sequence which may or may not be the same as any sort done for the purpose of grouping. See the next sample query.

The WHERE clause can be used to include or exclude certain rows from consideration *prior to* the formation of groups. The next query illustrates this point. It also explicitly specifies the sequence of the output display.

Sample Query 6.10:   For each department which offers courses, determine the average labfee of all three credit courses offered by the department. Display the output in ascending sequence by department id.

```
SELECT  CDEPT, AVG(CLABFEE)
FROM    COURSE
WHERE   CRED = 3
GROUP   BY CDEPT
ORDER   BY CDEPT
```

```
-------------------------------------------------
CDEPT                             COL1
-------------------------------------------------
CIS             125.000000000000
PHIL            116.666666666666
THEO             80.000000000000
```

Comments:

1. The example selected just the three credit courses for inclusion in the groups. We emphasize that this selection applied to individual rows (not the groups) and occurred before the formation of the groups.

2. Compare the output with that of the previous example. The average labfee for the CIS Department is unchanged because all its courses are worth three credits. However, the six-credit courses offered by the Philosophy and Theology Departments were excluded from the groups. Hence, their average labfee values differ from the previous example.

3. What if the selection criteria excludes every row from a group? Then no group is formed and none appears in the output display. See Sample Query 6.12.

4. The ORDER BY clause established the sort sequence. Again, because this sequence corresponds to that done by the system to establish the groups, the output would be the same if we omitted the ORDER BY clause. However, it is best to include it. We reiterate a point made in Chapter 2. The ORDER BY clause is always the last clause in a SELECT statement.

5. Recall that the ORDER BY clause can reference a column by its relative position. The ORDER BY clause could have been written as "ORDER BY 1". However, the GROUP BY clause must explicitly reference a column by its name (i.e., "GROUP BY 1" is *invalid*).

Exercises:

6E. For each department which offers courses, display the department id followed by the total number of credits offered by the department.

6F. Do not consider six-credit courses. For each department which offers courses, display the department id followed by the total of the labfees for courses offered by the department.

Sometimes a particular group may consist of just one row. The next query illustrates this situation.

Sample Query 6.11:   For each distinct labfee value, determine the total number of credits for courses having this labfee value. Sort the result by labfee in descending order.

```
SELECT  CLABFEE,  SUM(CRED)
FROM    COURSE
GROUP   BY CLABFEE
ORDER   BY CLABFEE DESC
```

```
-----------------------------------
    CLABFEE        COL1
-----------------------------------
    500.00            3
    200.00            9
    150.00            3
    100.00            9
     90.00            3
     50.00            6
      0.00           15
```

Comments:

1. There are seven distinct CLABFEE values recorded in the COURSE table. The system formed a group corresponding to each of the seven values. The CLABFEE values of 90.00, 150.00, and 500.00 only occurred once in the table. Therefore, the system formed a group consisting of one row for each of these values. The sum of the credits for such values is what you would expect, namely, just the credit value itself.

2. The ORDER BY clause was used to establish a sort sequence which is probably different from the one done by the system for the purpose of grouping.

Sometimes a situation occurs where the selection criteria implies that no rows are selected for a particular group. This simply means that the group is never formed. Hence, the output will not contain a row corresponding to any such group.

Sample Query 6.12: For each department which offers six-credit courses, display the average labfee of the six-credit courses.

```
SELECT  CDEPT, AVG(CLABFEE)
FROM    COURSE
WHERE   CRED = 6
GROUP   BY CDEPT
```

```
-------------------------------------------------
CDEPT                              COL1
-------------------------------------------------
PHIL                      0.000000000000
THEO                    200.000000000000
```

Comments:

1. The WHERE clause eliminated any three-credit courses from consideration. Hence, the group formed for the CIS Department, which only offers three-credit courses, was empty. The system does not display information about such groups in the output.

2. Note that because the Philosophy and Theology Departments each offer just one six-credit course, the PHIL and THEO groups each contained just one row. If you wanted to know the number of rows for each group, you could apply the COUNT(*) function.

HAVING Clause

The absence of a CIS group in the previous example occurred because the WHERE clause "just happened" to exclude every CIS row from the group. Sometimes we want to explicitly include just certain identifiable groups in the output display. The HAVING clause is used for this purpose. *We emphasize that the HAVING clause only applies to groups, whereas the WHERE clause only applies to individual rows.*

Sample Query 6.13:   Display the department id and average labfee for any department where that average exceeds $100.

```
SELECT  CDEPT, AVG(CLABFEE)
FROM    COURSE
GROUP   BY CDEPT
HAVING AVG(CLABFEE) > 100
```

```
-------------------------------------------------
CDEPT                          COL1
-------------------------------------------------
CIS              125.000000000000
THEO             110.000000000000
```

Comments:

1. We have introduced another clause in the SELECT statement called the HAVING clause. Its function is to specify conditions for groups similar to the way the WHERE clause specifies conditions for rows. In row-level processing the WHERE clause identifies conditions which must be met for a row to be retrieved. Any row which does not meet the conditions will not be retrieved, and is removed from any further processing. The HAVING clause works in a similar manner, but with regard to groups rather than to rows. The GROUP BY clause is used to specify how groups are formed. After the groups have been formed, a group must match the condition specified by the HAVING clause in order to be displayed.

2. Syntax: The HAVING clause can only be present if the statement contains a GROUP BY clause. The HAVING clause must immediately follow the GROUP BY clause.

3. The condition specified on the HAVING clause contains a reference to the function value, AVG(CLABFEE). This is almost always the case. In the current example, the HAVING clause condition cannot reference a specific column at the row level. For example, "HAVING CLABFEE = 0" would result in an error. This occurs because the CLABFEE value is not present in the group after the AVG function has been applied. The condition can only reference a value which is present after the group has been formed.

4. As with WHERE conditions we can use NOT to exclude certain groups from the display. For example, the following HAVING clause would display those groups with an average labfee which is not greater than $100.

```
HAVING NOT AVG(CLABFEE) > 100
```

Exercise:

6G. Display the department id and maximum labfee for any department which offers a course where the labfee exceeds $300.

6H. Display the department id and total number of credits offered by the department if that total exceeds 15.

A statement can contain both a WHERE clause and a HAVING clause. The WHERE clause will initially select rows for inclusion into groups and a HAVING clause will subsequently select just certain groups for display. The following query is a modification of the previous, which excludes the Theology Department from consideration.

Sample Query 6.14: For every department, except the Theology Department, which has an average labfee over $100, display its department id followed by its average labfee.

```
SELECT  CDEPT, AVG(CLABFEE)
FROM    COURSE
WHERE   NOT CDEPT = 'THEO'
GROUP   BY CDEPT
HAVING  AVG(CLABFEE) > 100
```

```
-----------------------------------------------
CDEPT                           COL1
-----------------------------------------------
CIS                 125.000000000000
```

Comment:

It is important that you understand the logical sequence of the operations SQL follows in response to this statement. First, the WHERE clause prohibits the formation of a group for the Theology Department (even though its average labfee does exceed $100). This means that the intermediate result consists of two groups corresponding to the Philosophy and Computer Science Departments. Thereafter, the HAVING clause selects the CIS Department for display because, unlike the Philosophy Department, its average labfee exceeds $100. This process is outlined in Figure 6.2.

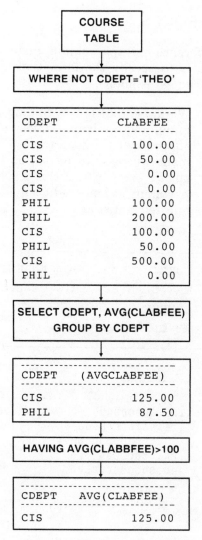

Figure 6.2   Logical sequence of operations for Sample Query 6.14.

Exercises:

6I.   Only consider three-credit courses. Display the department id and total labfee for courses offered by each department if the total is less than or equal to $150.

6J.   Do not consider courses with a labfee over $400. Display
the department id and maximum labfee charged by the
department if that maximum exceeds $175.

MULTILEVEL GROUPS

It is possible to reference multiple column names in the GROUP BY clause. The intent is to specify the formation of subgroups within groups. Consider the next example.

Sample Query 6.15:   We are interested in finding the average, maximum, and minimum labfee values for all courses offered by each department. Within each department we need to have this information broken out for each distinct credit value. Display the department id and credit value followed by the requested statistics.

```
SELECT  CDEPT, CRED, AVG(CLABFEE),
        MAX(CLABFEE), MIN(CLABFEE)
FROM    COURSE
GROUP   BY CDEPT, CRED
```

CDEPT	CRED	COL1	COL2	COL3
CIS	3	125.000000000000	500.00	.00
PHIL	3	116.666666666666	200.00	50.00
PHIL	6	.000000000000	.00	.00
THEO	3	80.000000000000	150.00	.00
THEO	6	200.000000000000	200.00	200.00

Comments:

1. The sample query requested two levels of grouping to be applied. First, all courses had to be grouped by department. This was accomplished by specifying the CDEPT column in the GROUP BY clause. Second, within each of the department groups smaller groups needed to be formed based on like credit values. This was accomplished by specifying the CRED column after the CDEPT column in the GROUP BY clause. In the same way that we are able to specify different levels of ordering with the ORDER BY clause, we can also specify different levels of grouping with the GROUP BY clause. The maximum number of columns allowed in a GROUP BY clause is, for all practical purposes, unlimited.

   One major difference between the GROUP BY and the ORDER BY clauses is that all columns identified in the ORDER BY clause must also appear in the SELECT clause. This is not necessary with the GROUP BY clause. However, if the grouping columns are not selected, the result may be confusing or ambiguous.

2. It can be observed from the results that all of the CIS Department courses have the same CRED value of 3. This is apparent because there is only a single row produced with a CDEPT value of "CIS". Remember that a column function always produces a single row for each group of records to which it is applied.

   In the cases of the PHIL and THEO departments, two rows were returned, indicating that these departments have courses with two different CRED values, 3 and 6.

The HAVING clause can be used with multilevel grouping to select just certain groups for display.

Sample Query 6.16:   Extend the previous query by retrieving the average, maximum, and minimum labfee values by credit within department only for those groups which have a maximum labfee value greater than zero.

```
SELECT CDEPT, CRED, AVG(CLABFEE),
       MAX(CLABFEE), MIN(CLABFEE)
FROM   COURSE
GROUP  BY CDEPT, CRED
HAVING MAX(CLABFEE) > 0
```

CDEPT	CRED	COL1	COL2	COL3
CIS	3	125.000000000000	500.00	.00
PHIL	3	116.666666666666	200.00	50.00
THEO	3	80.000000000000	150.00	.00
THEO	6	200.000000000000	200.00	200.00

Comment:

An examination of the query results reveals that the HAVING clause has eliminated one row from the output display. This is the row corresponding to the six-credit philosophy group which consisted of one row having a zero labfee. Hence, the maximum labfee of this group did not match the HAVING condition.

In Chapter 3 we learned that the WHERE clause can contain multiple conditions connected with the Boolean operators (AND and OR). Likewise, a HAVING clause can have multiple conditions connected by Boolean operators. Again, the only difference is that the conditions pertain to group values.

Sample Query 6.17: What is the average department labfee value for those departments where this average is greater than $100 and the department offers fewer than six courses?

```
SELECT  CDEPT, AVG(CLABFEE)
FROM    COURSE
GROUP   BY CDEPT
HAVING  AVG(CLABFEE) > 100
AND     COUNT(*) < 6
```

```
-------------------------------------------------
CDEPT                          COL1
-------------------------------------------------
THEO              110.000000000000
```

Comment:

From this example query we see that it is possible to specify more than one condition in a HAVING clause. Both conditions reference column functions which are applied to the groups formed by the GROUP BY clause. Both of these conditions must be met by any group if it is to be displayed because AND was used to connect the conditions. The same rules of logic and hierarchy of Boolean operators apply to the HAVING clause with multiple conditions as apply to the WHERE clause.

FINAL COMMENTS ON THE COLUMN FUNCTIONS

HAVING Clause

The HAVING clause specifies a condition applied to groups which must be met in order for that group to be displayed. The HAVING condition must reflect a group level value, something common to all rows in the group. Therefore, in most cases it is necessary to specify a column function in the HAVING clause. It is also possible, however, to specify the name of a grouping column and some condition which that column must meet for all rows in the group. Such cases would be statements like:

```
SELECT CDEPT, CLABFEE
FROM   COURSE
GROUP  BY CDEPT, CLABFEE
HAVING CLABFEE > 0

SELECT CDEPT, AVG(CLABFEE)
FROM   COURSE
GROUP  BY CDEPT
HAVING CDEPT LIKE '_ H _ _'
```

These queries are acceptable to the system because the column values are common to all rows in the group. Hence, they are group level values.

Null values

A column function might return a questionable result if it is executed with any column argument which contains null values. Because the COURSE table has no null values, the previous sample queries avoided this complexity. This topic will be discussed in detail in Chapter 10.

Limitations of Grouping

When the column functions are applied to groups, the values of the individual rows are no longer available for display. Many reports show both detail lines (corresponding to rows in the table) and summary lines (corresponding to the group statistics). For example, we might like to see the following output.

```
-----------------------
CDEPT     CLABFEE
-----------------------
CIS         50.00
CIS        100.00
CIS          0.00
CIS          0.00
CIS        100.00
CIS        500.00
          ----------
           750.00
```

However, because the column functions "compress" the individual row values, such reports cannot be directly generated by SQL. Again, the host system interface can serve to generate such control break summary reports. You would use SQL to select the individual rows. The host system interface, for example QMF, would be used to display the detail lines corresponding to the rows and the summary lines at specified control breaks.

SCALAR BUILT-IN FUNCTIONS

We now turn our attention to the SQL scalar functions. Unlike the column functions, the scalar functions do not operate at the group level. (i.e., they don't "compress" a group of rows into a single row). Instead these functions operate at the row level. A scalar function simply modifies values in an intermediate result or output display. There are three categories of scalar functions:

1. Data type conversion

2. String manipulation

3. Date/time processing

The present chapter shall cover almost all scalar functions in the first two categories. The date and time functions will be discussed in Chapter 7.

Data-Type Conversion Functions

In Chapter 5 we saw that we had to be sensitive to the data types of values involved in arithmetic operations. There were circumstances where we had to "play games" with a value by adding 0.0 or multiplying by 1.0 to establish an intermediate decimal data type. It is best to avoid such implicit game playing where possible. The scalar functions can help by providing explicit facilities for data-type conversion.

Scalar conversion functions provide a means of converting the value of data from one data type to another. This is not a permanent change to the internal representation of the stored data. Instead, these functions modify the data type of a column for the purposes of adjusting the format of the output or to facilitate arithmetic operations. Most of the functions allow different numeric data types to be converted to other numeric data types. One function allows numeric data to be converted to a character string representation.

We note that we are discussing data types prior to our discussion of the CREATE TABLE command, which initially defines the data type for each column. This should not present any problem for the professional programmer. Other readers may find this topic a little more difficult to understand. Nonprogrammers are encouraged to read all the sample queries except 6.19 on the HEX function and 6.20 on the VARGRAPHIC function. They are also encouraged to reread this section after studying the CREATE TABLE command presented in Chapter 8.

String Manipulation Functions

Thus far, the only thing we have done with character string data is to display it. What if the current length or format of the character string is not compatible with the desired output format? Then consider use of the scalar string manipulation functions. These functions provide a means of manipulating character string data. (Some of these functions can accept numeric arguments. However, you will find greatest application with character string data.) We will discuss all string manipulation functions with the exception of the VALUE function, which we defer until Chapter 10.

Conversion Functions: INTEGER, FLOAT, DECIMAL, and DIGITS

The next sample query illustrates the more useful data conversion functions. Subsequent sample queries will present more practical applications of these functions.

Sample Query 6.18: Use data conversion functions to display each CIS labfee (defined as a five-digit decimal with two positions after the decimal point) as an integer, a floating-point number, a seven-digit decimal with three positions after the decimal point, and a character string.

```
SELECT  CLABFEE,
        INTEGER(CLABFEE),  FLOAT(CLABFEE),
        DECIMAL(CLABFEE,7,3),  DIGITS(CLABFEE)
FROM    COURSE
WHERE   CDEPT = 'CIS'
```

CLABFEE	COL1	COL2	COL3	COL4
100.00	100	+1.000E+02	100.000	10000
50.00	50	+5.000E+01	50.000	05000
.00	0	+0.000E+00	.000	00000
.00	0	+0.000E+00	.000	00000
100.00	100	+1.000E+02	100.000	10000
500.00	500	+5.000E+02	500.000	50000

Comments:

1. COL1: INTEGER(CLABFEE)

   The INTEGER function produces an integer representation of its numeric argument. Only the integer (whole number) part of the argument is included in the result even if a decimal number is input to the function. This means the decimal component of the argument is truncated. Therefore, if a CIS course had a CLABFEE value of 499.99, the conversion would yield 499. Note that COL1 above contains integer values without leading zeros.

2. COL2: FLOAT(CLABFEE)

The FLOAT function produces a floating-point representation of its numeric argument. COL2 above shows the result of displaying the floating-point equivalent of the CIS labfee values.

3. COL3: DECIMAL(CLABFEE,7,3)

The DECIMAL scalar function allows any numeric data type to be specified as the first operand and converted to a decimal value. The second and third operands are optional. The second operand, if present, must be in the range of 1 to 15 and indicates the precision of the result. The third operand, if present, must be in the range of 0 to the total precision of the number, and indicates the scale. A scale of 0 is assumed if the third operand is omitted. If the second operand is not present, the precision is determined by the data type of the first operand. To determine the default precision, a value of 15 is used if the number being converted is either a floating-point number or a decimal number. A value of 11 is used if the value is an integer, and a value of 5 if it is a small integer.

4. COL4: DIGITS(CLABFEE)

The DIGITS function produces a character string representation of the digits in the data item. We have already noted that the CLABFEE column consists of a total of five positions. The result of the DIGITS function was to display all five digits, without regard to the scale of the number (there is no decimal point in the result). If the input to the function was a negative number there would be no sign in the result. The function produces the digits of the absolute value of the argument. Observe that leading zeros are not suppressed. The entire length of the column is used to display the digits. When the argument of the function is a small integer, the result is five digits. When the argument is an integer, the result is 10 digits. Finally, as the current example illustrates, when the argument is a decimal value (CLABFEE), the result contains as many digits as are in the precision of the number.

Later we will discuss the string manipulation functions which only operate on character data. If you want to use these functions with numeric data, first apply the DIGITS function to convert the numeric data to character format. Then apply the string manipulation functions. (See Sample Query 6.25.)

HEX Function

The HEX and VARGRAPHIC functions are probably of interest to professional programmers only. We cover them briefly here for the sake of completeness. (If you are not acquainted with the basic concepts pertaining to the internal machine representation of data, you should skip ahead to Sample Query 6.21.)

The HEX function produces a character string result which shows the hexadecimal representation of each byte of the argument. Each set of two hexadecimal digits in the resulting string represents one byte in the argument. The HEX conversion function can accept any data type as an argument. The only restrictions which apply to the argument are that if it is a character string, it cannot have a maximum length that is greater than 254 and if it is a graphic string, its maximum length cannot be greater than 127.

Sample Query 6.19: For each CIS course, display its CRED, CLABFEE and CDEPT value along with their corresponding hexadecimal representations.

```
SELECT  CRED, HEX(CRED), CLABFEE,
        HEX(CLABFEE), CDEPT, HEX(CDEPT)
FROM    COURSE
WHERE   CDEPT = 'CIS'
```

CRED	COL1	CLABFEE	COL2	CDEPT	COL3
3	0003	100.00	10000C	CIS	C3C9E240
3	0003	50.00	05000C	CIS	C3C9E240
3	0003	.00	00000C	CIS	C3C9E240
3	0003	.00	00000C	CIS	C3C9E240
3	0003	100.00	10000C	CIS	C3C9E240
3	0003	500.00	50000C	CIS	C3C9E240

Comments:

1. COL1 of the result is a hexadecimal representation of CRED, which is defined as a small integer value.

2. The values in COL2 of the result are the hexadecimal representations of the CLABFEE values. These are the internal representations of decimal numbers. The "10000C" in the first row is actually the digits "10000" (note that there is no decimal point) followed by a "C" which is the sign of the number.

3. COL3 in the result shows the hexadecimal representation of a character string. These hexadecimal numbers are the EBCDIC representation of the characters in the string.

VARGRAPHIC FUNCTION

The input to the VARGRAPHIC function is a character string and the result is a varying length graphic string of double-byte character set (DBCS) characters. DBCS characters are used by national languages such as Japanese, which have more symbols than can be represented in the 256 representations of EBCDIC.

Sample Query 6.20:   Display "CIS" and its corresponding DBCS character code.

```
SELECT CDEPT, VARGRAPHIC(CDEPT)
FROM    COURSE
WHERE   CNO = 'C11'
```

```
--------------------
CDEPT     COL1
--------------------
CIS     -C-I-S
```

NESTING OF SCALAR FUNCTIONS

A powerful aspect of the scalar functions is the ability to nest them within other scalar functions. (Recall we cannot nest a column function within a column function.) Not only can a scalar function be nested within another scalar function, but a column function may be nested within a scalar function. In fact, as the next sample query illustrates, many practical applications will have a column function nested within a scalar function.

Sample Query 6.21: Display the average labfee for each department followed by (1) an integer representation of the average and (2) a character string representation of this integer value.

```
SELECT CDEPT, AVG(CLABFEE),
       INTEGER(AVG(CLABFEE)),
       DIGITS(INTEGER(AVG(CLABFEE)))
FROM COURSE
GROUP BY CDEPT
```

CDEPT	COL1	COL2	COL3
CIS	125.000000000000	125	0000000125
PHIL	87.500000000000	87	0000000087
THEO	110.000000000000	110	0000000110

Comments:

1. COL1: AVG(CLABFEE)

   The average labfee is shown in COL1 as a decimal value. This is because a column function returns a data type that is the same as that of its argument. CLABFEE is decimal and therefore the AVG(CLABFEE) is decimal.

2. COL2: INTEGER(AVG(CLABFEE))

   This illustrates the nesting of the AVG function within the INTEGER function. The result of AVG(CLABFEE) is first obtained. Then the INTEGER function converts the averages to the value shown in COL2.

3. COL3: DIGITS(INTEGER(AVG(CLABFEE)))

   This example illustrates nesting to a second level. The AVG function is nested within the INTEGER function which is itself nested within the DIGITS function. Observe the "inside out" order of execution. AVG first generates a decimal result. Then INTEGER converts this to an integer. Finally, DIGITS converts this integer to a character string.

4. Syntax: Note that each function requires a balanced pair of parentheses.

5. What happens if one of the nested functions produces a null result? Then, the outer function returns a null result. All of the scalar functions presented to this point will produce the null value as their result if their argument is a null value. The VALUE scalar function, to be described in Chapter 10, allows you to define an alternate result for a null agrument.

Exercise:

6K. Recall that a column built-in function returns a value which has the same data type as its argument. This means that using the AVG function with an integer argument will return an integer value. Decimal accuracy is lost. Display the department id followed by the average number of course credits offered by each department. Do not lose decimal accuracy.

String Manipulation Functions: LENGTH and SUBSTR

The final category of scalar functions presented in this chapter pertains to string manipulation. These functions are LENGTH and SUBSTR. We will also discuss the concatenation operator, which is frequently used with these functions.

Sample Query 6.22:   What is the actual length of the CNO and CDESCP values for CIS courses? Display each CNO value followed by its length, and each CDESCP value followed by its length.

```
SELECT  CNO, LENGTH(CNO),
        CDESCP, LENGTH(CDESCP)
FROM    COURSE
WHERE   CDEPT = 'CIS'
```

CNO	COL1	CDESCP	COL2
C11	3	FOR ROOKIES	11
C22	3	VERY USEFUL	11
C33	3	ABSOLUTELY NECESSARY	20
C44	3	AH HA!	6
C55	3	VON NEUMANN'S MACH.	19
C66	3	THE ONLY WAY TO GO	18

Comments:

1. The LENGTH function returns the actual length of its argument. The result is returned as an integer.

2. In this query the scalar function was applied to columns of different character data types: a fixed length character column, and variable length character column. For a fixed length string, the function returns a value equal to the length of the string including any trailing spaces. The CNO column is defined as a length of 3 and will always return a value of 3 when used as the argument to the LENGTH function.

   For a variable length column, such as CDESCP, the function will return a value indicating the actual length of the data value. Note the range of values returned in the current output. If there are any trailing blanks stored in the variable string, they will be counted in determination of the length of the string.

3. If the argument of the function is a null value, then the result is a null value.

   The COURSE table does not have any null values. However, you can force a null result to demonstrate this point. Remember that the result of a column function is a null value when there are no values in a group. Hence, the average labfee for a nonexistent department is null. You can use this null value as input to the LENGTH function to illustrate its behavior.

   ```
   SELECT  LENGTH(AVG(CLABFEE))
   FROM    COURSE
   WHERE   CDEPT = 'HIST'
   ```

   Execution of this statement yields a null result.

Exercise:

6L. What is the actual length of each course name for courses offered by the Theology Department?

The LENGTH function is primarily used to determine the actual length of a variable length character string. However, it can also be used with a numeric argument.

Sample Query 6.23:   For each CIS course, display the CRED value followed by its length, and the CLABFEE value followed by its length.

```
SELECT CRED, LENGTH(CRED),
       CLABFEE, LENGTH(CLABFEE)
FROM COURSE
WHERE CDEPT = 'CIS'
```

CRED	COL1	CLABFEE	COL2
3	2	50.00	3
3	2	.00	3
3	2	.00	3
3	2	100.00	3
3	2	500.00	3

Comments:

The following comments reference internal representations which will be meaningful to professional programmers. Other readers will probably find this information more understandable after reading Chapter 8, which describes the CREATE TABLE command.

1. CRED is defined as a small integer (SMALLINT). LENGTH will always return a value of 2 for any such column because the value is stored in 2 bytes as a binary number.

    A large integer (INTEGER) argument will always return a value of 4 because 4 bytes are used to store its binary value.

2. CLABFEE is a decimal argument. Its length is determined based on the following formula.

    ```
    LENGTH(decimal) = INTEGER(precision / 2) + 1
    ```

    The CLABFEE column has a precision of 5. The length of this column is 3. If the precision was 8, the length of the column would be 5.

3. The COURSE table does not have any floating-point data, but we omment on their lengths. A single precision floating-point argument produces a length of 4, while a double precision floating-point argument produces a length of 8.

SUBSTR FUNCTION

There may be times when it is desirable to extract only a portion of a string, such as the first letter of a name to be used as an initial. The SUBSTR scalar function allows us to perform just such an operation.

Sample Query 6.24:   What is the first letter of each CIS course name? Also, what characters are present in the third, fourth, fifth, sixth, and seventh positions of those course names? Finally, display the course number values with the exception of the first character.

```
SELECT SUBSTR(CNAME, 1, 1),
       SUBSTR(CNAME, 3, 5),
       SUBSTR(CNO, 2)
FROM COURSE
WHERE CDEPT = 'CIS'
```

COL1	COL2	COL3
I	TRO T	11
D	TA ST	22
D	SCRET	33
D	GITAL	44
C	MPUTE	55
R	LATIO	66

Comments:

1. Syntax: The first argument of the SUBSTR function identifies the string from which the substring is extracted. The second argument indicates the starting position in the first argument string where the extracted string is to begin (i.e., the first position of the substring). The range of allowable values for this argument is from 1 to the length of the first argument string.

    The third argument is optional. When it is absent, the system begins its extraction at the start position and continues until the end of the string.

    When the third argument is present, it indicates the length of the substring. The length must identify a value which, when added to the start position, does not exceed the length of the string. For example, suppose we specify the start position as the third character in the CDEPT column. Because the CDEPT column can have four characters, the third argument must be in the range of 0 to 2.

2. The functions in the sample query are interpreted as follows.

    ```
    COL1: SUBSTR(CNAME, 1, 1)
    ```
    Start in position 1 of CNAME and extract 1 character.
    ```
    COL2: SUBSTR(CNAME, 3, 5)
    ```
    Start in position 3 of CNAME and extract 5 characters. (Note that an imbedded blank is treated as a character.)
    ```
    COL3: SUBSTR(CNO, 2)
    ```
    Start in position 2 of CNO and extract the rest of the string.

3. Important: The SUBSTR function cannot extract characters from a numeric argument. However, there is a way around this restriction, which will be presented in the next sample query.

Exercise:

6M. Display the first five characters of the course description for those courses offered by the Philosophy Department.

The next example illustrates a practical application of the nesting of scalar functions. We just learned that the SUBSTR function cannot operate on numeric arguments. However, you might need to extract a string of digits from a numeric value. This can be done by using the DIGITS function in conjunction with the SUBSTR function. The trick is to first apply DIGITS to the numeric argument to produce an intermediate character string representation of the numeric value, and then apply SUBSTR to this character representation. This involves the nesting of the DIGITS function within the SUBSTR function.

Sample Query 6.25: Display the course numbers of all CIS courses followed by the tens (second) digit of the corresponding labfees.

```
SELECT  CNO, SUBSTR(DIGITS(CLABFEE), 2, 1)
FROM    COURSE
WHERE   CDEPT = 'CIS'
```

```
-------------------
CNO     COL1
-------------------
C11     0
C22     5
C33     0
C44     0
C55     0
C66     0
```

Comment:

The DIGITS function is executed first, which produces a character string representation of the labfee. (Recall that this does not include the decimal point and leading zeros are attached where necessary.) The intermediate result produced by DIGITS(CLABFEE) is

```
10000
05000
00000
00000
10000
50000
```

Each of these character strings then becomes the first argument for the SUBSTR function, which begins at the second character position and extracts a string of length one (i.e., the character corresponding to the tens position in the CLABFEE's numeric representation). These characters correspond to the second column of the displayed result.

Exercises:

6N. Display the last character of course name for those courses with a labfee over $200.

6O. Display the last three characters of the course name for all courses in the COURSE table.

6P. Display just the cents amount for labfees of courses offered by the CIS Department.

CONCATENATION OPERATOR (||)

The SUBSTR function is used to extract a portion of a string, a kind of string subtraction. SQL also provides a method of putting two strings together, a kind of string addition. This is called "concatenation" and is specified by placing two vertical bars (||) between the strings to be connected. We note that the concatenation operator (||) is an operator, similar to the arithmetic operators (+, -, *, /). It is not a built-in function.

Sample Query 6.26:   Concatenate the CDESCP and CDEPT values, in that order, for all computer science courses. Follow this by the concatenation of CDEPT and CDESCP, in that order.

```
SELECT  CDESCP || CDEPT, CDEPT || CDESCP
FROM    COURSE
WHERE   CDEPT = 'CIS'
```

```
----------------------------------------------------------------
COL1                           COL2
----------------------------------------------------------------
FOR ROOKIESCIS                 CIS FOR ROOKIES
VERY USEFULCIS                 CIS VERY USEFUL
ABSOLUTELY NECESSARYCIS        CIS ABSOLUTELY NECESSARY
AH HA!CIS                      CIS AH HA!
VON NEUMANN'S MACH.CIS         CIS VON NEUMANN'S MACH.
THE ONLY WAY TO GOCIS          CIS THE ONLY WAY TO GO
```

Comments:

1. The concatenation operator works only with string data. It cannot be used with numeric data. In this query, one of the strings was fixed in length and the other was variable in length. There is no problem in concatenating a mixture of strings like this.

2. The resulting string produced by the operation has a length which is dependent on the lengths and types (fixed or variable) of both arguments. If both arguments are fixed length, then the result is fixed length equal to the sum of the two lengths. If either or both operands is a variable length string, the result is a variable length string with a maximum length equal to the sum of the maximum lengths of both strings. In our example, the CDEPT column is fixed length with a length of 4. The CNAME column is variable length with a maximum length of 25. The result of concatenating a string with values from these two columns is a variable length string with maximum length of 29.

3. Important to note in the result is what happens when the different type strings are united. When the variable length string is first, the fixed length string is appended immediately at the end of the string. There are no spaces in the newly formed string (unless there are explicitly defined trailing spaces in the variable length string). When the fixed length string is first, the result shows a space between the two values. This is because there is a space at the end of the fixed length string. The value of "CIS" occupies only the first three of the four character positions defined for the CDEPT column. The space in the fourth position is actually part of the string. If we had selected the PHIL or THEO department, the result would not show any space between the two strings.

4. If either of the strings being concatenated is the null value, the result of the concatenation is the null value. (If you are familiar with other string processing languages, you should note that this behavior implies a real difference between the concept of empty string as specified in those languages and null value as specified in SQL.)

Exercise:

6Q. Concatenate the CNO and CNAME columns in that order.

The last sample query illustrates the use of the concatenation operator to edit a numeric value. The built-in functions decompose the numeric value into character strings and the concatenation operator reassembles these strings for the output display.

Sample Query 6.27:   What is the labfee for each CIS course? Display the result as a character string with leading zeros having the "$" as a prefix.

```
SELECT  '$' ||
        SUBSTR(DIGITS(CLABFEE), 1, 3) || '.' ||
        SUBSTR(DIGITS(CLABFEE), 4, 2)
FROM    COURSE
WHERE   CDEPT = 'CIS'
```

```
--------------------
      COL1
--------------------
    $100.00
    $050.00
    $000.00
    $000.00
    $100.00
    $500.00
```

Comment:

1. Because the concatenation operator works only with string data, it was necessary in this query to convert the numeric value of the CLABFEE column into a string value. This was accomplished through the DIGITS scalar function. This string value was then manipulated by the SUBSTR function to extract the integer (dollar) portion of the labfee by specifying that the substring was to begin at the first position of the string and contain three characters. The decimal component was obtained by using SUBSTR again to extract the last two characters. The dollar sign and decimal point were then concatenated with these substrings to form the final result. This query illustrates how to generate expanded strings using the concatenation operator and how to contract strings by using the SUBSTR function. These two facilities offer some flexibility in string manipulation.

2. We are not limited to a single concatenation operator in an expression. In fact, for all practical purposes there is no limit to the length of the string formed by concatenation. (The limit is 32,754 for character strings and 16,382 for graphic strings.)

3. The example shows the editing of numeric values. In practice, you will find it easier to use the edit facilities of the host system interface to achieve this objective.

Exercises:

6R. Display a permutation of the CNO values in the COURSE table where the first character position of CNO is shown after the second and third characters (e.g., "C11" is displayed as "11C".)

6S. Concatenate the CNO and CRED values, in that order, for those courses offered by the CIS Department.

SUMMARY EXERCISES

The following exercises refer to the STAFF table. Recall that the column names are ENAME, ETITLE, ESALARY, and DEPT.

6T. Display the sum and average of all staff member salaries along with the largest and the smallest individual salary.

6U. How many staff members are employed by the Theology Department?

6V. How many different kinds of job titles apply to the current staff members?

6W. Assume a total of $5000 is allocated for staff member raises. What is the new total for all staff member salaries?

6X. Assume all members of the Theology Department will have their salaries reduced by $20. What is the new average salary for members of this department?

6Y. For all DEPT values found in the STAFF table, display the department identifier followed by the average salary for that department.

6Z. Consider only staff members whose current salary exceeds $600. For each department which has any such staff member, display the department id followed by the total amount paid to these staff members. Sort the result in alphabetical sequence by department id.

7

Processing Date and Time Information

This chapter introduces the SQL special facilities for processing data which represent date and time information. Previous chapters introduced and emphasized the differences between two "standard" data types, numeric and character. Traditional data processing systems use some form of numeric or character data to encode date and time information. This requires the user or some application program to go through extra effort to decode this data. This approach is aggravated by the multitude of different formats for date and time information. In fact, this approach was required for the early releases of DB2 and SQL/DS. Now SQL has special facilities to simplify the storage and manipulation of date/time information. While these facilities will reduce the effort required for programming tasks involving date/time information, the logic of such tasks can be inherently complex. Hence, the SQL date/time facilities are relatively sophisticated (and complex). For this reason, this book will only introduce some of the more basic concepts and facilities of handling date/time information. This chapter will restrict its attention to displaying date/time information which is present in some table.

DATE AND TIME DATA TYPES

Chapter 8 will introduce the CREATE TABLE command where you will see how each column in a newly created table is assigned a specific data type. There you will learn that, in addition to specifying the different variations of numeric and character data described in earlier chapters, it is possible to specify that a given column can only contain date and/or time values. To be specific, SQL supports "primitive" date/time data types. These are DATE, TIME, and TIMESTAMP which are described in Figure 7.1. We emphasize the fact that the system has its own internal representation for these data types; they need not concern us because these codes will automatically be converted to a character string representation when we display them. The following sample queries will describe a variety of formats for these character strings.

The availability of primitive data types for date and time information means that such information does not need to be represented as some form of numeric or character string value. It also means that the system recognizes a column as containing date/time data and supports certain useful operations which can be applied to this data. In effect, date/time data represents a third category of data distinct from numeric and character string data. The special built-in functions and other SQL facilities introduced in this chapter can only reference columns which contain date and/or time data. The COURSE table does not have any columns with date/time information. For this reason, we introduce the REGISTRATION table which has one column with date values and another column with time values.

DATE: An internal code representing a date as "yyyymmdd"

TIME: An internal code representing a time as "hhmmss"

TIMESTAMP: An internal code representing a combination of both date and time as
"yyyymmddhhmmss nnnnnn"
(nnnnnn = microsecond value)

Figure 7.1   Date/time data types.

THE REGISTRATION TABLE

In our mythical educational database we represent a course as a row in the COURSE table. We now assume that a student, who is identified by a student number (SNO), can take any of these courses.

Because a department chairperson may choose to offer multiple sections of the same course, each class is identified by a combination of its course number (CNO) and a section number (SEC). Students can register for one or more classes by executing an application program which asks the student to enter his student number and the course/section numbers of the classes he wants to attend. The program will use this information to update the REGISTRATION table. It will insert one row for each class the student wants to attend.

The REGISTRATION table contains the following columns.

CNO: Course number (a character string, length = 3)

SEC: Section number (a character string, length = 2)

SNO: Student number (a character string, length = 3)

REG_DATE: Registration date (DATE data type)

REG_TIME: Registration time (TIME data type)

This table contains a row for each class the student hopes to attend. Because some classes have a limited class size, a first-come–first-serve acceptance policy applies. Therefore, the application program must store the date and time of the student's registration in the table. This is the purpose of the REG_DATE and REG_TIME columns. The process by which the application program uses embedded SQL to insert rows in the REGISTRATION table is beyond the scope of this text. We assume that the program has been executed a number of times and that the REGISTRATION table now contains some number of rows that you would like to examine. The following sample queries illustrate some of the facilities for displaying date/time data.

DISPLAYING DATE/TIME DATA

We stated above that date/time information has a special internal data representation. However, whenever such information is displayed, you will observe the date/time values displayed as simple character strings. This is because the system will automatically convert the internal date/time code to a character string prior to display. The first sample query will display the REG_DATE and REG_TIME values which will appear as simple character strings.

Sample Query 7.1: Display all information in the REGISTRATION table.

```
SELECT  *
FROM    REGISTRATION
```

CNO	SEC	SNO	REG_DATE	REG_TIME
C11	01	325	1988-01-04	09.41.30
C11	01	800	1987-12-15	11.49.30
C11	02	150	1987-12-17	09.32.30
P33	01	100	1987-12-23	11.30.00
P33	01	800	1987-12-23	11.23.00
T11	01	100	1987-12-23	11.21.52
T11	01	150	1987-12-15	11.35.30
T11	01	800	1987-12-15	14.00.00

Comments:

1. Observe the REG_DATE and REG_TIME columns. The displayed values appear as character string data formatted according to the International Standard's Organization (ISO) format. This format is "yyyy-mm-dd" for date and "hh.mm.ss" for time. Again, we note that the internal representation of the date/time values is a special notation which is different from the displayed character string. The choice of the ISO format is made by the systems administrator. It is possible to display date/time values using formats other than the ISO date/time format. Sample Query 7.3 will illustrate how to specify alternate formats. The other formats are presented in Figure 7.2.

2. It is possible to display just the year, month and day components of a date value or the hour, minute and second components of a time value. The next sample query demonstrates the use of built-in functions to realize this objective.

FORMAT CODE	DATE FORMAT	TIME FORMAT
ISO	yyyy-mm-dd	hh.mm.ss
USA	mm/dd/yyyy	hh:mm (AM or PM)
EUR	dd.mm.yyyy	hh.mm.ss
JIS	yyyy-mm-dd	hh:mm:ss
LOCAL	(special installation-defined format)	

Figure 7.2   Date/time format options.

SOME DATE/TIME BUILT-IN FUNCTIONS

SQL has scalar built-in functions which can be used to extract individual components of date/time values. The functions YEAR, MONTH, and DAY accept a date or timestamp value as an argument and return the appropriate year, month, or day value. The functions HOUR, MINUTE, and SECOND accept a time or timestamp value as an argument and return the appropriate hour, minute or second value. Finally, the MICROSECOND function accepts a timestamp value as an argument and returns the microsecond component of the timestamp as a result. The next example illustrates the use of some of these functions.

Sample Query 7.2:   Display the month, day, hour, and minute that the student identified by student number 150 registered for section 02 of course C11.

```
SELECT  MONTH(REG_DATE), DAY(REG_DATE),
        HOUR(REG_TIME), MINUTE(REG_TIME)
FROM    REGISTRATION
WHERE   SNO = '150'
AND     CNO = 'C11'
AND     SEC = '02'
```

COL1	COL2	COL3	COL4
12	17	9	32

Comment:

These functions conform to the standard syntax rules and behavior of scalar functions as described in the previous chapter. Each function actually returns a numeric integer value. This means that any of the functions could be included within an arithmetic expression. [ex. SELECT DAY(REG_DATE)+10 ...]

DATE AND TIME FORMATS

As mentioned earlier, the ISO date/time format is not the only one available. Figure 7.2 summarizes the different formats which can be used to display date/time information. When displaying date/time information, you can specify the desired format by using the CHAR built-in function. This function accepts a date/time value as its first argument and any of the format codes shown in Figure 7.2 as its second argument. It returns the date/time value as a character string in the specified format.

Sample Query 7.3: Display all information in any row of the REGISTRATION table having a SNO value of 100. Display date and time information using the USA format.

```
SELECT  CNO, SEC, SNO,
        CHAR(REG_DATE,USA),
        CHAR(REG_TIME,USA)
FROM    REGISTRATION
WHERE   SNO = '100'
```

CNO	SEC	SNO	COL1	COL2
P33	01	100	12/23/1987	11:30 AM
T11	01	100	12/23/1987	11:21 AM

Comment:

The CHAR function has other uses which are beyond the scope of this text.

Exercises:

7A. Display the date on which student 800 registered for course number C11. Use the EUR format.

7B. Display the date and time for all registrations for course number T11. Use the JIS format.

COMPARING DATE/TIME VALUES

The previous examples only referenced date/time columns in the SE-LECT clause for the purpose of displaying such information. It is also possible to reference date/time columns in the WHERE clause for the purpose of selecting rows for display based on date/time values. We can also sort the output based on date/time values. The next sample query demonstrates these points.

Sample Query 7.4:   Display the student number and time of registration of any student who registered for a course on December 15, 1987, anytime between 11:30 a.m. and 1:30 p.m. Sort the result by registration time.

```
SELECT  SNO, REG_TIME
FROM    REGISTRATION
WHERE   REG_DATE = '1987-12-15'
AND     REG_TIME
        BETWEEN '11.30.00' AND '13.30.00'
ORDER   BY REG_TIME
```

SNO	REG_TIME
150	11.35.30
800	11.49.30

Comments:

1. The WHERE clause allows for the specification of "date/time constants." These constants are character strings which the system will convert to the internal date/time code representation for the purpose of performing the comparison. The system is intelligent enough to do this because it recognizes the other operands (REG_DATE and REG_TIME) as date/time values. Any date/time constant must conform to the format of a valid date or time as shown in Figure 7.2.

2. All time values are based on a 24-hour clock and have real significance only within the 24 hours of the particular date in which they occur. In the present sample query all information was for a particular day; therefore, ordering by time values made sense. If information had been retrieved for more than one day, ordering the result by time values alone would lack meaning. All 9:00 registrations would be displayed together regardless of the dates on which they occurred. A two-level sort on date followed by time would resolve this concern. Another solution could have been addressed when the table was created. The date and time values could have been consolidated into a single column with the timestamp data type. Note that the timestamp data type consists of a date portion followed by a time portion. Ordering by a timestamp would accomplish the two-level sort through a single column.

3. Note that we are not allowed to use LIKE when comparing date/time data. It might have been tempting to try the phrase WHERE REG_TIME LIKE '11%' to cover all times during the hour of 11 o'clock. This would result in an error because LIKE is strictly for use with character data.

Exercise:

7C. Display the student number and date of registration for all students who registered for course C11 during the month of December. Present the result in order by date.

SPECIAL REGISTERS

Users of DB2 and SQL/DS can access "current" date and time information by referencing one of three special registers called CUR-
RENT DATE, CURRENT TIME, and CURRENT TIMESTAMP.
These registers always contain the current date, time, and
timestamp values which can be used for purposes of display (as in
the next sample query) or to store a date/time value in a row of a
table. For example, the next query references CURRENT DATE and
CURRENT TIME to establish a historical record about information
in a table prior to modifying the contents of the table.

Sample Query 7.5:   In anticipation of changes to labfees for courses
offered by the CIS Department, you would like to
display and subsequently print (using the host
system print facility) the current CNO, CNAME,
and CLABFEE values for CIS courses followed by
the date and time of the execution of this query.

```
SELECT  CNO, CNAME, CLABFEE,
        CURRENT DATE, CURRENT TIME
FROM    COURSE
WHERE   CDEPT = 'CIS'
```

CNO	CNAME	CLABFEE	COL1	COL2
C11	INTRO TO CS	100.00	1988-07-14	08.56.27
C22	DATA STRUCTURES	50.00	1988-07-14	08.56.27
C33	DISCRETE MATHEMATICS	.00	1988-07-14	08.56.27
C44	DIGITAL CIRCUITS	.00	1988-07-14	08.56.27
C55	COMPUTER ARCH.	100.00	1988-07-14	08.56.27
C66	RELATIONAL DATABASE	500.00	1988-07-14	08.56.27

Comments:

1. Upon examination of the output display you can deduce that this SELECT statement was executed at 08:56:27 on 07/14/1988. Note that this same date and time is shown in all selected rows. (This is not the typical approach of showing the date/time information just once in the output display. Again, this illustrates the fact that SQL is a just a query language. You would have to use the report generation facilities of the host system to achieve this objective.)

2. The special registers can be used as arguments to the afore-mentioned date/time functions. For example, if you only wished to see the hours and minutes components of the time, you could have expressed this query as

```
SELECT CNO, CNAME, CLABFEE,
       HOURS(CURRENT TIME), MINUTES(CURRENT TIME)
FROM   COURSE
WHERE  CDEPT = 'CIS'
```

Exercise:

7D. Display the course name and description for course number C11. Attach a timestamp to this display.

DATE AND TIME DURATIONS

It is possible to add and subtract date and time values. In particular, the subtraction of two dates produces a result which is called a "date duration." Likewise, the subtraction of two time values produces a "time duration." SQL also allows for the specification of labeled durations (YEARS, MONTHS, DAYS, HOURS, MINUTES, SECONDS, and MICROSECONDS) and unlabeled durations (not described in this text). There are a number of details and restrictions on calculations with date/time values and durations which you can find in the IBM reference manuals.

Sample Query 7.6:   (Assume the current date is December 29, 1987.) Display the CNO, SEC, and SNO values for any registration which occurred 12 days earlier. For verification purposes, also display the registration date and the current date.

```
SELECT CNO, SEC,
       SNO, REG_DATE, CURRENT DATE
FROM   REGISTRATION
WHERE  REG_DATE =
       CURRENT DATE - 12 DAYS
```

```
-----------------------------------------------------------
CNO    SEC    SNO    REG_DATE      COL1
-----------------------------------------------------------
C11    02     100    1987-12-17    1987-12-29
C11    02     150    1987-12-17    1987-12-29
```

Comment:

The WHERE clause shows a labeled duration (12 DAYS) being subtracted from a special register (CURRENT DATE). The result is a date value which is compared to the REG_DATE value of each row. Rows matching this value are selected.

Previous examples have indicated that a duration can be added to or subtracted from a date/time value to produce a new date/time value. The next query shall show how a date can be subtracted from another date to produce a duration.

Sample Query 7.7: Assuming that today's date is February 14, 1988, how long ago did students 100 and 800 register for courses? In other words, how much time has elapsed from the date these students registered until today's date?

```
SELECT  CURRENT DATE, REG_DATE,
        CURRENT DATE - REG_DATE
FROM    REGISTRATION
WHERE   SNO IN ('100', '800')
```

```
-------------------------------------------
COL1               REG_DATE    COL2
-------------------------------------------
1988-02-14         1987-12-15  130
1988-02-14         1987-12-17  128
1988-02-14         1987-12-23  122
```

Comments:

1. The computed duration is an integer value with a maximum of eight digits representing YYYYMMDD. Leading zeroes are suppressed.

   The result of the present query shows durations of 1 month and 30 days, 1 month and 28 days, and 1 month and 22 days.

2. Two time values may participate in a subtraction operation. This may not be as useful or practical as with dates, for to have any meaning the two values must occur on the same date. However, the result of such an operation would be a six digit number in the form of HHMMSS.

3. A negative duration can occur if a more recent date is subtracted from an earlier date.

Sample Query 7.8:   What are the latest and earliest dates on which a student registered for a course and what is the duration between these dates?

```
SELECT  MAX(REG_DATE), MIN(REG_DATE),
        MAX(REG_DATE) - MIN(REG_DATE)
FROM    REGISTRATION
```

COL1	COL2	COL3
1988-01-04	1987-12-15	20

Comments:

1. The present sample query illustrates how the MAX and MIN functions can be applied to columns defined with date/time data. Because comparisons are made using the internal formats, chronological significance is retained. Therefore, the "1988" date is greater than the "1987" date.

2. A word of caution: We have seen that functions can be nested and it holds true with date/time data. If we needed to present the result in the USA format, we would use the CHAR function. The result is dependent on which function we nest. If we convert the date with CHAR and then apply the MAX function, MAX(CHAR(REG_DATE),USA), the result is "12/23/1987". This is because the CHAR conversion is applied first and produces a character string. This causes the date to lose its chronological significance. However, if we apply CHAR to the value returned from the MAX function, CHAR(MAX(REG_DATE),USA), the result is "01/04/1988".

3. The SUM and AVG functions are not valid with date/time data. These functions apply strictly to numeric data.

SUBTLETIES OF DATE/TIME ARITHMETIC

There are certain instances regarding date/time arithmetic which might be considered peculiar. To avoid surprises, it is important to be aware of the types of situations in which the data types behave somewhat unexpectedly. We now address some of these subtleties.

When adding a number of days to a date there are no surprises. The results are as you might expect. The same is true of subtraction. In the following examples, the system accurately handles the 29 days of February in the computation.

> 01/31/1988 + 30 DAYS produces 03/01/1988
>
> 03/01/1988 − 30 DAYS produces 01/31/1988

However, when adding units of MONTH and YEAR, peculiarities arise.

> 01/31/1988 + 1 MONTH produces 02/29/1988
>
> 02/29/1988 − 1 MONTH produces 01/29/1988

In the first instance, the system recognized the 31st day of January as the last day of the month and correctly produces the 29th as the last day of February. The system deals strictly with MONTH units and not increments of 30/31 DAYS. Problems arise due to these varying number of days in any given month.

A similar situation is that of adding and subtracting units of YEARS.

> 02/29/1988 + 1 YEAR produces 02/28/1989
>
> 02/28/1988 − 1 YEAR produces 02/28/1988

The issue of concern is that of inverses. Adding a quantity and subtracting the same quantity should result in the original value. With dates this may or may not be the case. There is another scalar function which applies to dates, which we mention in passing, that will allow the correct result with regard to inverses. The DAYS function returns an integer representation of a date which reflects the number of days elapsed from December 31, 0000. To accurately determine the duration between two dates, use the following:

> DURATION = DAYS(DATE1) − DAYS(DATE2)

Use of the 24 hour clock causes an interesting situation as well. The two times of "00:00:00" and "24:00:00" represent the same time of day, but this is not recognized by the system. These two times are not considered equal. The following situations illustrate this issue.

00:00:00 + 24 HOURS produces 24:00:00
00:00:00 − 24 HOURS produces 00:00:00
24:00:00 + 24 HOURS produces 24:00:00
24:00:00 − 24 HOURS produces 00:00:00

SUMMARY

This chapter presented an overview of the date/time processing facilities available with DB2 and SQL/DS. A significant feature is the ability to define primitive data types of DATE, TIME and TIMESTAMP. Columns containing such date/time data values can serve as arguments to certain built-in functions.

The functions YEAR, MONTH, DAY, HOUR, MINUTE, SECOND, and MICROSECOND can be used to extract individual components of date/time values. The CHAR function can be used to display date/time values in a variety of different formats (ISO, USA, EUR, JIS, or LOCAL).

Current date/time information can be obtained by referencing the special registers CURRENT DATE, CURRENT TIME, and CURRENT TIMESTAMP. Date/time values can be referenced in a WHERE clause for the purpose of selecting rows based on date/time values. Date/time values can also be used with the addition and subtraction operations which allow the calculation of date and time durations.

In conclusion, we emphasize that our treatment of date/time processing is not comprehensive. This is a rather specialized SQL feature which generally is used by professional application programmers writing programs with embedded SQL. This audience is referred to the IBM literature for a more detailed discussion of this topic.

II

Data Definition and Manipulation

This part of the text introduces the SQL database definition and update statements. We could have completed our discussion of the SELECT statement prior to introducing these topics. However, many subtle points associated with complex data retrieval pertain to decisions which are made during database design and subsequently implemented using SQL's data definition and update statements. Potentially embarrassing data retrieval errors can be avoided by understanding the key concepts of database definition and update. This is especially true for SELECT statements which must reference multiple tables or process columns which contain null values. For this reason, the fundamental concepts of data definition and update are presented in this part of the text before describing the more complex variations of the SELECT statement in Part III.

ORGANIZATION OF CHAPTERS

Chapter 8 introduces two important SQL data definition statements: CREATE TABLE and CREATE INDEX. Typically the database administrator executes these statements (among others) to initially establish the database. Unless you plan to use DB2 or SQL/DS as a personal system (the way many users and programmers utilize microcomputer database systems), you will probably never have to execute either of these statements. If this is the case, you can skim over the details of syntax. However, you should understand the conceptual substance of this chapter. The CREATE TABLE statement, in addition to defining the structure of a table, also establishes database integrity constraints by (1) specifying primary and foreign keys and (2) allowing or prohibiting null values in specified columns. In Chapter 9 you will learn that these constraints impact the proper formulation of update statements. In subsequent chapters we will see that a query which references multiple tables usually is premised upon a semantic relationship corresponding to the definition on some foreign key. From a conceptual point of view, this is a very important chapter because it shows how an application design using DB2 or SQL/DS is more than just a collection of tables. We emphasize that the design is actually a semantically meaningful collection of interrelated tables which should adhere to specified integrity constraints. The semantic relationships usually are the basis of a multi-table query, and the integrity constraints are used to evaluate the validity of update statements.

Chapter 9 is a comprehensive presentation of SQL's data manipulation statements: INSERT, UPDATE and DELETE. You will find the syntax for these statements to be quite straightforward. However, these statements are potentially dangerous because erroneous execution can cause the loss of valuable data. The examples illustrate interactive execution of the statements. However, for corporate (vs. personal) databases, these statements are usually embedded within application programs. Therefore, professional programmers should master the subject matter of this chapter. Those users who will not modify data can skip this chapter.

Chapter 10, which returns to the SELECT statement, is presented in this part of the text for a very important reason. Our intention is to emphasize the potential problems which can occur when a column is allowed to contain null values. If the CREATE TABLE statement does not prohibit null values, and subsequent INSERT or UPDATE statements actually store such values in a table, then special consideration must be given to the proper formulation of SELECT statements and to the interpretation of the output. The sample queries will show that the presence of null values increases the possibility of error. Therefore, both users and professional programmers should understand the content of this chapter. Hopefully it will also encourage the prohibition of null values where appropriate.

MORE SAMPLE TABLES

Below we describe the structure and content of other tables which are present in the educational database. These tables will be used for subsequent sample queries and exercises. The next chapter will describe how these tables are created and how some of the semantic relationships between the tables can be defined by the CREATE TABLE statement. Again we note that Appendix E shows a brief summary of the educational database design. We briefly describe the name and content of tables that will appear in the next few chapters. These tables are shown in Figure P2.1.

DEPARTMENT — Has one row for each academic department. Contents: Department id, building and room location, and department chairperson faculty number.

COURSE — Same as described in Part I of this text.

CLASS — Has one row for each class offering of a particular course. Contents: Course number, section number, faculty number of instructor, day and time, building and room location.

STUDENT — Has 1 row for each student enrolled in the college. Contents: Student number, name, address, phone number, birthdate, IQ, faculty number of advisor, and department major.

REGISTRATION — When a student registers for a class, one row is entered in this table to record the event. Review previous discussion in Chapter 7. Contents: Course number, section number, student number, date the student registered, and time of day that the student registered.

FACULTY — Has one row for each faculty member of the college. Contents: Faculty number, name, address, date of hire, number of dependents, salary, and department id of the associated department.

STAFF — Has one row for each non-faculty employee of the college. Contents: Name, title, salary, and department id of the associated academic department.

DEPARTMENT

DEPT	DBLD	DROOM	DCHFNO
THEO	HU	200	10
CIS	SC	300	80
MGT	SC	100	—
PHIL	HU	100	60

STAFF

ENAME	ETITLE	ESALARY	DEPT
LUKE	EVANGLIST3	53	THEO
MARK	EVANGLIST2	52	THEO
MATTHEW	EVANGLIST1	51	THEO
DICK NIX	CROOK	25001	PHIL
HANK KISS	JESTER	25000	PHIL
JOHN	EVANGLIST4	54	THEO
EUCLID	LAB ASSIST	1000	MATH
ARCHIMEDES	LAB ASSIST	200	ENG
DA VINCI	LAB ASSIST	500	—

FACULTY

FNO	FNAME	FADDR	FHIRE DATE	FNUM DEP	FSALARY	FDEPT
06	KATHY PEPE	7 STONERIDGE RD	1979-01-15	2	35000.00	PHIL
10	JESSIE MARTYN	2135 EAST DR	1969-09-01	1	45000.00	THEO
08	JOE COHN	BOX 1138	1979-07-09	2	35000.00	CIS
85	AL HARTLEY	SILVER SREET	1979-09-05	7	45000.00	CIS
60	JULIE MARTYN	2135 EAST DR	1969-09-01	1	45000.00	PHIL
65	LISA BOBAK	77 LAUGHING LN	1981-09-06	—	36000.00	THEO
80	BARB HLAVATY	489 SOUTH ROAD	1982-01-16	3	35000.00	CIS

CLASS

CNO	SEC	CINSTRFNO	CDAY	CTIME	CBLD	CROOM
C11	01	08	MO	08:00-09:00A.M.	SC	305
C11	02	08	TU	08:00-09:00A.M.	SC	306
C33	01	80	WE	09:00-10:30A.M.	SC	305
C55	01	85	TH	11:00-12:00A.M.	SC	306
P11	01	06	TH	09:00-10:00A.M.	HU	102
P33	01	06	FR	11:00-12:00A.M.	HU	210
T11	01	10	MO	10:00-11:00A.M.	HU	101
T11	02	65	MO	10:00-11:00A.M.	HU	102
T33	01	65	WE	11:00-12:00A.M.	HU	101

STUDENT

SNO	SNAME	SADDR	SPHNO	SBDATE	SIQ	SADVFNO	SMAJ
325	CURLEY DUBAY	CONNECTICUT	203-123-4567	780517	122	10	THEO
150	LARRY DUBAY	CONNECTICUT	203-123-4567	780517	121	80	CIS
100	MOE DUBAY	CONNECTICUT	203-123-4567	780517	120	10	THEO
800	ROCKY BALBOA	PENNSYLVANIA	112-112-1122	461004	99	60	PHIL

Figure P2.1   Sample tables.

8

Data Definition

The primary focus of this chapter is the CREATE TABLE statement. This statement is used to establish an "empty" table. Thereafter, rows can be stored in the table by executing the INSERT statement. We postpone discussion of the INSERT statement and other update statements (UPDATE and DELETE) until the next chapter.

The CREATE TABLE statement creates an "object" (the table) within the system. We will also discuss another system object, an index, which is established by executing the CREATE INDEX statement. Both DB2 and SQL/DS contain tables and indexes. However, each system also contains other objects. Because DB2 and SQL/DS are different systems, these other objects, while conceptually similar, have different names and are established by executing different statements.

This chapter will present simplified versions of the CREATE TABLE and CREATE INDEX statements. The simplified versions of these statements are the same for both DB2 and SQL/DS. Differences exist in the complete versions because each has distinct clauses which reference system specific objects. Fortunately, users and application programmers rarely need to be familiar with these objects. For this reason, a comprehensive discussion of the complete versions of these statements is beyond the scope of this text.

CREATE TABLE STATEMENT

We begin our discussion by presenting the CREATE TABLE statement which was used to create the COURSE table. The following comments will elaborate on the SQL keywords and related concepts.

Sample Statement 8.1: Create a table called COURSE which has six columns with the following names and descriptions.

1. **CNO**: A fixed length character string. Length = 3.

2. **CNAME**: A variable length character string.
   Maximum length = 22.

3. **CDESCP**: A variable length character string.
   Maximum length = 25.

4. **CRED**: A small integer.

5. **CLABFEE**: A decimal value with a precision of 5 and a scale of 2.

6. **CDEPT**: A fixed length character string. Length = 4.

   Furthermore,

   a. CNO should be specified as the primary key.

   b. CDEPT should be specified as a nonnull foreign key referencing the DEPARTMENT table.

   c. Default values should be specified for CNAME and CDESCP.

```
CREATE TABLE COURSE
   (CNO     CHAR(3) NOT NULL,
    CNAME   VARCHAR(22) NOT NULL WITH DEFAULT,
    CDESCP  VARCHAR(25) NOT NULL WITH DEFAULT,
    CRED    SMALLINT,
    CLABFEE DECIMAL(5,2),
    CDEPT   CHAR(4) NOT NULL,
 PRIMARY KEY (CNO),
 FOREIGN KEY (CDEPT)
         REFERENCES DEPARTMENT
         ON DELETE RESTRICT)
```

System Response:

The CREATE TABLE statement is not a query. Hence, there is no explicit display of data as with a SELECT statement. Contingent upon the host system you are using, you should receive some system-generated message which effectively states that the table was successfully created. An error message would imply that you violated one of the rules to be described below.

Comments:

The present example illustrates the general syntax of the CREATE TABLE statement. The general format of this statement is outlined in Figure 8.1. (This figure does not include other clauses which reference system specific objects.) Before addressing the details of syntax we enumerate the objectives of the CREATE TABLE statement.

Objectives of CREATE TABLE Statement:

1. Establish a new table and give it a name.

2. Give a name to all the columns in the table.

3. Specify the data type of each column.

4. Specify the default column sequence.

5. Specify which columns cannot accept null values.

6. Specify the primary key.

7. Specify any foreign keys.

8. Update the system catalog.

The following pages elaborate on each of these eight points.

```
CREATE TABLE name-of-table
(column1-name   data-type [NOT NULL [WITH DEFAULT]],
 column2-name   data-type [NOT NULL [WITH DEFAULT]],

                    .
                    .
                    .

 columnN-name   data-type [NOT NULL [WITH DEFAULT]],
 [primary-key-clause],
 [foreign-key-clause])
```

• primary-key-clause:

```
PRIMARY KEY (column1 [, column2, ..., columnN])
```

• foreign-key-clause:

```
FOREIGN KEY (column1 [, column2, ..., columnN])
REFERENCES (table-name)

                    ⎧ RESTRICT ⎫
[ON DELETE  ⎨ SET NULL ⎬ ]
                    ⎩ CASCADE  ⎭
```

Figure 8.1   CREATE TABLE statement.

1. Table Names

A table name may be one to 18 characters long. It must begin with a letter. This letter may be followed by other letters, digits, or underscore characters. The table name is specified immediately after "CREATE TABLE" in the statement. The example shows "COURSE" as the specified table name.

The CREATE TABLE statement and previous SELECT statements referenced this table as "COURSE". However, "COURSE" is not the complete name. This is because DB2 and SQL/DS are multiuser systems and it is possible for different users to specify "COURSE" in different CREATE TABLE statements used to create different tables. To handle this situation, the system will automatically attach each user's authorization id as prefix to the table name. This means that the complete name of any table consists of two parts.

1. Authorization-id: This is typically the sign-on id used to sign onto the host system. (Ex. U48989)

2. Table-name: This is the name specified in the CREATE TABLE statement. (Ex. COURSE)

Therefore, assuming your authorization-id is "U48989", the complete table name is "U48989.COURSE". This scheme of naming tables allows different users to specify the same name in a CREATE TABLE statement. For example, assume another user with an authorization-id of "U99999" issued the following statement.

```
CREATE TABLE COURSE
    (XXX CHAR(100),
     YYY DECIMAL (8,1))
```

If user U99999 inserted rows into this table and subsequently entered the statement "SELECT * FROM COURSE", the system would automatically attach his authorization-id as a prefix to the table name and execute "SELECT * FROM U99999.COURSE". Likewise, whenever you enter "SELECT * FROM COURSE", the system converts this to "SELECT * FROM U48989.COURSE".

There are occasions where you are required to explicitly specify a complete table name in a statement. For example, it is possible for user U99999 to grant you permission to access his COURSE table. (Chapter 17 will describe how this permission is granted.) You could then enter the following command to examine his COURSE table.

```
SELECT YYY, XXX
FROM    U99999.COURSE
ORDER  BY  XXX
```

Observe that the complete table name is specified and column names refer to those contained within the U99999.COURSE table.

2. Column Names

Column names are formulated according to the same syntax rules as table names. Column names must be unique within a given table; but it is possible to have the same column name specified within multiple tables. For example, both the COURSE table and the REGISTRATION table contain a column named "CNO". There is no ambiguity when a SELECT statement refers to CNO because the FROM clause indicates the appropriate table.

Chapter 11 will introduce the join operation which references multiple tables in the same SELECT statement. If two tables have a column with the same name, then a column name must be qualified by specifying a table name as a prefix. For example, you would specify "COURSE.CNO" to reference the CNO column of the COURSE table and "REGISTRATION.CNO" to reference the CNO column of the REGISTRATION table. Chapter 11 will present sample queries where the use of the table name as a prefix is required.

3. Data Types

The data type of each column is specified after the column name. We have seen that the type of data in a column can affect how conditions are formulated in a WHERE clause. For example, character strings, unlike numeric constraints, must be enclosed within apostrophes. Calculations can only be performed on numeric data, and pattern recognition only applies to string data. Also, the specification of different numeric data types can affect the accuracy of a calculated result. For these reasons. serious consideration should be given to the choice of data type. We present a comprehensive overview of available data types later in this chapter.

4. Default Column Sequence

The example shows the column definitions specified in a certain order. CNO is defined first, CNAME second, etc. This order establishes the default left-to-right column sequence to be displayed when a SELECT statement uses an asterisk to indicate the display of all columns. (SELECT * FROM ...)

5. NULL Values

The next chapter will present examples of the INSERT statement where values are not specified for some columns. When a row is inserted into a table, and a column value is not specified, the system provides a default value or a special "null" value. The null value is interpreted as "value unknown."

There are circumstances where null values may be unreasonable. For example, CNO serves as a unique identifier (the primary key) for a course. Also, it is academic policy that every course be sponsored by some academic department. For these reasons, the NOT NULL clause is entered with the CNO and CDEPT column definitions. In effect, specifying NOT NULL helps maintain database integrity. The presence of this clause will instruct the system to reject any update to the COURSE table which would produce a null value anywhere in the CNO or CDEPT columns.

The example shows "NOT NULL WITH DEFAULT" specified for the CNAME and CDESCP columns. (This clause can only be specified in DB2.) It is similar to "NOT NULL" because it prevents null values from occurring in a column. However, it does not require that an actual value be specified during an insert operation. Instead, the omission of a column value means that the system will automatically supply a default value. The default value will be blanks for fixed length character data, an empty string for variable length character data, zero for numeric data, and CURRENT DATE (TIME or TIMESTAMP) for date/time data.

The CRED and CLABFEE columns will accept null values. However, null values can be confusing and require that greater attention be given to query formulation. (This issue will be discussed in Chapter 10.) Attaching NOT NULL to a column definition eliminates potential problems pertaining to null values. It is strongly suggested that NOT NULL be specified wherever appropriate.

6. Primary Key

The following comments on primary keys (and foreign keys in the next section) pertain to the general topic of "referential integrity," which is presented later in this chapter. We introduce this topic with a few comments about the PRIMARY KEY clause in the current example.

It is recommended, but not required, that every table have some column or group of columns specified as the primary key of the table. The primary key is a value which is always (1) nonnull and (2) unique within the table. The current example shows CNO as the primary key of the COURSE table. The "PRIMARY KEY" clause is followed by "CNO" within parentheses. Also, because CNO is designated as the primary key, the NOT NULL clause must be specified for the CNO column definition.

7. Foreign Key

Foreign keys, like primary keys, enhance database integrity. In the previous discussion of null values we noted that a school policy of each course being sponsored by some academic department means that NOT NULL should be specified for the CDEPT column. However, the NOT NULL clause only keeps null values out of the CDEPT column. It would not prohibit any "garbage" four-character string values like "WXYZ" or "ART " from being stored in this column. A more desirable objective is to restrict CDEPT values to those found in the DEPT column of the DEPARTMENT table. This objective is realized by specifying CDEPT as a foreign key which references the DEPARTMENT table.

A foreign key is a column or group of columns whose value equals some primary key value in a specified table. The current example shows "FOREIGN KEY (CDEPT) REFERENCES DEPARTMENT" in the CREATE TABLE statement used to create the COURSE table. This means that CDEPT, as a foreign key within the COURSE table, references the DEPARTMENT table because any value in the CDEPT column must equal some existing primary key value in the DEPARTMENT table. Assuming that the CREATE TABLE statement for DEPARTMENT designates DEPT as its primary key, then all CDEPT values must equal some existing DEPT value in the DEPARTMENT table. (Figure 8.2 illustrates each CDEPT foreign key referencing a DEPT value.)

The system will take a specified action in response to any update operation which would violate this policy. The example shows "ON DELETE RESTRICT" which instructs the system to reject any DELETE operation for a DEPARTMENT row which has a DEPT value equal to one or more CDEPT values. For example, given the current content of the COURSE table, the system will reject any attempt to delete the CIS, PHIL, or THEO rows from the DEPARTMENT table. Also, the system will automatically reject the insertion of any row into the COURSE table if its CDEPT value does not match any existing DEPT value. This example illustrates the use of a foreign key to implement "referential" integrity. This topic will be described later in this chapter.

8. System Catalog

Both DB2 and SQL/DS maintain a catalog which contains information about the existence of database tables, columns, primary keys, and foreign keys. When a CREATE TABLE statement is executed, each system stores the table, column, and key information in its catalog. When the system processes a query, it examines this catalog to validate the presence of any referenced table and column names. It also examines the catalog to enforce database integrity as indicated by any primary and foreign keys. A comprehensive knowledge of the structure of the catalog is required by database administrators. However, users of interactive SQL and most application programmers can function very well with a limited knowledge of the catalog.

The general structure of the catalog is the same for DB2 and SQL/DS. Each is a collection of tables about tables, columns, indexes, views, etc. These tables can be examined by using a SELECT statement. However, the detail content of the DB2 catalog is different from the SQL/DS catalog. This text will only make an occasional reference to the system catalog. After you understand SQL, it is easy to read the IBM reference manuals to learn how to examine either the DB2 or SQL/DS catalog.

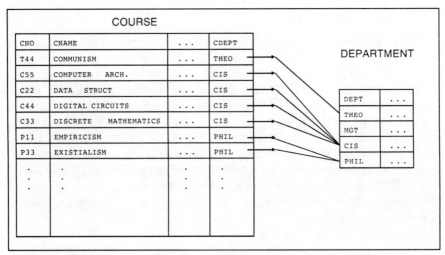

Figure 8.2   Foreign key (CDEPT) references (the primary key of) the DEPARTMENT Table.

SQL DATA TYPES

SQL supports a variety of data types. Each data type can be placed in one of three categories: (1) character string data, (2) numeric data, and (3) date/time data. We describe each category and its associated data types below.

Character String Data

There are six different character string data types. These are enumerated in Figure 8.3. The first three data types, CHAR, VARCHAR, and LONG VARCHAR, represent each alphanumeric character as 1 byte using the EBCDIC code. The remaining string data types use the DBCS ("Double Byte Character Set") code. These special data types are used to represent graphical character sets. A discussion of the graphical character codes is beyond the scope of this text.

You will find the greatest use for the CHAR and VARCHAR data types which are specified respectively for fixed and variable length character strings. Data values stored in a fixed length CHAR column will always have the same length. This means the system will append trailing blank characters if an insert operation attempts to store a string which is less than the defined length of the column. Data values stored as a variable length VARCHAR column will contain just those characters specified during an insert operation. The system will not append any trailing blanks. We can perform pattern recognition and use any of the string functions on either of these data types.

The LONG VARCHAR data type is used to store long (typically greater than 4046) character strings. These strings have many limitations with respect to comparison and function reference. In particular, such columns cannot be referenced in a WHERE, ORDER BY, or GROUP BY clause. They are primarily used to store and subsequently display long text strings. Finally, recall that arithmetic cannot be done with any of the string data types.

Name	Description
CHAR(n) or CHARACTER(n)	Fixed length character strings represented using EBCDIC. n is in the range of 1 to 254. All values in the column are of the same length, n. If n is omitted, a value of 1 is assumed.
VARCHAR(n)	Variable length character strings represented using EBCDIC. n is greater than 0 and less than a number determined by the installation page size (typically 4K). The values in the column may have different lengths not to exceed a maximum of n.
LONG VARCHAR	Variable length character strings represented using EBCDIC. The maximum length is determined by the system.
GRAPHIC(n)	Fixed length graphic strings containing DBCS data. n is in the range of 1 to 127 and indicates the number of characters in the string.
VARGRAPHIC(n)	Variable length graphic strings containing DBCS data. n is greater than 0 and less than a number determined by the installation page size.
LONG VARGRAPHIC	Variable length graphic strings containing DBCS data. The maximum length is determined by the system.

Figure 8.3   SQL Character String Data Types.

Numeric Data:

Numeric data types are defined for data items which will be used in arithmetic operations. Figure 8.4 presents the numeric data types. Recall that Chapters 5 and 6 presented a number of subtle points on the issues of decimal accuracy and overflow conditions. Selecting the appropriate data type can help avoid many of the potential problems described in those chapters.

Name	Description	Range of values
SMALLINT	Binary integer of 16 bits	-32768 to +32767
INTEGER or INT	Binary integer of 32 bits	-2147483648 to +2147483647
FLOAT(n) or REAL	Single precision floating-point number. n is in the range of 1 to 21. If n is omitted the column has double precision. The number is defined using 32 bits.	range of magnitude is 5.4E-79 to 7.2E+75
FLOAT(n) or DOUBLE PRECISION	Double precision floating-point number. n is in the range of 22 to 53 (default is 53). The number is defined using 64 bits.	range of maginitude is 5.4E-79 to 7.2E+75
DECIMAL(p,s) or DEC(p,s)	Decimal number with precision p and scale s. Precision is the total number of digits and must be between 1 and 15. The scale is the number of digits in the fractional part and must be between 0 and the number of the precision. If s is omitted a value of 0 is assumed. If s is omitted then p may be omitted in which case a alue of 5 is assumed.	-999999999999999 to +999999999999999

Figure 8.4   SQL Numeric data types.

Date/Time Data:

Most of the aforementioned data types are found in traditional high-level programming languages (i.e., COBOL, FORTRAN, etc.). Programmers would often use one of the traditional data types to encode a value which represented a date or a time. This is still possible. However, SQL has "primitive" date and time data types which can help avoid the complexity of the encoding process and can be utilized as arguments to the date/time functions presented in Chapter 7. These data types are DATE, TIME, and TIMESTAMP. Their values are stored in a special internal format (not described here) which is automatically converted to or from the following standard formats:

Format	Date	Time
ISO	1988-11-15	13.30.05
USA	11/15/1988	1:30 pm
EUR	15.11.1988	13.30.05
JIS	1988-11-15	13:30:05

These data types are described in Figure 8.5. They facilitate storing chronological information which can be operated upon for comparisons and computations using date/time functions and calculations.

Name	Description
DATE	Values consist of three parts for year, month, and day The range of values is 0001-01-01 to 9999-12-31.
TIME	Values represent a time of day in hours, minutes, and seconds. The range of values is 00.00.00 to 24.00.00.
TIMESTAMP	Values consist of seven parts representing a year, month, day, hour, minute, second, and microsecond. The range of values is 0001-01-01.00.00.00.000000 to 9999-12-31-24.00.00.000000.

Figure 8.5   SQL Date/time data types.

Entity Integrity and Referential Integrity

Sample Statement 8.1 introduced the PRIMARY KEY and FOREIGN KEY clauses which are used to implement entity and referential integrity. The purpose of this section is to elaborate on these concepts. The identification of primary and foreign keys occurs during database design when the semantic issues of entities, relationships, and database integrity are explicitly considered. A comprehensive discussion of database design is beyond the scope of this text. This is a very complex topic which requires attention to many issues which transcend SQL. But, it is impossible to present the CREATE TABLE or CREATE INDEX statements without touching on design issues. The following discussion offers some insight into the notions of entity and referential integrity. This is necessary to provide a context for a more detailed discussion the PRIMARY KEY and FOREIGN KEY clauses.

Entity (Primary Key) Integrity:

A row in a table usually corresponds to an instance of an entity type which the database is modeling. An entity may be described as any identifible object. For example, the COURSE table represents a type of entity, "course," and each row in the COURSE table corresponds to a particular course offered by the college. Because each real-world course entity is uniquely identifible, it is desirable that each corresponding row in the COURSE table also be uniquely identifible by some column or group of columns. This is called entity integrity and is the purpose of defining a primary key. Consider the ambiguity which occurs when a table contains two or more rows which cannot be distinguished from each other. There would be a loss of entity integrity because the one-to-one correspondence between a course entity and its corresponding row would be destroyed. By identifying CNO as the primary key we are stating that a course number can always be used to uniquely identify a course. Also, there are circumstances where the proper formulation of a SQL statement requires that a WHERE clause only select one row. And, if you write the statement so that multiple rows are actually selected, an error will occur. (Future sample queries will show such examples. Also, this is an especially important consideration when embedding SQL code in an application program.) The specification of CNO in the PRIMARY KEY clause instructs the system to reject any update operation which will result in a null or duplicate value in the CNO column. Therefore any statement containing "WHERE CNO = value" can never select more than one row.

Sometimes it is necessary to specify more than one column value in order to uniquely identify a row in a table. For example, if we assume that multiple sections of the same class may be offered during a given semester, then the CLASS table can have multiple rows with the same CNO value. For this reason, a "compound" primary key would be specified to include the CNO and SEC columns. In this case the PRIMARY KEY clause would be written as "PRIMARY KEY (CNO, SEC)".

Occasionally there will exist more than one choice for a primary key. For example, assume it is school policy that every course has a unique name. Then you could choose either CNO or CNAME as the primary key of the COURSE table. But only one primary key can be specified. How would you choose? A choice of CNO could be based upon the fact the school established course numbers for the purpose of uniquely identifying courses. However, choosing CNAME would not be wrong. And, it would even be a better choice if there were significantly more queries which selected rows based on CNAME values than CNO values. This is because you are required to create an index for the primary key which helps the system perform more efficient retrieval of rows. We will return to this issue in our discussion of the CREATE INDEX statement.

Referential (Foreign Key) Integrity:

Sample Statement 8.1 used the FOREIGN KEY clause to specify the CDEPT column in the COURSE table as a foreign key which references the DEPARTMENT table. We continue with this example to introduce terminology relevant to referential integrity.

Parent Table: A table which is referenced by some foreign key. DEPARTMENT is a parent table because it is referenced by the CDEPT foreign key. A primary key, such as DEPT in DEPARTMENT, must be specified for the parent table. This is because any nonnull foreign key (CDEPT) value must be equal to some existing primary key (DEPT) value. We say a foreign key references the parent table. It does so by identifying some primary key value in the parent table.

Dependent Table: A table which contains a foreign key. COURSE, which contains CDEPT as a foreign key, is a dependent table. It is dependent upon DEPARTMENT, the parent table. The academic policy requiring every course to be sponsored by some department means that courses are dependent upon departments. At the database level this means every dependent (COURSE) row is dependent upon some parent (DEPARTMENT) row. A dependent row cannot exist with a foreign key (CDEPT) value unless that value exists as some primary key (DEPT) value in the parent table.

Descendant Table: It is possible for a table which is dependent on one table to be the parent of another table. For example, assume it is school policy that every class correspond to some course. This means that every CNO value in the CLASS table must equal some existing CNO value in the COURSE table. Hence CNO in the CLASS table would be defined as a foreign key referencing COURSE. [In this example the foreign key (CNO) happens to be part of the primary key (CNO,SEC) for CLASS. This will occur often in practice.] This relationship means that COURSE becomes a parent table for CLASS in addition to being a dependent for DEPARTMENT. It also means that CLASS is dependent upon COURSE which is in turn dependent upon DEPARTMENT. Under this circumstance we say that CLASS is a descendant of DEPARTMENT. Figure 8.6 illustrates the relationship among these three tables.

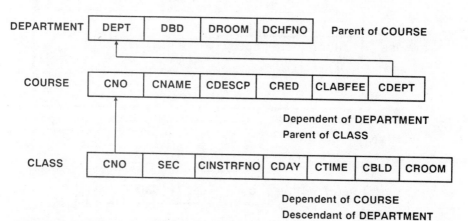

Figure 8.6   Parent, dependent and descendant tables.

Independent Table: A table without any foreign keys. For example, the CREATE TABLE for the STAFF table will not have a FOREIGN KEY clause specified for any column. (Note that the DEPT column in the STAFF table will contain department id values. However, this column is not specified as a foreign key because it may contain values not found in the primary key column of the DEPARTMENT table.)

A table may have multiple parent and/or dependent tables. Consider the REGISTRATION table, originally introduced in Chapter 7, which identifies which students registered for which classes. The primary key of this table is a composition of three columns (CNO, SEC, SNO). To ensure referential integrity we would specify two foreign keys in this table. The compound foreign key (CNO, SEC) would reference the CLASS table. And the SNO foreign key would reference the student table. Hence REGISTRATION is dependent on two tables, CLASS and STUDENT. Also, assume that all students must major in a subject corresponding to some existing academic department. This means the CREATE TABLE statement for STUDENT would specify SMAJ as a foreign key referencing DEPARTMENT. Hence DEPARTMENT is the parent of two tables, COURSE and STUDENT. Figure 8.7 reflects this expanded view of the design.

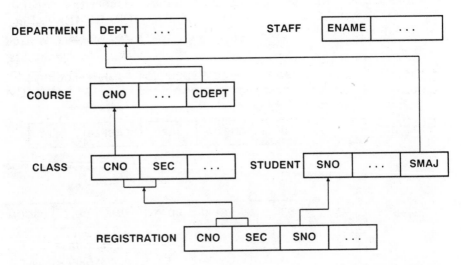

Figure 8.7   Expanded view of database design.

Cycle: Foreign keys can be defined so that a cyclic relationship is established. Assume it is school policy that each faculty member is assigned to some academic department. Then the FDEPT column in the FACULTY table would be specified as a foreign key referencing DEPARTMENT. (DEPARTMENT is the parent table and FACULTY is the dependent table.) Also assume that the chairperson of each academic department is some faculty member. Then the DCHFNO value in the DEPARTMENT is specified as a foreign key referencing FACULTY. (Here, FACULTY is the parent table and DEPART-MENT is the dependent table.) Figure 8.8 illustrates this relationship.

Sometimes a cycle involves more than two tables. TABLE1 could be the parent of TABLE2 which is the parent of TABLE3 which is the parent of TABLE4 which is the parent of TABLE1. In general, a cycle is formed if a dependent or descendant of any table becomes the parent of that table.

Self-Referencing Cycle: In DB2 (but not SQL/DS) it is possible for a table to be the parent and dependent of itself. In other words, the table contains a foreign key which references itself. For example, assume that some courses have at most one prerequisite course which students must take before registering for a class on the course. We could denote the prerequisite course in the COURSE table by altering this table to include a new column, PCNO, which contains the course number of the prerequisite course. Then the CREATE TABLE command for course would contain an additional FOREIGN KEY clause specifying PCNO as a foreign key referencing COURSE. Figure 8.9 illustrates this relationship. This self-referencing cycle is sometimes called a "recursive" relationship.

The data type and width of each component of a foreign key must be the same as the primary key. But a foreign key, unlike a primary key, may be allowed to contain null values (i.e., it is not necessary to specify NOT NULL for a foreign key column.) For example, there are many introductory courses which do not have a prerequisite course. Rows for such courses could have a null value in the PCNO column. Another example is the SMAJ column in the STUDENT table. If we assume that some students do not have to declare a major, then corresponding SMAJ values could be null. Also, note that if any part of a compound foreign key is null, then the entire foreign is considered to be null.

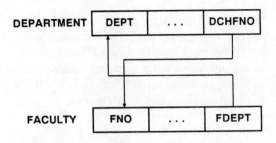

Figure 8.8   A cycle.

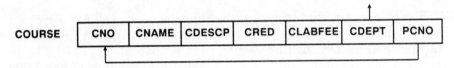

Figure 8.9   Self-referencing cycle.

Thus far, only the structural aspect of referential integrity has been considered. We now outline some of the processing rules which specify the system response to SQL data manipulation statements which reference primary and/or foreign key values. These statements (INSERT, UPDATE, and DELETE) will be described in Chapter 9.

Insert of Primary Key: The system will verify that the primary key value is unique. If it is not, the insert is rejected.

Insert of Foreign Key: The system will verify that any nonnull foreign key value equals some existing primary key in the referenced table. If it does not, the insert is rejected.

Update of Primary Key: The system will reject the update if there exists a dependent row referencing the primary key value.

Update of Foreign Key: The system will verify that the new foreign key value equals some existing primary key in the referenced table. If it does not, the update is rejected.

Delete of Primary Key: The ON DELETE clause can be included with the FOREIGN KEY clause. This clause directs the system response to the deletion of a row having a primary key value equal to some corresponding foreign key value. The available options are:

- RESTRICT: The system will reject the delete operation. This is the default action if the ON DELETE clause is not specified.
- SET NULL: The system will automatically substitute null values for the corresponding foreign key values. (This assumes the foreign key can accept null values.)
- CASCADE: The system will automatically delete any dependent rows having a foreign key value equal to the primary key value.

If there do not exist any foreign key values equal to the primary key value, then the ON DELETE clause does not apply and the delete is permitted.

Delete of Foreign Key: No restrictions (unless the foreign key is part of a primary key where other restrictions apply).

The database designer must give careful consideration to these processing rules. There are further restrictions and implications for descendent tables, especially those involved in cyclic relationships, which are not examined in this text.

Exercises:

For each of the following exercises refer to the descriptions of the tables as presented in the introduction to Part II of this text.

8A. Write the CREATE TABLE statement used to create the STUDENT table. Define SNO as the primary key, SMAJ as a foreign key referencing the DEPARTMENT table, and SADVFNO as a foreign key referencing the FACULTY table.

8B. Write the CREATE TABLE statement used to create the REGISTRATION table. Define (CNO, SEC, SNO) as a compound primary key. Also, define (CNO, SEC) as a foreign key referencing the CLASS table and SNO as a foreign key referencing the STUDENT table.

CREATE INDEX

The CREATE INDEX statement is used to create a database object called an index. Before introducing this statement we present the fundamental objectives and concepts of database indexes.

What is an index?

An index is an internal structure which the system can use to find one or more rows in a table. Figure 8.10 presents the general idea of an index. In effect, a database index is conceptually similar to an index found at the end of this or any other textbook. In the same way that a reader of a book would refer to an index to determine the page locations of a specified topic, a database system would read an index to determine the disk locations of rows selected by a SQL query. Simply put, the presence of an index can help the system process some queries in a more efficient manner.

A database index is created for a column or group of columns. Figure 8.10 shows an index (XCNAME) for the CNAME values found in the COURSE table. Observe that the index, unlike the COURSE table, represents the CNAME values in sequence. Also, the index is small relative to the size of the table. Therefore it is probably easier for the system to search the index to locate a row with a given CNAME value than to scan the entire table in search of that value. For example, the XCNAME index might be helpful to the system when it executes the following SELECT statement:

```
SELECT *
FROM    COURSE
WHERE   CNAME = 'EXISTENTIALISM'
```

Because the WHERE clause references CNAME, the system would consider using the XCNAME index. Now consider the statement:

```
SELECT *
FROM    COURSE
WHERE   CDESCP = 'FOR THE GREEDY'
```

The XCNAME index is of little use when searching for CDESCP values. Therefore, the system would probably not reference it.

There are many complex issues pertaining to database indexes. Some of these issues will be introduced below. However, we first present an example of the CREATE INDEX statement which is used to create the CNAME index.

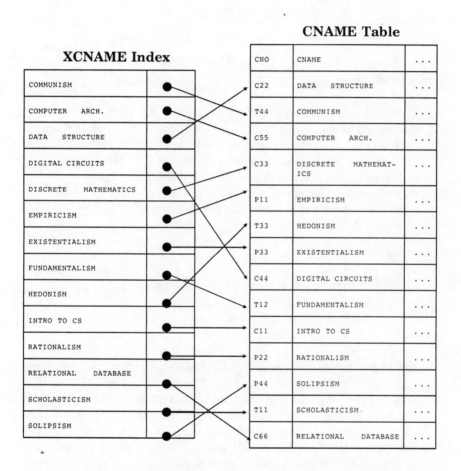

Figure 8.10   Index (XCNAME) based on CNAME column in COURSE table.

Sample Statement 8.2: Create an index on the CNAME column of the COURSE table. Call this index XCNAME.

```
CREATE INDEX XCNAME
ON COURSE (CNAME)
```

System Response:

Like the CREATE TABLE statement, the CREATE INDEX statement is not a query and hence there is no output display. Instead, the system returns a message which (presumably) indicates the successful creation of the XCNAME index. This index will be conceptually like that shown in Figure 8.10. We do not need to be concerned with its actual internal structure, which is considerably more complex.

Comments:

1. Syntax: A simplified version of the general syntax is:

```
CREATE INDEX index-name
ON table-name (column-name)
```

An index is given a name (XCNAME) according to the same rules that apply to table names. The name must begin with a letter which may be followed by one or more letters, digits, or underscore characters. Its length cannot exceed 18 characters. The examples of this text follow a common convention of choosing "X" as the first letter followed by the name of the column. However, this naming convention is not a system requirement.

The ON clause must reference a valid table name. The column name must be enclosed within parentheses and refer to a valid column name within the specified table.

2. In this example, the COURSE table already has rows stored in it. The system will scan this table to obtain the CNAME values and corresponding row locations to construct the index. In practice it is better to issue the CREATE INDEX statement before any rows are actually inserted into the table. However, as the example illustrates, an index may be created for a table which already has rows in it.

3. Once the index is created, the system will automatically maintain it. For example, if you issue an INSERT statement to place a new row in the COURSE table, the system will automatically determine the CNAME value and location of the new row and place a new entry in the XCNAME index. Simply put, once you create the index, the system does the rest.

4. Like the CREATE TABLE statement, the CREATE INDEX statement will cause an update to the system catalog. In this case, the system will record the presence of a new index (XCNAME) and its dependence on the COURSE table.

Do indexes force a change to the SELECT statement?

There is absolutely no change to the coding of a SELECT statement due to the presence or absence of an index. The syntax of all SELECT statements remains the same. Therefore, most users of the system can remain ignorant about the existence of any database indexes. Whenever a SELECT statment is submitted by a user, the system uses a special internal module called the "optimizer" to analyize the statement to determine if using an index would be beneficial. If this is the case, the system consults the catalog to determine if an index is available. If it is, the system utilizes the index. If it is not, the system performs a scan operation for the desired rows.

The use of an optimizer to determine the most efficient access path means the system possesses the desirable characteristic of physical data independence. The database administrator can modify internal data structures without forcing changes to previously written application programs. In particular, indexes can be created and dropped without affecting the validity of any existing or future SELECT statements.

What are the advantages of indexes?

The system can use an index to enhance machine efficiency in a number of circumstances. Some of these are described below.

1. **Direct access to a specified row:** Assuming an index is defined on the appropriate column, the system can avoid a scan to locate rows identified by a WHERE clause.

2. **Sorting:** Note that Figure 8.10 shows the CNAME values in alphabetical (really EBCDIC) sequence. The system can use this index to retrieve the COURSE table rows in CNAME sequence. In the absence of an index, the system must initiate an internal sort routine which can be costly, especially for a large number of rows. Current versions of DB2 and SQL/DS will consider using an index whenever the SELECT statement contains any of the following keywords or clauses: ORDER BY, DISTINCT, GROUP BY, or UNION.

3. **Join Operation:** The join operation is presented in Chapter 11. At this point we simply state that the join operation can be expensive and indexes can reduce the cost of this process.

4. Below we introduce special types of indexes (compound, unique, and clustered) which provide additional advantages.

How many indexes can be created?

Any number of indexes can be created for a given table. However, there is a cost associated with each index which may offset its advantages.

What are the disadvantges of indexes?

There are two cost factors associated with database indexes which prohibit their unlimited use. These are:

1. **Disk space used by the index:** An index, although it is smaller than the table, can occupy a considerable amount of disk storage. A table with many rows means that the index will have many entries. If the table has many indexes, the total disk space used by all the indexes could exceed the size of the table itself.

2. **Update costs:** While indexes expedite the retrieval process, they penalize the update process. Whenever a new row is inserted into or deleted from a table, the sytem must make the corresponding change to the indexes. If, for example, a table has five indexes, then an insert or delete operation forces an update to the five indexes. This could severely impact response time.

Will the system always use the index?

The optimizer may decide not to use an index even if it is defined on an appropriate column. This can occur under a number of circumstances. Some of these are:

1. **The table is very small:** Because it takes time to read the index itself, the optimizer may decide that it is quicker to simply scan the entire table.

2. **The index is not selective enough:** The optimizer might estimate that so many rows will eventually be selected that it is more efficient to perform a scan operation to find the desired rows.

There is no way to explicitly tell the system to use an index. The decision to use an index to access the data is made by the optimizer. (However, it is possible to modify certain catalog information to influence the optimizer to specify an access path which uses an index. This might be done by a database administrator or an application programmer who is using embedded SQL in a program which will be executed many times.)

Compound Indexes, Unique Indexes, and Clustered Indexes

The CREATE INDEX statement provides other advantages in addition to those specified above. By including special keywords in the statement (to be described below) any of the following special type indexes can be created.

1. **Compound index:** An index can be created on multiple column names. A simple example of such an index is a name-address (e.g., FNAME-FADDR) index for a table containing a column for faculty name and another column containing faculty address. Note that a compound index is just a single index where the key is composed of data found in multiple columns. Also note that the order of the index components is significant. For example, a name-address (FNAME-FADDR) index is different from an address-name (FADDR-FNAME) index. Current versions of DB2 and SQL/DS allow up to sixteen columns to be specified for a compound index.

2. **Unique index:** A unique index is an index which cannot contain any duplicate values. The presence of a unique index causes the system to reject any update to the table which will result in duplicate values in the column(s) specified by the index. *A unique index must be created for the primary key column(s).* (In SQL/DS the system automatically generates this index.) Although only one primary key can be specified for a table, any number of unique indexes can be specified for a table. For example, if you wanted the system to enforce uniqueness on CNAME values, you could have included the keyword "UNIQUE" in the CREATE INDEX statement shown in Sample Statement 8.1.

3. **Clustered index:** One index for each table may be designated as a clustered index. When the load or reorganization utility is executed, the system will store the table's rows in the physical sequence according to the key of the clustered index. For certain queries the optimizer can capitalize on the knowledge that the rows are stored in a specified sequence. (This does not conflict with our earlier comment that tables do not have any predefined sequence. There is still *no necessary sequence* which the system relies on. Even though inserts to the table may cause the sequenced rows to get out of sequence, the optimizer can still find some access path to satisfy any valid query.)

The above types of indexes are not mutually exclusive. It is possible for a single index to have all the above characteristics. Next, we consider a more general syntax of the CREATE INDEX statement which can be used to establish the above special types of indexes.

General Syntax of CREATE INDEX

A more general version of the CREATE INDEX statement is shown in Figure 8.11. This figure shows the syntax and keywords necessary to establish a compound, unique, or clustered index. Note that this figure does not represent the most general form of the CREATE INDEX statement which will be different for DB2 and SQL/DS. Again, this is because the most general forms of the statement can reference objects which are system specific. We comment on the details of syntax in the following example.

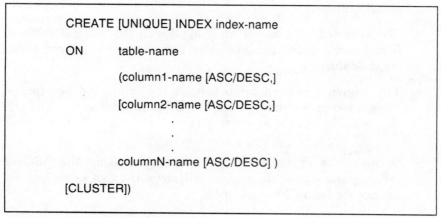

Figure 8.11   CREATE INDEX statement.

Sample Statement 8.3: Create a unique compound clustered index for the CLASS table. The index should reference the CNO and SEC columns which constitute the primary key.

```
CREATE UNIQUE INDEX XCNOSEC
    ON CLASS (CNO, SEC)
    CLUSTER
```

Comments:

1. The keyword "UNIQUE" is specified prior to "INDEX." This causes the system to reject any update which would cause multiple rows to have the same CNO-SEC combination.

2. The index is a compound index because it is defined for more than one column (CNO, SEC). Note that the order specified is significant.

3. The keyword "CLUSTER" only applies to DB2. In SQL/DS the first index created automatically becomes the clustered index for the table.

4. The sequence of each component of the compound key can be designated as ascending (ASC) or descending (DESC). The ON clause could have been written as

   ON CLASS (CNO ASC, SEC ASC)

   Because the example did not explicitly specify the ASC or DESC parameters, the system will default to an ascending sequence for both CNO and SEC.

Exercise:

8C. Create a unique clustered index for the SNO primary key of the STUDENT table. Also, create an index for the SMAJ foreign key in this table.

ALTER Statement

Assume that after you created the STUDENT table and inserted some rows, you decide that the database should include each student's height and weight. This means that two new columns containing student heights and weights need to be attached to the STUDENT table. This is the purpose of the ALTER statement. It can be used to add one or more new columns to an existing table. The next example illustrates this statement.

Sample Statement 8.4: Add two new columns to the STUDENT table. The first is called SHT which represents student weight in pounds and the second is called SWT which represents student height in inches. Represent both these values as decimals with a precision of 4 and a scale of 1. Establish zero as the default values for these new columns.

```
ALTER TABLE STUDENT
    ADD SHT DECIMAL(4,1)
        NOT NULL WITH DEFAULT
    ADD SWT DECIMAL(4,1)
        NOT NULL WITH DEFAULT
```

Comments:

1. The SHT and SWT columns are appended to the right-hand side of the STUDENT table. The NOT NULL WITH DEFAULT clause means that any rows subsequently inserted into the table with unspecified SHT and SWT values will cause these values to default to zero. It also means that the SHT and SWT columns for any existing rows will be set to zero. If this clause was not specified, the SHT and SWT for existing values would be set to null. For this reason, the NOT NULL clause cannot be specified for any columns defined in the ALTER TABLE statement.

2. SQL has other ALTER statements to modify certain physical characteristics of indexes and other system objects. These statements are not covered in this text.

OTHER DATABASE OBJECTS

This chapter has presented an overview of two types of database objects, tables and indexes. DB2 and SQL/DS also have other types of database objects in common. These are synonyms and views which will be described in later chapters. The other objects supported by each product are specific to the product. We briefly describe these objects for the sake of completeness. Again, the reader should recognize that the creation of these system specific objects is the responsibility of the database administrator.

DB2 Objects:

A DB2 table must reside within an object called a tablespace which is created with a CREATE TABLESPACE statement. The CREATE TABLE statement can assign a table to a specific tablespace by using the IN clause. The absence of this clause implies that the table will reside in a default tablespace. A tablespace may contain one or more tables. However, a table must reside within a single tablespace.

An index resides within an object called an indexspace. Because an indexspace can contain only one index, the CREATE INDEX statement automatically creates an indexspace for each new index.

Both tablespaces and indexspaces reside within a higher-level object called a database. The CREATE DATABASE statement is used to establish a new database. Usually this statement is executed once for each major application system and will contain all the data for that system. The DB2 system can support multiple databases.

Databases, tablespaces, and indexspaces, like tables and indexes, are logical objects. Tablespaces and indexspaces are assigned to a collection of direct access storage devices (DASD) called a storagegroup. The CREATE STOGROUP statement is used to identify the devices by volume name. Figure 8.12 illustrates an overview of the above DB2 objects.

SQL/DS Objects:

In SQL/DS a table must reside within an object called a dbspace. The ACQUIRE DBSPACE statement defines a dbspace and associates it with another object, a storage pool. A storage pool is a collection of DASD, the counterpart of the storagegroup in DB2. The CREATE TABLE statement can assign a newly created table to a specific dbspace using the IN clause. The absence of this clause in the previous examples implies that the newly created table was assigned to a default dbspace. A dbspace may contain one or more tables. However, a table must reside within a single dbspace.

An index will reside within the same dbspace as the table that it references. The CREATE INDEX statement does not explicitly reference this dbspace. The system will use the catalog to determine the dbspace for the specified table and then place the index in that same dbspace. Figure 8.13 illustrates an overview of these SQL/DS objects.

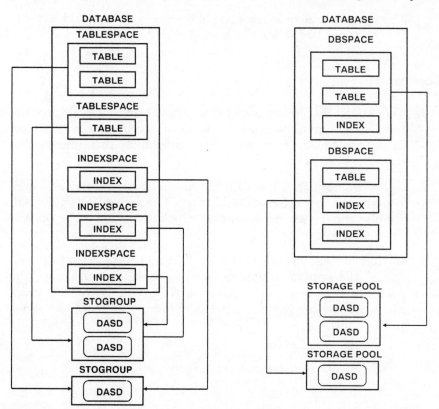

Figure 8.12   DB2 objects.   Figure 8.13   SQL/DS objects.

DROP Statement

All of the aforementioned database objects can be removed from the system by the DROP statement. This statement is the inverse of the CREATE statement. It is executed whenever the created object no longer serves any purpose in the application environment. We illustrate this command with two examples.

Sample Statement 8.5: Remove the XCNOSEC index.

```
DROP  INDEX  XCNOSEC
```

System Response:

The system will produce some message which should confirm that the specified index has been dropped.

Comments:

1. The XCNOSEC index is based on the CLASS table. Note that the DROP command does not need to specify the table name. This is because the system can determine this information from the system catalog.

2. Again we note that the CLASS table still exists and any queries against this table will still work. The system optimizer will simply choose an access path which does not rely on the dropped index.

3. Earlier it was noted that the CREATE INDEX statement causes the system to update the system catalog to record the presence of a new index. Likewise, the DROP INDEX statement causes the system to delete information about the index from the catalog.

Sample Statement 8.6: Drop the COURSE table. (Do not actually execute this statement if you are testing the examples shown in this text.)

```
DROP TABLE COURSE
```

System Response:

The system would display some message which confirms that the table has been dropped.

Comments:

1. Execution of the DROP TABLE statement not only deletes all rows from the table, it removes the very definition of the table from the system catalog. This means that a subsequent attempt to insert rows into the table would fail. The DELETE statement (described in the next chapter) is used to delete some or all rows in a table without removing the table definition. Obviously, the DROP TABLE statement is potentially dangerous, which is why we advised you not to actually execute the above statement. If you did, you would have to go through the effort of recreating the COURSE table and inserting its rows.

2. Whenever a table is dropped any indexes based on the table are also automatically dropped. For example, if the COURSE table is dropped, the system would automatically drop the XCNAME index.

3. SQL does not have any statement which can be used to remove just selected columns from a table (i.e., there is no "drop column" statement). To realize this objective a new table must be created with just the desired columns. Chapter 9 will show a variation of the INSERT statement which can be used to copy data from selected columns in the original table to the new table.

SUMMARY

This chapter has introduced some of SQL's most useful data defintion statements. These are

- CREATE TABLE: To create a new table.
- ALTER TABLE: To add columns to an existing table.
- CREATE INDEX: To create an index on an existing table.
- DROP INDEX: To remove an index.
- DROP TABLE: To remove a table.

In a production environment, where the database contains corporate data, these statements would only be executed by the database administrator. The database administrator would also execute other SQL statements not covered in this text because such statements would reference system specific physical objects. However, some users and programmers may have permission to create tables for personal data or testing purposes. This chapter has covered the above data definition statements in enough detail to realize these objectives.

SUMMARY EXERCISES

8D. Create a table called CISCOURSE. It should have four columns called CISCNO, CISCNAME, CISCRED, CISCLABFEE which, respectively, have the same attributes as the CNO, CNAME, CRED, and CLABFEE columns in the COURSE table. CISCNO is the primary key. There are no foreign keys. Also create a unique index for the primary key.

8E. Write the CREATE TABLE statement used to create the FACULTY table which was described in the introduction to Part II of this text. Also create a unique clustered index for the primary key and an index for each foreign key.

9

Data Manipulation

Chapter 8 introduced the CREATE TABLE statement which is used to create an empty table. We now turn our attention to SQL's data manipulation statements which are used to store rows in a table and subsequently modify and delete these rows. These are the INSERT, UPDATE, and DELETE statements.

The INSERT statement is used to store rows in a table. This statement could be used to store rows into an empty table or a table which already contains some number of rows. Thereafter, if you wish to change the contents of any existing rows, you must use the UPDATE statement. The DELETE statement is used to remove one or more rows from the table. This chapter will examine each of these statements. Again we emphasize that execution of these statements is potentially dangerous because errors could cause the loss of valuable data. If you are running the sample statements on a sample database, double check each statement before execution.

The INSERT Statement

There are two forms of the INSERT statement. The first form is used to insert exactly one row into a table. Using this form, data which currently does not exist in the database may be introduced into a table. The second form allows data from multiple rows already existing in some table to be inserted into another table. Both forms are shown in Figure 9.1. We introduce the first form of the INSERT statement by illustrating the addition of a new row into the COURSE table.

Sample Statement 9.1: Assume the CIS department offers a new course with the name "INTRODUCTION TO SQL". The course number is "C77". This course is worth 3 credits and its labfee is $150.00. The course description is "GOOD STUFF!". Insert a new row into the COURSE table corresponding to this course.

```
INSERT INTO COURSE
VALUES ('C77','INTRODUCTION TO SQL',
        'GOOD STUFF!',3,150.00,'CIS')
```

System Response:

The system will display a message which indicates that the system (1) successfully inserted the new row or (2) rejected the insert operation due to a syntax error or a violation of an integrity constraint. The specific response will vary according to the host system. Assuming that the insert operation is successful, you can further verify the presence of the new row by executing the following SELECT statement:

```
SELECT * FROM COURSE WHERE CNO = 'C77'
```

The system should display:

CNO	CNAME	CDESCP	CRED	CLABFEE	CDEPT
C77	INTRODUCTION TO SQL	GOOD STUFF!	3	150.00	CIS

Comments:

1. Syntax: INSERT Clause

    The name of the table, "COURSE" immediately follows "IN-SERT INTO". The table name must correspond to some previously created table.

2. Syntax: VALUES Clause

    The VALUES keyword is followed by a pair of parentheses which enclose the values to be placed in the fields of the newly inserted row. The example shows that the values are specified in the COURSE table's default left-to-right column sequence. Each value must comply with the data type of the corresponding column. The example shows apostrophes enclosing the character string values. Numeric values must not be enclosed within apostrophes. Each value must be separated by a comma which may or may not be followed by one or more spaces.

3. Recall that the relational model makes no assumptions about the ordering of rows within a table. This simplifies the insertion process because it is not necessary (in fact, it is not possible) to specify where the row actually gets placed in the table. Recall that the ORDER BY clause can be used in a SELECT statement to display rows in any desired sequence.

Format 1:

```
INSERT INTO name-of-table [(names-of-columns)]
VALUES (constant value/NULL/special-register)
```

Format 2:

```
INSERT INTO name-of-table [(names-of-columns)]
subselect-statement
```

Figure 9.1   SQL INSERT statement.

4. The previous chapter described the concepts of entity and referential integrity. If we assume that CNO is the primary key of the COURSE table and CDEPT is a foreign key referencing the DEPARTMENT table, then an error message indicating the violation of an integrity constraint could occur for two reasons. The first is that the CNO value in the new row equals some existing CNO value. The second is that the new CDEPT value does not match any existing DEPT value in the DEPARTMENT table. The system will reject the INSERT statement for either reason.

   Recall that the specification of a unique index on any column prevents the insertion of duplicate rows. If these features are not implemented the system will permit the insertion of duplicate rows. Duplicate rows are almost always undesirable. Therefore you should understand the integrity rules for any table before inserting rows into the table.

5. What if a certain value is unknown? For example, determination of a course labfee may require further financial analysis, but it still may be necessary to insert a row for a new course. Sample Statement 9.3 will illustrate use of the NULL keyword to handle this situation.

6. You must have permission (recognized by the system) to insert rows into the table. If you created the table, then you automatically have permission to insert rows into it. Otherwise, you must obtain INSERT privileges from the creator of the table. The process of granting privileges is described in Chapter 17.

7. The current example does not explicitly specify column names. Therefore, the VALUES clause must contain values for all columns specified in the default left-to-right column sequence. This requires that you know the data type and position of every column in the table. The next example will illustrate a variation of the INSERT statement which allows you to relate a value to a column by explicitly referencing the name of the column.

Sample Statement 9.2:   Same as previous example. This time specify the column names in the INSERT statement.

```
INSERT INTO COURSE
    (CNO, CNAME, CDESCP, CRED, CLABFEE, CDEPT)
VALUES ('C77','INTRODUCTION TO SQL',
        'GOOD STUFF!',3,150.00,'CIS')
```

System Response:

Same as the previous example.

Comment:

The specification of the column names requires extra typing. However, it forces you to confirm your understanding of the columns in the table. The specification of column names also allows for some flexibility. The column names may be specified in any left-to-right sequence as long as the values in the VALUES clause match the same sequence. The following INSERT statements would produce the same result.

```
INSERT INTO COURSE
        (CNAME, CNO, CDESCP, CRED, CLABFEE, CDEPT)
VALUES ('INTRODUCTION TO SQL',
        'C77','GOOD STUFF!',3,150.00,'CIS')

INSERT INTO COURSE
        (CRED, CNAME, CDEPT, CDESCP, CLABFEE, CNO)
VALUES (3,'INTRODUCTION TO SQL','CIS',
        'GOOD STUFF!',150.00,'C77')
```

Using this variation of INSERT eliminates the need to know the actual left-to-right sequence of the columns. However, it is still necessary to know the data types of the columns.

INSERTING ROWS WITH UNKNOWN VALUES

The previous INSERT statements specified values for all columns. However, there may be circumstances where some data values are unknown, yet you would still like to insert the row using just the known values. The next two examples illustrate techniques where only some column values are entered for a row. The column for any unknown value will be set to the null value or a default value.

Sample Statement 9.3:   Insert a row into the COURSE table with the following information. (Assume the course description, credit, and labfee values are unknown.)
- Course Number: C78
- Course Name: EMBEDDED SQL
- Department: CIS

```
INSERT INTO COURSE VALUES
('C78','EMBEDDED SQL',' ',NULL,NULL,'CIS')
```

Comments:

1. This example does not specify column names. Therefore, the VALUES clause must indicate all column values in the proper left-to-right sequence. (The absence of explicit column names is the same as naming all the columns.) Because the CRED and CLABFEE values are unknown, their values are specified by using the keyword NULL. The CDESCP value is also unknown, but NULL cannot be specified because NOT NULL WITH DEFAULT was declared in its definition. Specifying NULL for a column defined with the "NOT NULL" or "NOT NULL WITH DEFAULT" parameter would cause an error. Therefore, because CDESCP is implicitly named in the INSERT statement, a value (spaces in this example) must be provided. The system will insert the default value only when the column is not named in the column list and therefore no value is provided.

2. NULL is used for any data type, not just numeric values as shown in this example. Also, observe that NULL is not enclosed by apostrophes.

The next example illustrates another technique for inserting a row with just some known values.

Sample Statement 9.4:   Perform the same insert as in the previous example. This time explicitly identify the columns for which you are providing information.

```
INSERT INTO COURSE (CNO, CNAME, CDEPT)
VALUES ('C78', 'EMBEDDED SQL','CIS')
```

Comments:

1. This example specifies the column names and corresponding values for just those columns where the values are known. When column names are explicitly identified, it is not necessary to use the NULL keyword. This is because any unspecified column will be set to a null value or some default value. In this case the CRED and CLABFEE values are set to null and the CDESCP value defaults to spaces.

2. Again, note that the system will not let a column value default to the null value if that column was defined as "NOT NULL."

Exercises:

9A. Insert a row into the STAFF table with the following values:
  - ENAME: ALAN
  - ETITLE: LAB ASSIST
  - ESALARY: 3000
  - DEPT: CIS

9B. Insert a row into the STAFF table with the following values:
  - ENAME: GEORGE
  - DEPT: CIS

The ETITLE and ESALARY values are unknown.

The previous examples illustrated the first format of the INSERT statement which is used to insert exactly one row into a table. The next sample statement illustrates the second format of the INSERT statement which can be used to extract information from one or more rows in a table and use that information to insert one or more rows into another table.

The next sample statement assumes that the CISCOURSE table has been created. (See Exercise 8D) This table contains columns CISCNO, CISCNAME, CISCRED, and CISCLABFEE which have the same respective definitions as the CNO, CNAME, CRED, and CLABFEE columns in the COURSE table.

Sample Statement 9.5:   Copy the course number, course name, credits, and labfee for all CIS courses from the COURSE table into the CISCOURSE table.

```
INSERT INTO CISCOURSE
        SELECT CNO, CNAME, CRED, CLABFEE
        FROM    COURSE
        WHERE   CDEPT = 'CIS'
```

Comments:

1. Syntax: Like previous examples, this example begins with an INSERT clause ("INSERT INTO CISCOURSE"). Unlike previous examples, it does not have a VALUES clause. Instead, the INSERT clause is followed by a "good old SELECT statement" which conforms to the syntax rules presented earlier in this text. Considered in isolation, this SELECT statement is:

```
SELECT CNO, CNAME, CRED, CLABFEE
FROM    COURSE
WHERE   CDEPT = 'CIS'
```

A SELECT statement which follows an INSERT clause is called a "subselect" or a "subquery." (Chapters 13 and 15 will examine subqueries placed within other SELECT statements.)

Some restrictions exist when using the subquery form of INSERT. The subquery cannot reference the same table which the rows are to be inserted into. Also, the sequence in which the rows are to be inserted cannot be specified. This means that the ORDER BY clause cannot be used in the subquery.

2. Behavior: The subquery behaves like previous queries. It extracts the CNO, CNAME, CRED and CLABFEE columns for rows corresponding to the CIS Department. However, this time it does not display the selected data. Instead, the system inserts this data into the CISCOURSE table. The columns of rows selected by the subquery must be compatible with the columns of the CISCOURSE table. Observe that the left-to-right column sequence of the subquery is in the same order as the columns of the CISCOURSE table. The data types of corresponding columns are the same. If these conditions are not met, the system will reject the insert.

3. The example does not explicitly name the columns of the receiving table. The following INSERT statement shows this is valid. The result would be the same as the current example.

```
INSERT INTO CISCOURSE
        (CISCNO, CISCNAME, CISCRED, CISCLABFEE)
        SELECT  CNO, CNAME, CRED, CLABFEE
        FROM    COURSE
        WHERE   CDEPT = 'CIS'
```

4. The COURSE table is unchanged. After execution of the INSERT statement some duplication of data exists in the COURSE and CISCOURSE tables. This is potentially dangerous from a database integrity point of view because any changes to CIS rows in the COURSE table do not automatically carry over into the CISCOURSE table. (If data consistency is desirable, then the view mechanism should be used. Chapter 16 will present the CREATE VIEW command which can realize this objective. The above approach is useful if we want a copy of CIS rows which can be changed without affecting the original COURSE table.)

5. Although the CISCOURSE table was empty prior to this insert operation, this is not necessary. If the table already contained rows, the new rows would simply have been appended to the table.

The UPDATE Statement

The UPDATE statement can be used to change any value in a table. It must contain a SET clause to identify which columns are to be changed. And it may include a WHERE clause to identify the rows to be modified. The next sample statement simply changes one value in one row. Sample Statement 9.7 will illustrate how multiple row/column values can be changed by executing a single UPDATE statement.

Sample Statement 9.6:   Change the labfee for the course with course number "C77" to $175.00.

```
UPDATE COURSE
SET CLABFEE = 175.00
WHERE CNO = 'C77'
```

System Response:

The system will display a message which indicates (1) a successful update or (2) failure of the update operation due to a syntax error or a violation of an integrity constraint. The specific response will vary according to the host system. (Assuming that the update operation is successful, you can further verify the change by displaying the COURSE table.)

Comments:

1. The keyword "UPDATE" is followed by the name of the table (COURSE) to be changed.

2. The SET clause, which follows the UPDATE clause, specifies the column(s) to be changed. "SET CLABFEE = 175.00" means CLABFEE will be set to 175.00 in the row(s) identified by the WHERE clause. The previous CLABFEE value is lost. It is overlaid by the value of 175.00.

3. The WHERE clause, which follows the SET clause, identifies the row(s) to be changed. Knowing that CNO is the primary key gives us assurance that only the C77 row will be changed.

The previous example simply changed one value in a table. Figure 9.2 outlines the general syntax of the UPDATE statement which shows that the SET clause can reference many columns and the WHERE clause can specify any search condition. Both the SET and WHERE clauses are described below.

SET Clause

The SET clause identifies each column to be changed and specifies the value to be used in making the change. This value can be an expression which is evaluated. The expression can also be a simple constant, the NULL keyword, or one of the special date/time registers. More than one column can be changed in a single UPDATE statement by ending the first expression with a comma and following it with another column and expression.

WHERE Clause

The WHERE clause identifies the row(s) to be changed. The changes made by the SET clause will only apply to rows which match the condition specified in the WHERE clause. If the WHERE clause identifies multiple rows, then all such rows are updated. The WHERE clause is coded just like a WHERE clause in the SELECT statement. Its syntax is the same and can contain any of the Boolean operators.

The WHERE clause is optional. *However, we emphasize that the absence of a WHERE clause will cause every row in the table to be changed.* For example, if we wanted to change *all* CISCRED values to 9, we would execute:

```
UPDATE  CISCOURSE
SET     CISCRED=9
```

This behavior parallels that of the SELECT statement. The absence of a WHERE clause means that all rows are selected for display. The UPDATE statement without any WHERE clause is used to make a global change to every row in the table.

```
UPDATE name-of-table
   SET name-of-column-1 = expression-1,
       name-of-column-2 = expression-2,

             .
             .

       name-of-column-n = expression-n,
  [WHERE search-condition]
```

Figure 9.2   SQL UPDATE statement.

The next example illustrates the set level processing of SQL which allows many rows to be updated by execution of a single UPDATE statement.

Sample Statement 9.7:   Make the following changes to any COURSE row which has a course number beginning with "C7".
- Set the credit value equal to 6.
- Increase the labfee by 10%.
- Change the description to "THE LANGUAGE OF DB2"

```
UPDATE COURSE
SET CRED = 6,
    CLABFEE = CLABFEE * 1.10,
    CDESCP = 'THE LANGUAGE OF DB2'
WHERE CNO LIKE 'C7%'
```

Comments:

1. Previous examples inserted two rows into the COURSE table with course numbers C77 and C78. These are the only courses which match the WHERE condition. Hence two rows will be changed by the UPDATE command.

2. This example changes three columns in each target row. All changes are expressed in a the SET clause. Each expression except the final expression is terminated by a comma. If the comma is omitted, an error occurs.

   Both the CRED and CDESCP columns are assigned new values in the same manner as in the previous example. The new value assigned to the CLABFEE column is based on the value presently existing in the column. The result of the calculation replaces the existing value.

Exercise:

9C. Update the ESALARY value of any staff member assigned to the CIS Department. The new salary for all such individuals is $4000.

The DELETE Statement

The DELETE statement is used to remove an entire row or group of rows from a table. One cannot delete a column or just part of a row.

Sample Statement 9.8:   Delete all rows from the COURSE table which have a course number beginning with "C7". (Remove the two rows previously inserted into the COURSE table.)

```
DELETE
FROM   COURSE
WHERE  CNO LIKE 'C7%'
```

System Response:

The system responds with a message which (1) confirms the successful deletion or (2) rejects the deletion due to a syntax error or violation of an integrity constraint.

Comments:

1. Given the current status of the COURSE table, the WHERE clause identifies the C77 and C78 course for deletion. After deleting these rows, the contents of COURSE table becomes the same as it was prior to the execution of the data manipulation examples shown in this chapter.

2. Assume the "ON DELETE RESTRICT" clause is specified for the foreign keys (CNO,SEC) and (CNO,SEC,SNO) in the CLASS and REGISTRATION tables. Then, if either of these tables has a row with a CNO value of "C77" or "C78", the delete operation will be rejected to maintain referential integrity.

The general format of the DELETE statement is shown in Figure 9.3. The syntax is simple, but you should be careful to accurately specify the correct rows for deletion.

The DELETE keyword identifies the operation. The FROM clause is followed by the name of the target table.

The WHERE clause is used to identify the row(s) to be deleted. The search condition has the same structure as that of the SELECT and UPDATE statements. It can be used to identify many rows and is therefore subject to the same accuracy considerations. (The previous example illustrated the set level processing capabilities of the DELETE by selecting multiple rows for deletion.) Therefore, we again recommend caution in the coding of the WHERE clause to avoid the erroneous deletion of rows. If you want to delete just one row make certain the WHERE clause identifies the row by the primary key or some other column which has a unique index defined for it.

The WHERE clause is optional. *However, we emphasize that failure to include it will cause every row in the table to be deleted.* For example, the following statement will delete every row in the CISCOURSE table.

```
DELETE
FROM      CISCOURSE
```

Because the WHERE clause is omitted, all rows are deleted from the table. The table will still exist, but will not contain any rows. A subsequent reference to the CISCOURSE table in a SELECT statement would not cause an error, but would not return any rows.

Exercise:

9D. Delete all rows in the STAFF table corresponding to employees assigned to the CIS Department.

```
DELETE
FROM    name-of-table
[WHERE search-condition]
```

Figure 9.3   SQL DELETE Statement

SUMMARY

In this chapter we introduced the data manipulation statements of SQL which allow

- The insertion of new rows into a table using the INSERT statement
- The modification of data in existing rows of a table using the UPDATE statement
- The deletion of existing rows from a table using the DELETE statement

These statements may be executed in the interactive environment as demonstrated in this chapter. However, operations which affect the content of the database will usually be performed from within an application program using embedded SQL to ensure greater control and reduce the chance of error. In the event that database changes must be made interactively, there are precautionary measures which can be used to prevent a permanent change from being applied to the database until such changes are confirmed. This topic will be addressed in Chapter 18 which presents the concept of transaction processing as implemented by the COMMIT and ROLLBACK statements.

SUMMARY EXERCISES

9E. Create a table called EXPENSIVE with the columns EXPCNO, EXPCNAME, EXPCLABFEE, and EXPDEPT which respectively have the same data types and lengths as the CNO, CNAME, CLABFEE, and CDEPT columns in the COURSE table. (Do not specify any primary or foreign keys for this table.) Then, for every COURSE table row with a CLABFEE value over $100, copy the column information into the corresponding columns of the EXPENSIVE table.

9F. Update the EXPENSIVE table by subtracting $50 from the EXPCLABFEE column if its current value exceeds $400.

9G. Delete all rows in the EXPENSIVE table which correspond to courses offered by the Theology Department.

9H. Insert a new row into the EXPENSIVE table. The EXPCNO value is "X99" and the EXPDEPT value is "XXX". The EXPCNAME and EXPCLABFEE values are unknown.

9I. Change every EXPCNAME value in the EXPENSIVE table to "JUNK".

9J. Delete all rows from the EXPENSIVE table.

9K. Drop the EXPENSIVE table.

10

Processing Null Values

When we first encountered the STAFF table we observed that the DEPT value for the row describing Da Vinci contained a null value. This value implies that Da Vinci's department is unknown. All the previous sample queries and exercises involving the STAFF table were designed to avoid any potential problems which can result from the presence of null values. This chapter will describe these potential problems and present techniques for handling such problems.

In Chapter 8 we emphasized that the creator of a table should consider using the NOT NULL or the NOT NULL WITH DEFAULT options to prohibit any database operation from storing null values in a specified column. However, there will be circumstances when values are unknown. Chapter 9 described how the INSERT command allows a column to be assigned or default to a null value. Unless the designer uses the traditional default approach of using a specific value, typically blank or zero, to represent an unknown value (i.e., specifies NOT NULL WITH DEFAULT), null values may be present in database tables. When this occurs, the results produced by a SELECT statement may not be what you expect. This is because of the semantic subtleties associated with unknown values. This chapter presents sample queries which illustrate the behavior of the SELECT statement when it encounters null values. You may think that this behavior is unnecessarily complex and conclude, as others have, that null values are just not worth the trouble. However, null values can occur in DB2 and SQL/DS tables. Therefore, you should understand how to code SELECT statements which process them correctly.

To present sample queries on this topic we digress from our educational database design and introduce a special table which contains a spectrum of null values. The table's name is NULLTAB and its content is shown in Figure 10.1. In particular, note that NULLTAB has multiple rows where every value is null. This is most unusual, but it is nonetheless valid.

PKEY	COLA	COLB	COLC
1	10.00	20.00	5.00
2	30.00	30.00	5.00
3	160.00	–	10.00
4	–	170.00	5.00
5	–	–	10.00
6	10.00	40.00	5.00
7	30.00	60.00	5.00
8	–	–	–
–	–	–	–
–	–	–	–
–	–	–	–

Figure 10.1   NULLTAB table.

CALCULATING WITH NULL VALUES

Assume you were asked to add 10 to the winning number of tomorrow's Connecticut Million Dollar Lottery. Unfortunately, today you cannot guarantee to calculate the correct answer. Because the calculation involves at least one unknown value, the result of the calculation is unknown. SQL applies the same logic when it evaluates an expression involving an unknown value. The result is a null value.

Sample Query 10.1: Calculate the sum and the difference of the COLA and COLB values in NULLTAB.

```
SELECT PKEY, COLA, COLB,
       COLA + COLB, COLA - COLB
FROM   NULLTAB
```

```
--------------------------------------------------------
  PKEY      COLA       COLB       COL1       COL2
--------------------------------------------------------
    1      10.00      20.00      30.00     -10.00
    2      30.00      30.00      60.00       0.00
    3     160.00        -          -          -
    4        -       170.00        -          -
    5        -          -          -          -
    6      10.00      40.00      50.00     -30.00
    7      30.00      60.00      90.00     -30.00
    8        -          -          -          -
    -        -          -          -          -
    -        -          -          -          -
    -        -          -          -          -
```

Comment:

This example illustrates that any arithmetic expression will produce a null value if one or more of its operands is a null value.

Sample Query 10.2:   Find the sum, average, maximum, and minimum values of COLA in NULLTAB.

```
SELECT  SUM(COLA),  AVG(COLA),
        MAX(COLA),  MIN(COLA)
FROM    NULLTAB
```

COL1	COL2	COL3	COL4
240.00	48.00000000000	160.00	10.00

Comments:

1. This example demonstrates that built-in arithmetic functions ignore nulls in their calculation. These functions do not simply treat an unknown value as zero. If this were the case, the average of column COLA would be $240.00/11 = 21.82$. Instead, the AVG function only used the five known values to determine the result, $240.00/5 = 48.00$.

   We emphasize the apparent lack of symmetry in the way SQL handles null values. For the built-in functions, it ignores the null values and generates a nonnull result based upon the present known values. But, as Sample Query 10.1 illustrates, the presence of a null value causes an arithmetic expression to evaluate to null.

2. What if all values passed to a column function are null? Then the result produced by the function is also null.

We did not include the COUNT function in the previous example because its behavior is different from the other column functions. This is because the COUNT(*) function counts the number of rows selected. Unlike the other column functions, it does not examine the actual values, which may or may not be null, that are stored in the rows.

Sample Query 10.3:   How many rows does NULLTAB have?

```
SELECT COUNT(*)
FROM NULLTAB
```

```
----------
   COL1
----------
    11
```

Comment:

The result (11) is reasonable once we realize that the COUNT(*) function simply counts the number of selected rows. It does not consider whether any of the selected rows contain null values. In particular, a row consisting of all null values is still included in the count.

We stated above that null values are potentially dangerous. The next two sample queries demonstrate that the previous reasonable behavior of arithmetic expressions and built-in functions may generate confusing results when processing null values.

Sample Query 10.4:   Calculate the average of COLA two ways. Apply (1) the AVG function and (2) SUM and COUNT functions.

```
SELECT  SUM(COLA), COUNT(*),
        SUM(COLA)/COUNT(*), AVG(COLA)
FROM    NULLTAB
```

COL1	COL2	COL3	COL4
240.00	11	21.8	48.000000000000

Comment:

Note the difference in the averages. The third column was calculated as 240.00/11. The fourth column was calculated as 240.00/5. Which is correct? Regardless of how you answer this question, the example shows the subtleties of null values.

Exercise:

10A. Refer to the FACULTY table for this exercise. Display the average number of dependents and the total number of dependents for all faculty members together with the number of faculty members at our mythical college. Additionally, derive the average by dividing the total you retrieve by the number of faculty members. Compare the results of these calculations.

Sample Query 10.5: Calculate the overall total of the values found in COLA and COLB. Use two approaches. (1) Find the sum of COLA, then the sum of COLB, then add the results. (2) For each row, add the COLA and COLB values, then summarize these row totals.

```
SELECT  SUM(COLA) + SUM(COLB),
        SUM(COLA + COLB)
FROM    NULLTAB
```

```
------------------------------------
  COL1                 COL2
------------------------------------
 560.00               230.00
```

Comment:

Note the different results to two apparently equivalent mathematical expressions. In effect, they are only equivalent when all the COLA and COLB values are known. Review Sample Queries 10.1 and 10.2 to confirm your understanding of this example.

Exercise:

10B. Assume that each faculty member was awarded a $250 tuition credit for each dependent. What would be the total remuneration for each faculty member if this amount was added to his salary? In other words, display the total of the salary and $250 for each dependent for all faculty members. (Consider the above example when reviewing your solution.)

COMPARING WITH NULL VALUES

Assume you have $10 in your pocket and you pass a complete stranger on the street. If you were asked to compare your $10 to the presumably unknown amount the stranger has, the result is unknown. Again, SQL applies the same logic. When it does a comparison involving at least one null value, the result is null. And again, we will see that this reasonable behavior has potential pitfalls.

Sample Query 10.6: Display all rows from NULLTAB where the COLA value equals the COLB value.

```
SELECT  *
FROM    NULLTAB
WHERE   COLA = COLB
```

```
-----------------------------------------------
    PKEY      COLA      COLB      COLC
-----------------------------------------------
      2     30.00     30.00      5.00
```

Comments:

This query only returned one row. Consider why the WHERE clause resulted in a "no hit" for the other ten rows.

1. Rows corresponding to PKEY values of 1, 6, and 7 have known COLA and COLB values which are not equal to each other. Hence, it is clear why they are not selected.

2. Rows corresponding to PKEY values of 3 and 4 have one null value in either COLA or COLB. Because one value is unknown, the comparison results in a "no hit" and hence these rows are not selected. Note this is the case even though one of the unknown (null) values could possibly be equal to the known value. SQL only selects a row when it is certain that the WHERE condition evaluates to true.

3. Rows corresponding to PKEY values of 5, 8, and null have null values in both COLA and COLB. These rows are not selected. SQL does not consider two null values to be equal to each other. This is analogous to trying to deduce whether or not two complete strangers have the same amount of money in their pocket. The answer is "unknown," not "true." Again, SQL only selects a row when it is certain that the WHERE condition evaluates to "true." To emphasize the point, this means SQL does not consider "null = null" to be true.

4. The example uses the equals comparison operator. The same behavior applies to the other comparison operators. A greater than (>), less than (<), etc., comparision results in "unknown" if any value is null. In particular, "null <> null" is considered to be unknown.

Exercise:

10C. Display any row in NULLTAB where the COLA value is not equal to the COLB value. (If you execute this query, observe that only three rows are selected for this display. These correspond to PKEY values 1, 6, and 7. Because the sample query only selected one row, and there are 11 rows in NULLTAB, it might seem that this exercise should produce 10 rows. Why not? See the following Sample Queries for a discussion of this point.)

The next two examples together show the potential problems with
WHERE clauses involving null values.

Sample Query 10.7:   How many staff members are assigned to the
Theology Department?

```
SELECT COUNT(*) FROM STAFF
WHERE  DEPT = 'THEO'
```

```
----------
  COL1
----------
    4
```

Comment:

This query selected the four rows corresponding to Matthew,
Mark, Luke, and John.

Sample Query 10.8:   How many staff members are not assigned to the
Theology Department?

```
SELECT COUNT(*) FROM STAFF
WHERE DEPT <> 'THEO'
```

```
----------
  COL1
----------
    4
```

Comment:

This query selected the four rows corresponding to Dick Nix,
Hank Kiss, Euclid, and Archimedes.

The previous two queries show 4 members assigned to the Theology Department and 4 members not assigned to the Theology Department. Can we deduce that we have a total of 8 staff members? No! There are 9 rows in the STAFF table. Neither of the above queries had a match on the row corresponding to Da Vinci whose DEPT value is null. In particular, Sample Query 10.7 did not select Da Vinci's row because SQL could not conclude that Da Vinci is assigned to the Theology Department. Likewise, Sample Query 10.8 did not select Da Vinci's row because SQL concludes that he could be assigned to the Theology Department. The WHERE clause in both sample queries evaluates to "unknown" when considering Da Vinci's row. Again, SQL will select only those rows which evaluate to "true."

These sample queries illustrate the potential danger associated with using a WHERE clause to test for the presence or absence of a given value when a null value can occur. Sample Query 10.13 will introduce the use of "IS NULL" as a means of testing for the presence of a null value. Then, if we assume that a null DEPT value can be interpreted as "not assigned to any department, including the Theology Department," Sample Query 10.8 could be expressed as

```
SELECT COUNT (*) FROM STAFF
WHERE   DEPT <> 'THEO'
OR      DEPT IS NULL
```

The result of executing this statement is 5. Most users would consider this to be a better answer than 4. However, the choice of which answer is "correct" depends upon how you interpret the query objective.

THREE-VALUE LOGIC

Traditional database systems and traditional computing languages which manipulate them are based on a system of two-value logic. This simply means that any comparison will always result in a "true" or "false" conclusion. The source of the potential confusion in the aforementioned problems lies in the fact that null values force the introduction of a three-value logic system where a comparison reduces to a "true," "false" or "unknown" result. A three-value logic system is more complex and requires greater attention in entering SQL commands and interpreting the results of a query.

In Chapter 3 we presented the Boolean operators (AND, OR, NOT) in the context of the traditional two-value logic. Figure 10.2 summarizes the behavior of these operators in a three-value logic system. We do not explain the details of each comparison except to note that the evaluations of "true" (T), "false" (F) and "unknown" (U) are consistent with the notions of AND, OR and NOT as described earlier. The AND of two conditions only evaluates to "true" if both conditions are "true." The OR of two conditions evaluates to "true" if either or both of the conditions are "true." The NOT of a "true" condition is "false" and vice versa. The NOT of an "unknown" condition is "unknown."

| Logic of NOT: | condition   : T F U |
| | NOT condition : F T U |

Logic of AND:	AND : T F U
	T : T F U
	F : F F F
	U : U F U

Logic of OR:	OR : T F U
	T : T T T
	F : T F U
	U : T U U

Figure 10.2   Logical Connectors in three-value logic systems.

Sample Query 10.9:   Display any row from NULLTAB where COLA is equal to COLB, or COLA is greater than COLC.

```
SELECT  *
FROM    NULLTAB
WHERE   COLA = COLB
OR      COLA > COLC
```

PKEY	COLA	COLB	COLC
2	30.00	30.00	5.00
1	10.00	20.00	5.00
7	30.00	60.00	5.00
6	10.00	40.00	5.00
3	160.00	–	10.00

Comment:

You should work through the logic of this query to confirm your understanding of the three-way logic.

SORTING NULL VALUES

Null values sort high in an ascending sort sequence. The next example illustrates this point.

Sample Query 10.10:   Display all rows of NULLTAB in ascending sequence by COLA.

```
SELECT PKEY, COLA
FROM    NULLTAB
ORDER BY COLA
```

```
------------------------
   PKEY      COLA
------------------------
      6     10.00
      1     10.00
      2     30.00
      7     30.00
      3    160.00
      -         -
      -         -
      5         -
      4         -
      8         -
      -         -
```

Comments:

1. Null values appear at the bottom of the output display because they sort higher than any known value.

2. This raises another subtle semantic issue. Earlier we emphasized that a comparison involving a null value evaluates to "unknown." Sorting a collection of values involves comparing them, and if the system doesn't know a value (because it's null), how does it know where to put it in sequence? This is an apparent contradiction. It is resolved by noting that the displayed row must go somewhere. DB2 and SQL/DS decide to put it at the high end of the sequence. This is an arbitrary decision. Some other relational database systems place null values at the low end of the sequence.

SQL also treats null values like known values when it does internal sorting for the sake of removing duplicate values or forming groups. The next two examples illustrate this point.

Sample Query 10.11:   Display the unique values (including null) found in COLA of NULLTAB.

```
SELECT DISTINCT COLA
FROM    NULLTAB
```

```
----------
   COLA
----------
  10.00
  30.00
 160.00
    -
```

Comment:

We emphasize that DISTINCT considers null values equal to each other. Hence, only one null value is shown in the result. (Likewise the specification of a UNIQUE index on a column which allows null values will permit only one occurrence of a null value in the column.)

Exercise:

10D. Display the name, faculty number, and number of dependents for all faculty members. Arrange the result in descendng sequence by the number of dependents.

Sample Query 10.12:   Using the NULLTAB table, form groups of COLC values and display the sum of the COLA values for each group.

```
SELECT  COLC, SUM(COLA)
FROM    NULLTAB
GROUP BY COLC
```

COLC	COL1
5.00	80.00
10.00	160.00
-	-

Comment:

We emphasize that SQL treats null values as equal for the purpose of grouping. Hence, only one group is formed for the nulls found in COLC. The sum of the COLA values shown in COL1 for this group is null because all the corresponding COLA values are null and the sum of null values is null.

Exercise:

10E. Display the average salary of faculty members who have the same number of dependents.

SUMMARY OF THE PROBLEMS WITH NULL VALUES

The previous examples presented a number of situations where an unsophisticated user could easily misinterpret the contents of an output display. The general source of the problem is the more complex semantics of a three-value logic system. So again we encounter complexity which transcends the SQL language. To briefly consider the semantics, note that the "null value" is not really a "value" since its purpose is to designate the absence of a value. Sometimes, when performing calculations and comparisons, SQL behaves in a way which is consistent with this "absence of a value" concept. Under other circumstances, for example, when you use the ORDER BY, DISTINCT, and GROUP BY features, SQL ends up treating nulls as though they were values.

AVOIDING THE COMPLEXITY OF NULL VALUES

The easiest way to avoid the complexity described above is to simply keep nulls out of the database by using the NOT NULL or NOT NULL WITH DEFAULT option for every column of every table in the database. Many database designers adopt this approach. However, others say this is just sweeping the problem under the carpet. The real world presents situations where data is unknown and our database should reflect this reality. In this case, nulls should be allowed to appear in some columns of some tables. The remaining examples present some SQL techniques for handling null values when they are necessary.

IS NULL

It is possible to explicitly test for the presence of a null value in a row by using "IS NULL" in a WHERE clause.

Sample Query 10.13:   Display any row in NULLTAB which has a null value in COLA.

```
SELECT  *
FROM    NULLTAB
WHERE   COLA IS NULL
```

PKEY	COLA	COLB	COLC
-	-	-	-
8	-	-	-
-	-	-	-
5	-	-	10.00
4	-	170.00	5.00
-	-	-	-

Comments:

1. Only those rows with a null value in COLA are displayed.

2. You cannot use an equal sign with the NULL predicate (that is, "WHERE COLA = NULL" is invalid). You must specify "IS NULL".

Exercise:

10F. Display the names, number of dependents, and department numbers of all faculty members for whom it is not known whether they have any dependents.

IS NOT NULL

The NOT keyword can be used with the NULL predicate. The "IS NOT NULL" phrase is probably more useful than "IS NULL" because it allows you to bypass some of the aforementioned problems by explicitly excluding null values from consideration. The next sample query is a modification of Sample Query 10.4 where the presence of null values caused two different averages to be calculated.

Sample Query 10.14:   Calculate the average of COLA two ways. (1) Apply the AVG function and (2) use the SUM and COUNT functions. Exclude any null values such that both results are the same.

```
SELECT  SUM(COLA), COUNT(*),
        SUM(COLA)/COUNT(*), AVG(COLA)
FROM    NULLTAB
WHERE   COLA IS NOT NULL
```

COL1	COL2	COL3	COL4
240.00	5	48.00	48.000000000000

Comments:

1. The WHERE clause eliminated any row with a null COLA value from being selected. Hence, only five rows were selected and the average was calculated as 240.00/5 = 48.00. Most of the time it is a good idea to explicitly exclude null values from mathematical calculations.

2. Again, the not equal sign cannot be used with the NULL predicate (that is, "WHERE COLA <> NULL" is invalid).

VALUE Built-in Function

The previous examples showed the null value displayed as a hyphen (-). It is possible to substitute a more meaningful value for a null value in an output display. This is the purpose of the VALUE function.

Sample Query 10.15:   Display NULLTAB as described below.

1. Display COLC. Substitute 999.99 for any null values.

2. Display COLB. Substitute the value of COLC whenever the COLB value is null.

3. Display COLA. Whenever COLA is null substitute the COLB value. If COLB is also null, substitute the COLC value.

```
SELECT  PKEY, VALUE(COLC,999.99),
        VALUE(COLB,COLC),
        VALUE(COLA,COLB,COLC)
FROM    NULLTAB
```

PKEY	COLC	COLB	COLA
1	5.00	20.00	10.00
2	5.00	30.00	30.00
3	10.00	10.00	160.00
4	5.00	170.00	170.00
5	10.00	10.00	10.00
6	5.00	40.00	10.00
7	5.00	60.00	30.00
8	999.99	-	-
-	999.99	-	-
-	999.99	-	-
-	999.99	-	-

Comments:

1. You are advised to examine the NULLTAB table to verify the value substitutions shown in the output display.

2. The first argument of the VALUE function is a column or an expression which could possibly evaluate to null. The second argument is a (presumably nonnull) value to be substituted in the output display whenever the first arrument is actually null. For example, if we specified VALUE(COLA, 0), the system would display 0 instead of the standard null value symbol whenever COLA was null.

3. The VALUE function can have more than two arguments. This handles the case where the second argument is also null by substituting the value of the third argument. If the third argument is also null, but a fourth argument is present, it substitutes the value of the fourth argument, and so on. The standard null symbol is displayed only if all arguments evaluate to null. The primary restriction on the arguments is that they must have comparable data types.

4. The NULLTAB table contains all numeric values. Hence, all the substituted values were numeric. The other data types (character strings, date/time values) can be used as well in the VALUE function. For example, if the CDESCP column in the COURSE table could contain nulls, we could specify VALUE(CDESCP, "DESCRIPTION UNKNOWN"). The character string "DESCRIPTION UNKNOWN" would be displayed whenever CDESCP is null.

5. Sometimes a built-in function evaluates to null. For example, applying the SUM function to a column of null values produces a null result. Assume the sum of some COLX could be null. Then you could specify VALUE(SUM(COLX),0) to display a 0 whenever the sum is actually null.

SUMMARY

This chapter introduced the concept of null values. We examined the complexities of dealing with a three-value logic system incorporating the notion of an unknown value. The major points discussed were:

- A null value is a special value. It does not represent 0 or spaces, but indicates that the value is not known. This results in a three-value logic system.

- Because we do not have any knowledge about unknown values, two such values cannot be said to be equal or unequal. The same approach to handling null values is used by the system. This means that one null value is neither equal nor unequal to another. A special syntax is used to examine a column for null values. Rather than using "=" as the comparison operator, we must use "IS NULL", and in the negative sense, "IS NOT NULL".

- Null values affect the results of computations both in calculated expressions and in built-in functions. Null values do not participate in these operations and, therefore, may distort the results if you are not aware of their presence.

- The VALUE scalar function is used to prevent null values from appearing in a query result. It allows you to specify an alternative value to replace a null value in the result table.

- Null values sort higher than any other value when the system is required to order the result.

SUMMARY EXERCISES

10G. Display the name and department of any staff member who is not assigned to known department.

10H. For all departments, display the department name and the number of all staff members in the department.

More About the SELECT
Statement

In this part of the text we return to the task of data retrieval. The following chapters complete our exhaustive examination of the SELECT statement. As you progress through these chapters you will notice a shift in perspective. The logical considerations for most examples presented in PART I of the text were relatively simple. Our primary focus was on the syntax of the SELECT statement. In this part of the text you will find it easy to learn the new syntactical constructs. However, the sample queries and exercises become more complex because you will be required to give more thought to the logical dimension of the query objective. The complexity of these examples will pertain to the "conceptual navigation" required when multiple tables need to be referenced.

ORGANIZATION OF CHAPTERS

Chapter 11 presents the join operation which is probably the most important topic covered in this part of the book. The join operation is the most useful technique for referencing multiple tables. Many of the sample queries presented in subsequent chapters can also be solved using the join operation.

Chapter 12 introduces the CREATE SYNONYM statement to create synonyms (abbreviations) for table names. Because the statements become longer in this part of the text, you will appreciate the opportunity to reduce the number of necessary keystrokes.

Chapter 13 introduces subqueries. Most of the sample queries and exercises presented in this chapter can be solved using the join operation. (However, the converse is not true.) Subqueries serve a purpose because some users find it more "friendly" than the join operation. Also, this chapter provides a basis for understanding correlated subqueries presented in Chapter 15.

Chapter 14 introduces the union operation. This simple operation is very useful. Many reasonable queries could not be expressed if the UNION keyword was missing from SQL. This topic is covered before correlated subqueries because some of the more interesting correlated subquery examples also utilize the union operation.

Chapter 15 presents correlated subqueries. This type of subquery is important because, unlike those described in Chapter 13, they allow us to solve certain problems which could not be solved using the join operation. The logic of correlated subqueries is different from those presented earlier. This is our rationale for discussing them in a separate chapter.

11

Join Operation

This chapter introduces the join operation which allows a single SELECT statement to reference columns from more than one table. The join operation allows a query to specify the merging of columns from two or more tables by matching values found in columns from each table. The precise definition of this "merging" and "matching" will be described below. We begin by presenting three queries which could utilize the join operation. This is followed by a detailed explanation of the join operation and a number of sample queries which demonstrate its use.

Query 1:   For every employee who is known to be assigned to some existing department, select his or her name, title, salary and department id, along with the department building, room location, and department chairperson faculty number.

This query requires that the system display:

1.   all columns from the STAFF table and

2.   all columns from the DEPARTMENT table (with the possible exception of the DEPT column because each value would be identical to the matching DEPT value from the STAFF table).

This query is based upon the fact that some of the DEPT values in the STAFF table match the DEPT values in the DEPARTMENT table. These values match even though the DEPT column in the STAFF table is not a foreign key referencing the DEPARTMENT table. (Note this query is phrased to exclude Archimedes and Euclid who are assigned to nonexistent departments and Da Vinci whose department assignment is unknown.)

Query 2:   For every course with a labfee over $175, display the course name and labfee, along with the faculty number of the chairperson responsible for the course.

This query requires that the system display:

1.   CNAME and CLABFEE from the COURSE table, and

2.   DCHFNO from the DEPARTMENT table.

This query presumes that every CDEPT value in the COURSE table matches some DEPT value in the DEPARTMENT table. We can be certain of this fact because CDEPT is a foreign key which references the DEPARTMENT table.

Observe that neither of the above queries could be satisfied using just previously described SQL techniques. A join operation is necessary because the result of each query contains data from more than one table. However, there are other reasons for using the join operation. For example, we might want to display columns from one table, but specify row selection criteria relative to some other table. Consider the third query.

Query 3:   Display the name and title of every staff member who is
known to work in the Humanities Building.

This query displays the ENAME and ETITLE columns which are
both found in the STAFF table. However, the system must examine
the DEPARTMENT table to determine which departments are located in the Humanities Building. Only staff members assigned to
these departments will be selected. (Again, the query is phrased to
exclude Archimedes, Euclid and Da Vinci whose DEPT values do not
match any DEPT value in the DEPARTMENT table.)

You could satisfy this query with your current knowledge of SQL.
However, the process would be awkward because you must execute
two independent SELECT statements. The first would determine
which departments are located in the Humanities Building. This is

```
SELECT  DEPT
FROM    DEPARTMENT
WHERE   DBLD = 'HU'
```

The output would identify the "THEO" and "PHIL" values. You
would then use this information to construct the following SELECT
statement.

```
SELECT  ENAME, ETITLE
FROM    STAFF
WHERE   DEPT = 'THEO'
OR      DEPT = 'PHIL'
```

While this approach will work, it is not desirable for a couple of
reasons. The first is that the user must memorize or write down the
intermediate result (THEO and PHIL). This requires some effort, especially if the intermediate result is large. A second (usually less
important) reason this approach is undesirable is machine ineffi-
ciency. The execution of two separate SELECT statements is more
costly than executing a single equivalent statement

Each of the previous queries can be realized by issuing a single
SELECT statement which implements a join operation. The following pages explain the important concepts pertaining to the join operation. After you understand these concepts, the sample queries will
demonstrate that the SQL syntax for expressing the join operation is
relatively straightforward.

JOINING TWO TABLES

From a conceptual point of view, the join of two tables is the concatenation of rows from the two tables where values from a column in the first table match values from a column in the second table. The result of the join operation is a new table which has a row for each match which occurred between the original two tables. The original tables remain unchanged. This is best illustrated by an example.

Figure 11.1 shows two tables, TABLE1 and TABLE2, which will be joined to form a third table shown in Figure 11.2. The first step is to specify the "join column" for each table. Column C3 of TABLE1 and column CA of TABLE2 are specified as the join columns. This means that whenever the C3 value of a row in TABLE1 is equal to the CA value of a row in TABLE2, a new row is established in the resulting join table. This row is formed by concatenating the rows where the match occurred. We make the following observations about the join result.

- In TABLE1, the rows with C3 values of 45, 55 and 15 did not match any values in column CA of TABLE2. Hence, they do not appear in the join result.
- Likewise, in TABLE2, the rows with CA values of 35, 65 and 75 did not match any values in column C3 of TABLE1. Hence, they do not appear in the join result.
- There was one match on the value 10. This produced the first row of the join result.

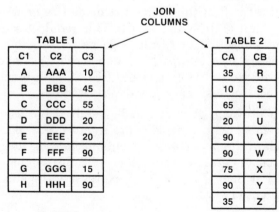

Figure 11.1   Tables to be joined.

- Both of the TABLE1 rows with a C3 value of 20 matched the CA value of 20 in TABLE2. These two matches produced the second and third rows in the join result.
- In TABLE1 there are two rows with a C3 value of 90. Each of these two rows matched the three rows in TABLE2 with CA values of 90. This is a total of six matches for the value of 90. It produced the last six rows of the join result.

Observe that neither of the join columns, CA and C3, is a primary key or a foreign key. Usually a foreign key in one table and its corresponding primary key in another table are specified as the join columns. However, as the example shows, this is not necessary. Any columns with comparable data types can be specified as join columns.

Subsequent sample queries will illustrate the syntax of a SELECT statement which implements a join operation. These will show both tables referenced in the FROM clause and the join columns specified in the WHERE clause. The SELECT statement to produce the join result of Figure 11.2 is

```
SELECT  *
FROM    TABLE1, TABLE2
WHERE   C3 = CA
```

We will postpone further discussion of syntax until the presentation of this chapter's sample queries. For the moment we return to the more important conceptual considerations.

C1	C2	C3	CA	CB
A	AAA	10	10	S
D	DDD	20	20	U
E	EEE	20	20	U
F	FFF	90	90	V
F	FFF	90	90	W
F	FFF	90	90	Y
H	HHH	90	90	V
H	HHH	90	90	W
H	HHH	90	90	Y

MATCHING
COLUMNS

Figure 11.2   Join result.

To reiterate a previously mentioned point, it is necessary to specify the join columns. We could have joined TABLE1 and TABLE2 on *any* two comparable columns. For example, we could have requested the system to join the tables by matching columns C1 and CB. In this case, no matches would occur, and the result would be an empty table. In most realistic situations we only join tables by matching columns which contain values based upon some common set of values. For example, we will be matching those columns which contain department id values in the COURSE and DEPARTMENT tables.

Observe that two extreme results can occur when joining any two tables. These are the:

1. "Empty Table" result: This is the case mentioned above where no matches occur.

2. "Worse Case" result: This occurs when every column of the first table matches every column of the second table. Figure 11.3 illustrates this situation. TABLE3 is joined with TABLE4 on columns C2 and CB. Every "X" value in column C2 matches every "X" value in column CB. Because TABLE3 has 3 rows and TABLE4 has 4 rows, the join result has 3 x 4 = 12 rows. This is the largest number of rows which could be generated. We call this the "worst case" because it takes more computer time to process a large join result than a small one.

TABLE 3

C1	C2
1	X
2	X
3	X

TABLE 4

CA	CB
9	X
8	X
7	X
6	X

JOIN RESULT

C1	C2	CA	CB
1	X	9	X
1	X	8	X
1	X	7	X
1	X	6	X
2	X	9	X
2	X	8	X
2	X	7	X
2	X	6	X
3	X	9	X
3	X	8	X
3	X	7	X
3	X	6	X

MATCHING
COLUMNS

Figure 11.3   "Worst case" join.

NULLS IN THE JOIN COLUMNS

The preceding examples referenced tables which did not contain null values. Recall that null means "value unknown." Therefore, a null cannot match with any other value; it does not even match another null value. Figure 11.4 shows TABLE1A and TABLE2A. These tables are similar to TABLE1 and TABLE2 except that nulls have replaced some values. The result of joining TABLE1A and TABLE2A on columns C3 and CA is shown in Figure 11.5. We make the following observations.

- The nonnull values match (or don't match) in the same way as occurred in the join of the original TABLE1 and TABLE2.
- The null values in the join columns did not match with any other values. In particular, note that the null values in the last row of each table did not match with each other.
- The only null value which appears in the join result is the null value which is present in column CB which is not a join column. Hence, it is treated like any other data value.

A final comment before presenting the sample queries. The term "match" is not very precise. In this chapter it usually means "equal to." From a formal point of view, the join operation described thus far is called "equijoin." This is the most common join operation used in practice. The SQL language allows for other types of joins where the join condition can include any of the comparison operators. These other join operations will be introduced in Sample Query 11.13.

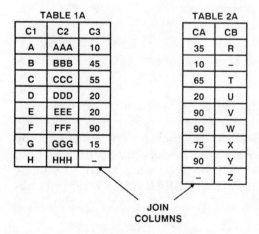

TABLE 1A

C1	C2	C3
A	AAA	10
B	BBB	45
C	CCC	55
D	DDD	20
E	EEE	20
F	FFF	90
G	GGG	15
H	HHH	–

TABLE 2A

CA	CB
35	R
10	–
65	T
20	U
90	V
90	W
75	X
90	Y
–	Z

JOIN
COLUMNS

C1	C2	C3	CA	CB
A	AAA	10	10	–
D	DDD	20	20	U
E	EEE	20	20	U
F	FFF	90	90	V
F	FFF	90	90	W
F	FFF	90	90	Y

MATCHING
COLUMNS

Figure 11.4   Nulls in join columns.

Figure 11.5   Join of TABLE1A and TABLE2A.

JOIN STAFF AND DEPARTMENT TABLES

The first sample query involving a join operation will join the STAFF and DEPARTMENT tables. The semantic relationship which justifies this join is the "employee works in department" relationship. The match is based upon join columns which happen to have the same name (DEPT). Although this query itself is not very realistic, it serves the purpose of illustrating a pure equijoin.

Sample Query 11.1: For all staff members assigned to existing departments, select all information about the staff members and their respective departments.

```
SELECT *
FROM    STAFF, DEPARTMENT
WHERE   STAFF.DEPT = DEPARTMENT.DEPT
```

ENAME	ETITLE	ESALARY	DEPT	DEPT	DBLD	DROOM	DCHFNO
HANK KISS	JESTER	25000	PHIL	PHIL	HU	100	60
DICK NIX	CROOK	25001	PHIL	PHIL	HU	100	60
MATTHEW	EVANGLIST1	51	THEO	THEO	HU	200	10
MARK	EVANGLIST2	52	THEO	THEO	HU	200	10
LUKE	EVANGLIST3	53	THEO	THEO	HU	200	10
JOHN	EVANGLIST4	54	THEO	THEO	HU	200	10

Comments:

1. Logic:

   Confirm your understanding of the join operation by observing that both DEPT columns have equal values. Also note the STAFF and DEPARTMENT rows which do not appear in the join result. STAFF rows corresponding to EUCLID, ARCHIMEDES and DA VINCI did not match on DEPT values; likewise, the MGT row from the DEPARTMENT table is absent for the same reason.

2. Syntax:

FROM clause:

The logic of the query requires that data be extracted from two tables. Therefore, both tables are referenced in the FROM clause. The table names must be separated by a comma. The table names can be specified in any order. A complex query could involve more than two tables. The general rule is simple. If any clause references any column of a table, the name of the table must be included in the FROM clause. (See Sample Query 11.9 which illustrates the join of three tables.)

WHERE clause:

The join columns are specified in the WHERE clause. The match is effected by specifying that the two join columns are equal. Our sample query illustrates

```
WHERE STAFF.DEPT = DEPARTMENT.DEPT
```

This condition is called the "join condition." Note that the column names are qualified. Qualification is required in this query because both join columns have the same name (DEPT). An error would occur if the join column names were not qualified.

SELECT clause:

The "SELECT *" means the same as in previous queries. In this example, the system will display all columns in the join result. Since the FROM clause references STAFF before DEPARTMENT, the columns of the STAFF table are displayed first (to the left of the DEPARTMENT table columns).

Observe that the result displays both DEPT columns which have the same values. In practice, we would not display redundant columns. The SELECT clause would specify just those columns we want displayed. See the next sample query.

DISPLAYING A SUBSET OF THE JOIN RESULT

We rarely want to see all rows and columns of a join result. For example, the previous equijoin result showed duplicate DEPT columns which are completely redundant. Usually our intention is to display only some of the row and column data present in the join result. This objective is achieved by applying previously described row/column selection techniques to the intermediate table produced as the result of the join operation. The next sample query shows that the syntax is the same as with previous queries that referenced just one table. The only difference is conceptual. The row and column selection criteria applies to the intermediate table produced as a result of the join operation.

Sample Query 11.2: For every staff member whose yearly salary exceeds $1000, display his or her name, salary, department id and building/room location.

```
SELECT  ENAME, ESALARY, STAFF.DEPT,
        DBLD, DROOM
FROM    STAFF, DEPARTMENT
WHERE   STAFF.DEPT = DEPARTMENT.DEPT
AND     ESALARY > 1000
```

ENAME	ESALARY	STAFF.DEPT	DBLD	DROOM
HANK KISS	25000	PHIL	HU	100
DICK NIX	25001	PHIL	HU	100

Comments:

1. Logic:

   Any query which involves a join requires that the user really understand the meaning of the data items. This is especially true of the relationships between the tables as reflected by the join columns. Consider the following semantic assumptions implicit in the SQL code for the current sample query.

   - Staff members always work in the same building and room where their department is located. (Is it possible for a staff member to work in a building other than the department's location?) We must confirm that department location and staff work location are the same thing.
   - We are not interested in information about staff members who are not assigned to existing departments. Rows corresponding to these staff members are "flushed out" by the join operation.

   These issues are logical. They transcend the SQL language. They must be addressed by the database administrator during the process of database analysis and design. This is beyond the scope of this text. However, it is mandatory that users properly interpret the meaning of the data and relationships implicit in the database design.

   The current sample query illustrates that there are potential pitfalls even with a simple database. Throughout the remainder of this text we will assume that the semantics of the sample queries are correct. This is necessary to focus on the SQL code and to avoid a long digression into issues of database analysis and design.

2. Syntax:

   (1) The FROM clause and join condition are identical to the previous sample query. This is

   ```
   FROM   STAFF, DEPARTMENT
   WHERE  STAFF.DEPT = DEPARTMENT.DEPT
   ```

2.   As mentioned above, there is no syntax change just because we are working with an intermediate join result.

- We only want some rows. These rows correspond to staff
members whose salary exceeds $1000. This implies that
another condition should be appended to the join condition. This is

```
AND ESALARY > 1000
```

- We only want some columns. These are explicitly named
in the SELECT clause. Columns from different tables can
be specified because the columns are selected from the
join result. Thus, we have

```
SELECT ENAME, ESALARY, STAFF.DEPT, DBLD, DROOM
```

Qualification of the DEPT column is necessary. We may
understand that both DEPT columns in the join result are
identical, but the system does not. If DEPT is not qualified, an error will occur. Either table name may be used
as the qualifier. The following SELECT clause would produce the same result.

```
SELECT ENAME, ESALARY, DEPARTMENT.DEPT, DBLD, DROOM
```

3. Physical Effiency:

Earlier we identified the "worst case" situation where all the
join column values match with each other. When we consider
that we usually want just some subset of rows and columns
from the join result, it seems that the system could incur the
cost of generating a large intermediate join result. This is not
necessarily the case. Both DB2 and SQL/DS have internal soft-
ware modules called "optimizers" which can usually avoid this
effort. In fact, the "AND ESALARY > 1000" clause will help the
optimizers. From a user's point of view, only two comments are
necessary.

a.   Don't worry about efficiency. That is the job of the optimizer. It is intelligent enough to avoid the unnecessary
generation of a large intermediate join result.

b.   Even though the system may not actually generate the
actual join table, it is helpful for you to think that it does.
This can simplify your thought process as described below.

4. Mental Steps: There are three basic steps which you can follow when you need to reference two tables.

   a. Join the Tables:

   Determine the tables to be joined and their respective join columns. Then construct the FROM clause and the join condition. In the current example, this leads to

   ```
   FROM      STAFF, DEPARTMENT
   WHERE     STAFF.DEPT = DEPARTMENT.DEPT
   ```

   b. Specify the Desired Columns:

   Construct the SELECT clause which identifies the columns that you want displayed. Don't forget any necessary qualification. In the current example, this yields

   ```
   SELECT ENAME, ESALARY, STAFF.DEPT, DBLD, DROOM
   ```

   c. Specify the Desired Rows:

   Use the AND connector to append other selection criteria to extract the desired rows from the join result. In the current example, this is

   ```
   AND ESALARY > 1000
   ```

These pieces of code are put together in the standard order of

```
SELECT  ---------
FROM    ---------
WHERE   ---------
AND     ---------
```

You are encouraged to apply these mental steps to future workshop exercises.

JOIN BASED UPON PRIMARY KEY AND FOREIGN KEY VALUES

The next sample query joins the COURSE and DEPARTMENT tables. The semantic relationship which justifies this join is the "course is offered by department" relationship. This example reflects a typical situation where the join operation matches the foreign key of the referencing table (CDEPT in COURSE) with the primary key of the referenced table (DEPT in DEPARTMENT). *Because every CDEPT value will be equal to some DEPT value, we can expect every row of the COURSE table to be present in the intermediate join result.*

Sample Query 11.3: For every course with a labfee over $175, display the course name, labfee and faculty number of the chairperson responsible for the course. Display the output in ascending sequence by course name.

```
SELECT  CNAME, CLABFEE, DCHFNO
FROM    COURSE, DEPARTMENT
WHERE   CDEPT = DEPT
AND     CLABFEE > 175
ORDER   BY CNAME
```

```
-----------------------------------------------------
CNAME                      CLABFEE  DCHFNO
-----------------------------------------------------
COMMUNISM                   200.00  10
EXISTENTIALISM              200.00  60
RELATIONAL DATABASE         500.00  80
```

Comments:

1. The course name and labfee are stored in the COURSE table, and the chairperson's faculty number is stored in the DEPART-MENT table. The join columns are CDEPT in the COURSE table and the DEPT column in the DEPARTMENT table. Hence, the example shows

    ```
    FROM    COURSE, DEPARTMENT
    WHERE   CDEPT = DEPT
    ```

    Note that, unlike the previous two examples, qualification of column names is unnecessary. The join columns have distinct names so there is no possible ambiguity. We could have qualified the names of the join columns. Then the WHERE clause would be

    ```
    WHERE COURSE.CDEPT = DEPARTMENT.DEPT
    ```

2. Unlike previous sample queries, neither of the two join columns, CDEPT and DEPT, are referenced in the SELECT clause. It is not necessary to display join columns.

3. Sorting the result requires use of the ORDER BY clause. Any column(s) from either table can be specified in this clause. All the variations of the ORDER BY clause described in Chapter 2 apply.

The next sample query displays columns from just one table (STAFF). This is not unusual. The purpose of the join is to permit row selection based on information found in a second table (DEPARTMENT).

Sample Query 11.4:   Display the name and title of every staff member who works in the Humanities Building.

```
SELECT  ENAME, ETITLE
FROM    STAFF, DEPARTMENT
WHERE   STAFF.DEPT = DEPARTMENT.DEPT
AND     DBLD = 'HU'
```

```
-------------------------------------
ENAME           ETITLE
-------------------------------------
HANK KISS       JESTER
DICK NIX        CROOK
MATTHEW         EVANGLIST1
MARK            EVANGLIST2
LUKE            EVANGLIST3
JOHN            EVANGLIST4
```

Comments:

1. Observe that both of the displayed columns are located in the STAFF table. The join operation is necessary to determine which departments are located in the Humanities Building.

2. Sample Query 13.8 will present an alternative solution to this problem. It will show a "nested subquery" solution which can only be applied because all the displayed columns come from a single table. This point will be emphasized in Chapter 13 when we introduce nested subqueries.

Recall that displaying just some columns of a table can produce an output display with duplicate rows. (The DISTINCT keyword was used to remove this duplication.) The next example shows that duplicate rows can occur in a result produced by a join operation.

Sample Query 11.5:   Where can I find an evangelist? More precisely, display the building and room of any academic department which employs a staff member whose title begins with "EVANGLIST".

```
SELECT  DBLD, DROOM
FROM    DEPARTMENT, STAFF
WHERE   DEPARTMENT.DEPT = STAFF.DEPT
AND     ETITLE LIKE 'EVANGLIST_'
```

```
----------------
DBLD    DROOM
----------------
HU      200
HU      200
HU      200
HU      200
```

Comment:

Because all four evangelists reside in the same room of the same building, the output display contains four duplicate rows. Duplicate rows can be removed from the output display by including DISTINCT in the SELECT clause. We rewrite the example including the DISTINCT keyword.

```
SELECT  DISTINCT DBLD, DROOM
FROM    DEPARTMENT, STAFF
WHERE   DEPARTMENT.DEPT = STAFF.DEPT
AND     ETITLE LIKE 'EVANGLIST_'
```

Exercises:

11A. Display the equijoin of the COURSE and DEPARTMENT tables where the join operation matches the CDEPT values in
COURSE with the DEPT values in DEPARTMENT.

11B. The "natural join" of two tables is the same as the equijoin
except that one of the duplicate columns present in the
equijoin is not displayed. Modify the previous exercise so that
it produces the natural join of the COURSE and DEPART-
MENT tables based upon the CDEPT and DEPT columns.
(You can display either the CDEPT column or the DEPT column from the join result, but not both columns.)

11C. For each course with a labfee over $100, display the course
name and its labfee along with the faculty number of the
chairperson of the department which offers the course.

11D. Display the course number and name of any course which is
offered by a department chaired by the person having the
faculty number of 60. Display the output result in descending
sequence by course number.

11E. Display the name and salary of any staff member assigned to
a department which is located in the Science Building.

11F. For any staff member who is assigned to an existing department and whose salary exceeds $200, display the building
and room location of the staff member. The output should not
display any duplicate rows.

Previous sample queries illustrated the use of familiar techniques to display a given row/column subset of a join result. We also saw that the DISTINCT keyword and ORDER BY clause apply. In fact, there do not exist any special display restrictions specific to a join result. You can treat an intermediate join result like any other table. In particular, you can perform computations with a join result. The next three sample queries illustrate some of the computational techniques originally presented in Chapters 5 and 6. This time the techniques are applied to intermediate join results.

Sample Query 11.6:   What is the total salary of staff members who work in Room 100 of the Humanities Building.

```
SELECT  SUM (ESALARY)
FROM    DEPARTMENT, STAFF
WHERE   DEPARTMENT.DEPT = STAFF.DEPT
AND     DBLD = 'HU'
AND     DROOM = '100'
```

```
--------------
      COL1
--------------
   50001
```

Comments:

1. There is really nothing new in this example. The FROM and WHERE clauses identify the join operation and row selection criteria. The SUM function is then applied to the ESALARY column. As usual, a column built-in function compresses the displayed output to a single row.

2. All the SQL built-in functions described in Chapter 6 apply. The function arguments may be any of the columns from the intermediate join result.

The next sample query joins the COURSE and STAFF tables. The semantic relationship which justifies this join is the "employee works in the department which offers the course" relationship. The join columns are CDEPT and DEPT, both of which contain department id values.

Note that the semantics of this relationship are more complex than the previously described "employee works in department" and "course is offered by department" relationships. This is because courses and employees are only indirectly related via the aforementioned direct relationships with department. Proper understanding of the next sample query requires that you comprehend these relationships and further assumptions specified below.

Assume that any staff member employed by an existing department is available and qualified to serve as tutor for any course offered by the department. Staff members not assigned to existing departments are not required to tutor. If a given department does not offer courses or does not have any staff members assigned to it, then that department does not offer tutoring services. The next few sample queries are based upon these assumptions.

Sample Query 11.7: For every staff member who has tutoring responsibilities, display his name and salary along with the course number and credits of any course he can tutor. Also, display the ratio of salary to credits for each staff member and course combination. Sort the output by course number within staff member name.

```
SELECT  ENAME, ESALARY, CNO, CRED, ESALARY/CRED
FROM    STAFF, COURSE
WHERE   DEPT = CDEPT
ORDER   BY ENAME, CNO
```

```
-------------------------------------------------------------
ENAME               ESALARY   CNO    CRED   COL1
-------------------------------------------------------------
DICK NIX             25001    P11       3   8333
DICK NIX             25001    P22       3   8333
DICK NIX             25001    P33       3   8333
DICK NIX             25001    P44       6   4166
HANK KISS            25000    P11       3   8333
HANK KISS            25000    P22       3   8333
HANK KISS            25000    P33       3   8333
HANK KISS            25000    P44       6   4166
JOHN                    54    T11       3     18
JOHN                    54    T12       3     18
JOHN                    54    T33       3     18
JOHN                    54    T44       6      9
LUKE                    53    T11       3     17
LUKE                    53    T12       3     17
LUKE                    53    T33       3     17
LUKE                    53    T44       6      8
MARK                    52    T11       3     17
MARK                    52    T12       3     17
MARK                    52    T33       3     17
MARK                    52    T44       6      8
MATTHEW                 51    T11       3     17
MATTHEW                 51    T12       3     17
MATTHEW                 51    T33       3     17
MATTHEW                 51    T44       6      8
```

Comments:

1. This example illustrates the generation of a column containing calculated values. This is the rightmost column produced by dividing ESALARY by CRED. The fact that these two columns come from different tables is incidental. They are both present in the intermediate join result and hence can be referenced in the expression to calculate the ratio.

2. The COL1 calculated result is integer because both operands (ESALARY and CRED) are defined as integer. Hence, decimal accuracy is lost.

The next sample query demonstrates grouping within the context of a join operation.

Sample Query 11.8: For every department which offers tutoring services, display the department id along with the average labfee of the courses it offers and the average salary of staff members who can tutor such courses. Sort the output by department id.

```
SELECT DEPT, AVG(CLABFEE), AVG(ESALARY)
FROM    STAFF, COURSE
WHERE   DEPT = CDEPT
GROUP   BY DEPT
ORDER   BY DEPT
```

DEPT	COL1	COL2
PHIL	87.50	25000
THEO	110.00	52

Comments:

1. Again, there is nothing new in this example. The example merely demonstrates the GROUP BY clause with values present in an intermediate join result. All the previously specified rules pertaining to grouping must apply. (See Chapter 6.)

2. The summary output of this example confirms our earlier observations regarding the content of the sample tables. Only the Philosophy and Theology Departments offer courses and have staff members assigned to them. Hence, only these departments appear in the output display.

Exercises:

11G. Display the smallest and largest labfees associated with any course offered by a department located in the Science Building.

11H. How many staff members are assigned to existing departments (i.e., those departments described in the DEPARTMENT table)?

11I. If a staff member can tutor a course, and the labfee for the course exceeds his salary by at least $52, then display the staff member's name and salary along with the course labfee and the difference between the labfee and the salary.

11J. For each department which employs staff members, display the department id followed by the total staff salary and average staff salary for the department.

11K. For those courses which have staff members available as tutors, display the course name followed by the number of available tutors for the course.

11L. Display the department id of any department described in the DEPARTMENT table which employs at least three staff members.

11M. For each department described in the DEPARTMENT table which employs at least one staff member, display the department id followed by the number of staff members assigned to the department.

JOIN OF THREE TABLES

The next sample query requires the join of three tables. Again, we rely on the previous assumptions about staff members tutoring courses offered by their departments.

Sample Query 11.9: For any course which has a staff member available to tutor students, display its number, the names and titles of the staff members who can serve as a tutor for the course, and their respective building and room locations. Sort the output by staff member name within course number.

```
SELECT  CNO, ENAME, ETITLE, DBLD, DROOM
FROM    COURSE, STAFF, DEPARTMENT
WHERE   CDEPT = STAFF.DEPT
AND     CDEPT = DEPARTMENT.DEPT
ORDER   BY CNO, ENAME
```

CNO	ENAME	ETITLE	DBLD	DROOM
P11	DICK NIX	CROOK	HU	100
P11	HANK KISS	JESTER	HU	100
P22	DICK NIX	CROOK	HU	100
P22	HANK KISS	JESTER	HU	100
P33	DICK NIX	CROOK	HU	100
P33	HANK KISS	JESTER	HU	100
P44	DICK NIX	CROOK	HU	100
P44	HANK KISS	JESTER	HU	100
T11	JOHN	EVANGLIST4	HU	200
T11	LUKE	EVANGLIST3	HU	200
T11	MARK	EVANGLIST2	HU	200
T11	MATTHEW	EVANGLIST1	HU	200
T12	JOHN	EVANGLIST4	HU	200
T12	LUKE	EVANGLIST3	HU	200
T12	MARK	EVANGLIST2	HU	200
T12	MATTHEW	EVANGLIST1	HU	200
T33	JOHN	EVANGLIST4	HU	200
T33	LUKE	EVANGLIST3	HU	200
T33	MARK	EVANGLIST2	HU	200
T33	MATTHEW	EVANGLIST1	HU	200
T44	JOHN	EVANGLIST4	HU	200
T44	LUKE	EVANGLIST3	HU	200
T44	MARK	EVANGLIST2	HU	200
T44	MATTHEW	EVANGLIST1	HU	200

Comments:

1. It is necessary to display CNAME (from the COURSE table), ENAME and ETITLE (from the STAFF table), and DBLD and DROOM (from the DEPARTMENT table). This requires the join of three tables based on columns containing the department identifiers. A SELECT statement may specify a maximum of 16 tables to be joined together.

2. A join of three tables requires two join conditions. The COURSE and STAFF tables are joined by

   ```
   WHERE CDEPT = STAFF.DEPT
   ```

   and the COURSE and DEPARTMENT tables are joined by

   ```
   AND CDEPT = DEPARTMENT.DEPT
   ```

3. The system behaves as follows.

   a. It joins two tables to establish an intermediate join result. If the first two tables are the COURSE and STAFF tables, COURSE rows corresponding to the CIS courses, and STAFF rows with "ENG," "MATH" and null values in the DEPT column will not match. They will not be part of the intermediate join result. Hence, they will not appear in the final result.

   b. If the next join operation is based on the condition "CDEPT = DEPARTMENT.DEPT" the system will join the DEPARTMENT table with the previous intermediate result (not just the COURSE table as the code might indicate.) Here the row for the MGT department will not match any value in the intermediate result. Hence, it will not appear in the final result.

   Item (1) above stated, "If the first two tables are the COURSE and STAFF tables." We said "If" because the system may, for reasons of efficiency, initially choose to join the COURSE and DEPARTMENT tables to establish an intermediate join result. Then it would join the STAFF table to the intermediate result. The result is the same. The order in which to join conditions are written has no effect. The optimizer will try to choose the most efficient approach.

CROSS PRODUCT

The next example has a FROM clause which references two tables, but there is no WHERE clause specifying a join condition. Usually someone writes such a statement by accident. They intend to perform a regular join operation, but forget to include the join condition. Then they are surprised by the large number of rows displayed. What they get is known as the "Cross Product" or the "Cartesian Product" where every row in the first table is paired with every row in the second table. This occurs because the join condition, which restricts the join result to matching values, is not present.

Sample Query 11.10:   Form the cross product of the STAFF table and the DEPARTMENT table.

```
SELECT *
FROM STAFF, DEPARTMENT
```

Comments:

1. Observe that the columns of the STAFF table are displayed to the the left of the columns of the DEPARTMENT table. This is because "STAFF" was referenced before "DEPARTMENT" in the FROM clause. The following statement would result in the DEPARTMENT columns being displayed to the left of STAFF columns.

    ```
    SELECT *
    FROM    DEPARTMENT, STAFF
    ```

2. The cross product coincides with the "worst case" join situation described earlier. The number of rows generated could be very large. For example, if two tables each had one thousand rows, their cross product would have one million rows. As indicated above, users rarely need a cross product. However, there are occasions where this operation is useful.

ENAME	ETITLE	ESALARY	DEPT	DEPT	DBLD	DROOM	DCHFNO
HANK KISS	JESTER	25000	PHIL	THEO	HU	200	10
DICK NIX	CROOK	25001	PHIL	THEO	HU	200	10
MATTHEW	EVANGLIST1	51	THEO	THEO	HU	200	10
MARK	EVANGLIST2	52	THEO	THEO	HU	200	10
LUKE	EVANGLIST3	53	THEO	THEO	HU	200	10
JOHN	EVANGLIST4	54	THEO	THEO	HU	200	10
DA VINCI	LAB ASSIST	500	-	THEO	HU	200	10
EUCLID	LAB ASSIST	1000	MATH	THEO	HU	200	10
ARCHIMEDES	LAB ASSIST	200	ENG	THEO	HU	200	10
HANK KISS	JESTER	25000	PHIL	MGT	SC	100	-
DICK NIX	CROOK	25001	PHIL	MGT	SC	100	-
MATTHEW	EVANGLIST1	51	THEO	MGT	SC	100	-
MARK	EVANGLST2	52	THEO	MGT	SC	100	-
LUKE	EVANGLST3	53	THEO	MGT	SC	100	-
JOHN	EVANGLIST4	54	THEO	MGT	SC	100	-
DA VINCI	LAB ASSIST	500	-	MGT	HU	100	-
EUCLID	LAB ASSIST	1000	MATH	MGT	HU	100	-
ARCHIMEDES	LAB ASSIST	200	ENG	MGT	HU	100	-
HANK KISS	JESTER	25000	PHIL	CIS	SC	300	80
DICK NIX	CROOK	25001	PHIL	CIS	SC	300	80
MATTHEW	EVANGLIST1	51	THEO	CIS	SC	300	80
MARK	EVANGLIST2	52	THEO	CIS	SC	300	80
LUKE	EVANGLIST3	53	THEO	CIS	SC	300	80
JOHN	EVANGLIST4	54	THEO	CIS	SC	300	80
DA VINCI	LAB ASSIST	500	-	CIS	SC	300	80
EUCLID	LAB ASSIST	1000	MATH	CIS	SC	300	80
ARCHIMEDES	LAB ASSIST	200	ENG	CIS	SC	300	80
HANK KISS	JESTER	25000	PHIL	PHIL	HU	100	60
DICK NIX	CROOK	25001	PHIL	PHIL	HU	100	60
MATTHEW	EVANGLIST1	51	THEO	PHIL	HU	100	60
MARK	EVANGLIST2	52	THEO	PHIL	HU	100	60
LUKE	EVANGLIST3	53	THEO	PHIL	HU	100	60
JOHN	EVANGLIST4	54	THEO	PHIL	HU	100	60
DA VINCI	LAB ASSIST	500	-	PHIL	HU	100	60
EUCLID	LAB ASSIST	1000	MATH	PHIL	HU	100	60
ARCHIMEDES	LAB ASSIST	200	ENG	PHIL	HU	100	60

JOINING A TABLE WITH ITSELF

All previous join operations involved two or more *different* tables. The next example illustrates that a table can be joined with itself. The SQL technique involves the use of an "alias" for a table name. In this case, we assign the STAFF table two distinct aliases which allows us to think of and reference this single table as two distinct tables. An alias is assigned to a table by placing it after the table name in the FROM clause. The following example assigns two aliases, ST1 and ST2, to the STAFF table. Then all reference to columns of the conceptually distinct STAFF tables is done by using the alias names for qualification.

The solution to this sample query is intentionally incomplete. There is a considerable amount of redundant information in the output. Our intention is to show the matching pattern which occurs when a table is joined with itself. Sample Query 11.12 will present a more precise solution which does not display redundant information.

Sample Query 11.11:   For each department referenced in the STAFF table, we would like to form a committee composed of two staff members from the department. For each possible pair of staff members, display their department id followed by the names of the two staff members. The result should contain a row for every possible pair of staff members.

```
SELECT  ST1.DEPT, ST1.ENAME, ST2.ENAME
FROM    STAFF ST1, STAFF ST2
WHERE   ST1.DEPT = ST2.DEPT
```

```
---------------------------------------------------------
ST1.DEPT          ST1.ENAME         ST2.ENAME
---------------------------------------------------------
ENG               ARCHIMEDES        ARCHIMEDES
MATH              EUCLID            EUCLID
PHIL              DICK NIX          DICK NIX
PHIL              DICK NIX          HANK KISS
PHIL              HANK KISS         DICK NIX
PHIL              HANK KISS         HANK KISS
THEO              JOHN              JOHN
THEO              JOHN              LUKE
THEO              JOHN              MARK
THEO              JOHN              MATTHEW
THEO              LUKE              JOHN
THEO              LUKE              LUKE
THEO              LUKE              MARK
THEO              LUKE              MATTHEW
THEO              MARK              JOHN
THEO              MARK              LUKE
THEO              MARK              MARK
THEO              MARK              MATTHEW
THEO              MATTHEW           JOHN
THEO              MATTHEW           LUKE
THEO              MATTHEW           MARK
THEO              MATTHEW           MATTHEW
```

Comments:

1. Syntax: An alias is placed after the table name in the FROM
    clause. One or more spaces must separate the table name from
    its alias. (Note that a comma should not be used to separate a
    table name from its alias. The separator comma follows the
    alias.)

    The word "alias" is not an official term in DB2 and SQL/DS.
    The precise term is "correlation variable." We will address the
    behavior of correlation variables in Chapter 15. However,
    within the context of this sample query, it is easier to work
    with the notion of an alias for a table name. An alias (correla-
    tion variable) can be up to 18 characters in length. It must
    begin with a letter and is followed by zero or more letters, dig-
    its or underscore characters.

2. Logic: After defining aliases in the FROM clause, we can conceptually operate under the assumption that there are two distinct tables with the names of ST1 and ST2 both of which happen to contain the same data as the STAFF table. (The system does not actually make two copies of the STAFF table. Our discussion of correlation variables in Chapter 15 will provide more insight into the actual process.) The WHERE clause specifies a join condition which joins the ST1 and ST2 "tables" by matching each of their DEPT columns.

Observe the duplication of information present in the result. This is less than desirable. Because every staff member's name and department id is in both ST1 and ST2, each row in ST1 matches with its corresponding row in ST2. Therefore, every staff member appears on the same committee with himself. In particular, ARCHIMEDES, who is the only staff member with "ENG" as a department id, can only be on a committee with himself. (Likewise for EUCLID.) Also, if MARK is in the same department as JOHN, then JOHN is in the same department as MARK. This means the result table will show two rows for each match of different staff members assigned to the same department. The joining of a table with itself produces these matches. The solution to the next sample query presents a trick to eliminate these undesirable rows from the result.

3. Do not confuse an alias with a synonym. Synonyms (to be described in CHapter 12) are established with the CREATE SYNONYM statement and remain in effect until explicitly dropped. An alias is temporary. It is in effect only while the query is being executed.

Sample Query 11.12:   Refine the previous sample query. For each department id referenced at least twice in the STAFF table, display a row for each possible combination of *distinct* staff member names. The row should contain the department id followed by staff member names.

```
SELECT  ST1.DEPT, ST1.ENAME, ST2.ENAME
FROM    STAFF ST1, STAFF ST2
WHERE   ST1.DEPT = ST2.DEPT
AND     ST1.ENAME < ST2.ENAME
```

ST1.DEPT	ST1.ENAME	ST2.ENAME
PHIL	DICK NIX	HANK KISS
THEO	JOHN	LUKE
THEO	JOHN	MARK
THEO	JOHN	MATTHEW
THEO	LUKE	MARK
THEO	LUKE	MATTHEW
THEO	MARK	MATTHEW

Comment:

The additional condition (ST1.ENAME < ST2.ENAME) removes redundant rows from the output. It also prohibits any staff member with a unique department id (e.g., ENG or MATH) from appearing in the result. Because this clause compares two columns from (conceptually) different tables, it could be considered as defining a second join condition where the comparison operator is "less than" instead of "equals" as in previous examples. This leads us into a discussion of the more general concept of "theta join" which is described in the following sample queries.

THETA-JOIN

SQL permits a join condition to be formulated with any of the standard comparison operators. The term "theta-join" is used to indicate this more general capability where "theta" represents a given comparison operator. The next sample query illustrates use of the "less than" operator to define a join condition.

Sample Query 11.13: Assume we would like to compare the salary of every staff member with every course labfee. Whenever the salary is less than the labfee, display the staff member name and salary followed by the corresponding course name and labfee.

```
SELECT  ENAME, ESALARY, CNAME, CLABFEE
FROM    COURSE, STAFF
WHERE   ESALARY < CLABFEE
```

Comments:

1. Syntax: The syntax is consistent with all previous rules pertaining to the syntax of a join operation. The FROM clause identifies the names of the tables, and a WHERE clause specifies the join condition. The join condition can use any of the comparison operators. This example used the "<" operator.

2. Logic: The process is similar to previous join examples. The only difference in this example is that comparison is based upon the "less than" operator. Examination of each row in the output shows the ESALARY value is less than the corresponding CLABFEE value. The definition of what we mean by a "match" has to be expanded to incorporate all the comparison operations.

3. Equi-join is just a special case of theta-join where theta represents the "equals" operator. Because equi-join has greatest application, the term "join" usually implies "equi-join". However, to be precise, join in the general sense is really theta-join and therefore encompasses all the comparison operators.

ENAME	ESALARY	CNAME	CLABFEE
MATTHEW	51	SCHOLASTICISM	150.00
MATTHEW	51	FUNDAMENTALISM	90.00
MATTHEW	51	COMMUNISM	200.00
MATTHEW	51	EMPIRICISM	100.00
MATTHEW	51	EXISTENTIALISM	200.00
MATTHEW	51	INTRO TO CS	100.00
MATTHEW	51	COMPUTER ARCH.	100.00
MATTHEW	51	RELATIONAL DATABASE	500.00
MARK	52	SCHOLASTICISM	150.00
MARK	52	FUNDAMENTALISM	90.00
MARK	52	COMMUNISM	200.00
MARK	52	EMPIRICISM	100.00
MARK	52	EXISTENTIALISM	200.00
MARK	52	INTRO TO CS	100.00
MARK	52	COMPUTER ARCH.	100.00
MARK	52	RELATIONAL DATABASE	500.00
LUKE	53	SCHOLASTICISM	150.00
LUKE	53	FUNDAMENTALISM	90.00
LUKE	53	COMMUNISM	200.00
LUKE	53	EMPIRICISM	100.00
LUKE	53	EXISTENTIALISM	200.00
LUKE	53	INTRO TO CS	100.00
LUKE	53	COMPUTER ARCH.	100.00
LUKE	53	RELATIONAL DATABASE	500.00
JOHN	54	SCHOLASTICISM	150.00
JOHN	54	FUNDAMENTALISM	90.00
JOHN	54	COMMUNISM	200.00
JOHN	54	EMPIRICISM	100.00
JOHN	54	EXISTENTIALISM	200.00
JOHN	54	INTRO TO CS	100.00
JOHN	54	COMPUTER ARCH.	100.00
JOHN	54	RELATIONAL DATABASE	500.00
ARCHIMEDES	200	RELATIONAL DATABASE	500.00

MULTIPLE JOIN CONDITIONS

It is possible to facilitate a join operation where multiple columns from each table are compared to determine the join result. All that is required is the specification of multiple join conditions. Consider the next example which is a refinement of the previous sample query.

Sample Query 11.14: We want to compare the salary of every staff member with the labfee of every course offered by their respective department. Whenever a staff member has a salary which is less than the labfee of a course offered by his department, display the department id, followed by the staff member name and salary, and the corresponding course name and labfee.

```
SELECT  DEPT, ENAME, ESALARY, CNAME, CLABFEE
FROM    STAFF, COURSE
WHERE   ESALARY < CLABFEE
AND     DEPT = CDEPT
```

DEPT	ENAME	ESALARY	CNAME	CLABFEE
THEO	MATTHEW	51	SCHOLASTICISM	150.00
THEO	MARK	52	SCHOLASTICISM	150.00
THEO	LUKE	53	SCHOLASTICISM	150.00
THEO	JOHN	54	SCHOLASTICISM	150.00
THEO	MATTHEW	51	FUNDAMENTALISM	90.00
THEO	MARK	52	FUNDAMENTALISM	90.00
THEO	LUKE	53	FUNDAMENTALISM	90.00
THEO	JOHN	54	FUNDAMENTALISM	90.00
THEO	MATTHEW	51	COMMUNISM	200.00
THEO	MARK	52	COMMUNISM	200.00
THEO	LUKE	53	COMMUNISM	200.00
THEO	JOHN	54	COMMUNISM	200.00

The final sample query in this chapter utilizes the techniques introduced in the previous four sample queries. It joins a table with itself based upon multiple join conditions.

Sample Query 11.15:   Assume the dean is considering moving the administrative office of the Management Department. The intention is to combine its administrative facilities with those of another department which is located in the same building (which is unknown to the dean). To evaluate all possible options, display all information about the Management Department followed by all information about any other department which is located in the same building.

```
SELECT *
FROM    DEPARTMENT D1, DEPARTMENT D2
WHERE   D1.DBLD = D2.DBLD
AND     D1.DEPT <> D2.DEPT
AND     D1.DEPT = 'MGT'
```

DEPT	DBLD	DROOM	DCHFNO	DEPT	DBLD	DROOM	DCHFNO
MGT	SC	100	-	CIS	SC	300	80

Comment:

Again, we have not introduced any new SQL techniques. Previous techniques were applied to solve this problem. Any complexity pertains to the logical dimension of the query.

SUMMARY

The basic structure of a SELECT statement which joins two or more tables is essentially the same as one which references just one table. For two tables this is

```
SELECT  col1, col2, col3, ...
FROM    table1, table2
WHERE   table1.joincol1 = table2.joincol2
AND     (other row selection conditions)
ORDER   BY (any displayed columns)
```

The logic of a join condition is another matter. You must understand the relationship between the tables as reflected in the join columns. Sometimes the database design can simplify the situation. For example, every CDEPT value in the COURSE table matches some DEPT value in the DEPARTMENT table. Also there were no null values in the CDEPT column. Therefore, every COURSE row will be present in a join of these two tables. There is no chance of an undetected COURSE row missing from an output display. Desired rows are explicitly selected (or undesired rows explicitly rejected) by coding conditions in the SELECT statement. It is possible for a designer to establish this simplified situation by (1) using the NOT NULL option for the CDEPT column when creating the COURSE table and (2) defining CDEPT as a foreign key referencing the DEPARTMENT table.

Very often the application environment does not permit the designer to incorporate the above procedures. We mirrored this complexity in the STAFF and DEPARTMENT tables. Some departments might not have chairpersons, staff or courses. Some staff members might not have department assignments or be assigned to nonexisting departments. This created a situation where the join of the DEPARTMENT and STAFF tables caused no-match situations, which removed certain rows from the join result. The key point is that users of SQL must be sensitive to this situation. Otherwise, incorrect output displays could be generated. Once again, we emphasize that this issue transcends the SQL language. Simply, users must understand the semantic structure of their database.

SUMMARY EXERCISES

11N. . Display the faculty number of any faculty member who chairs a department which offers a six-credit course.

11O. Display the course number, name and section of every class which is offered on a Monday.

11P. Display the course number and name of every course that student 800 is registered for.

11Q. Display all information about any scheduled class which has a labfee less than $100 and is not offered on a Friday.

11R. Display the student number and date of registration from all students who registered for at least one course offered by the Theology Department.

11S. How many students are registered for all sections of the EXISTENTIALISM course?

11T. How many students have registered for classes offered by the Philosophy Department?

11U. Display the name and number of every faculty member who teaches a class which meets on a Monday or a Friday. Do not display duplicate rows.

The following exercises are more of a challenge. They require that you use techniques presented toward the end of this chapter.

11V. Display the name of any faculty member who chairs a department which offers a six-credit course.

11Wa. Produce a class list for the first section of the EXISTENTIALISM course. Display the course number, section number, course name and faculty number of the instructor followed by the student number of every student registered for the class.

11Wb. Modify the previous "class list" query. Display each student's name after his or her student number.

11Wc. Make another modification to the "class list" query. Display the faculty name instead of faculty number.

11X.   This is a "paper and pencil" exercise. Verify that any of the following join sequences involving three tables will produce the same result.

    a.   Join the COURSE and STAFF tables to get an intermediate result. Then join this with the DEPARTMENT table.

    b.   Join the COURSE and DEPARTMENT tables to get an intermediate result. Then join this with the STAFF table.

    c.   Join the STAFF and DEPARTMENT tables to get an intermediate result. Then join this with the COURSE table.

11Y.   Form the cross product of the COURSE and FACULTY tables.

11Z.   Display the department identifiers of each pair of departments which are located in the same building.

11Za.   Compare the salaries for each pair of staff members. Whenever the salary of the first staff member exceeds the salary of the second staff member by more than $1000, display the name and salary of both staff members followed by the difference in salaries.

11Zb.   Modify the previous "salary comparison" query. Only compare the salaries of staff members who have the same department id value specified in the STAFF.DEPT column.

11Zc.   Make another modification to the "salary comparison" query. This time, only compare salaries of staff members who are assigned to existing departments which are located in the Humanities Building.

12

Synonyms

This chapter is dedicated to those with poor typing skills who will appreciate the opportunity to reduce the number of keystrokes required to express a SQL statement. One such oppportunity is the creation of synonyms for table names. Synonyms can serve as abbreviations for long table names. For example, a number of queries in the previous chapter referenced the DEPARTMENT table. We will create a synonym, "D", to be used as an abbreviation for this table. This will be done by executing a CREATE SYNONYM statement which will associate D with DEPARTMENT. Thereafter, D can be substituted for DEPARTMENT in any SQL command where a table name would be specified.

Sample Statement 12.1:   Create a synonym called "D" for the DE-
PARTMENT table.

```
CREATE SYNONYM D FOR DEPARTMENT
```

System Response:

- The system should display a message indicating successful creation of the synonym.

Comment:

Now that the synonym has been created, it can be used like
any valid table name in a SQL statement. Consider the following sample query where "D" is used in place of "DEPART-
MENT."

Sample Query 12.2:   Display the building and room location for the
Philosophy Department.

```
SELECT DBLD,  DROOM
FROM    D
WHERE   DEPT = 'PHIL'
```

```
-------------------
DBLD     DROOM
-------------------
HU        100
```

Comments:

1. Synonyms are local to a sign-on id. This means that if another
user (a person using a different authorization id) has access to
the DEPARTMENT table, that user cannot validly reference
the synonym D unless that user explicitly issues the same
CREATE SYNONYM command. This other user could also create a different synonym for the same table. For example, assume this other user issued the following command.

```
CREATE SYNONYM DEP FOR DEPARTMENT
```

Under this circumstance, the system would recognize the other user's DEP synonym and reject references to D by that user. Likewise, it would recognize your D synonym, but reject your reference to DEP. Note that, because synonyms are local, there is no problem when multiple users create synonyms which happen to have the same name. This means another user could also create a D synonym which may be associated with the DEPARTMENT table or an entirely different table.

Aside: We have yet to discuss the GRANT command which enables one user to permit another user access to his table. Chapter 17 is devoted to this topic. Once you understand the GRANT command, the above discussion can be summarized by noting that privileges on synonyms cannot be granted. Users must explicitly create their own synonyms.

2. The system remembers your synonyms for the entire terminal session, even after you sign off. The same synonyms are available the next time you sign on. You do not have to reissue the CREATE SYNONYM command.

3. What if you forget your synonyms? There is an easy way to ask the system to display your current synonyms. The section on the SYSSYNONYMS catalog table will address this topic.

4. What if you no longer need a particular synonym? Synonyms can be dropped the same way that tables and indexes were dropped in Chapter 8. The following command would remove the D synonym.

```
DROP SYNONYM D
```

5. The system will let you create multiple synonyms for the same table. However, it will reject any attempt to create the same synonym for two different tables.

SYNONYMS AS COLUMN QUALIFIERS

The use of synonyms can be even more helpful in queries which involve the join operation. Consider the following.

Sample Query 12.3: Display the name, title, department id, and room location of every staff member who works in the Humanities building. (Same as Sample Query 11.4)

```
SELECT  ENAME, ETITLE, D.DEPT, DROOM
FROM    STAFF, D
WHERE   STAFF.DEPT = D.DEPT
AND     DBLD = 'HU'
```

```
------------------------------------------------------------
ENAME           ETITLE          D.DEPT      DROOM
------------------------------------------------------------
HANK KISS       JESTER          PHIL        100
DICK NIX        CROOK           PHIL        100
MATTHEW         EVANGLIST1      THEO        200
MARK            EVANGLIST2      THEO        200
LUKE            EVANGLIST3      THEO        200
JOHN            EVANGLIST4      THEO        200
```

Comments:

1. In addition to referencing the synonym D in the FROM clause, this sample query uses D as a table qualifier in the SELECT clause and the join condition. A synonym can be placed anywhere in the SELECT statement that the corresponding table name can be placed. This means it can be used to qualify column names.

2. The current sample query uses a synonym for the DEPARTMENT table, but not for the STAFF table. A query can reference multiple synonyms.

SYSSYNONYMS TABLE

Earlier we noted that there is a way to determine which synonyms are currently in effect. This is helpful in case you forget the names of any synonyms which you created during a previous terminal session. We will see the process is straightforward, but some preliminary comments are necessary.

All the tables presented in this book have been "application" tables which contain data relating to a business application. Our business application contains data necesssary to manage a mythical college. This data is of direct interest to the user. These application tables are explicitly created with the CREATE TABLE command. In addition to application tables, DB2 and SQL/DS each maintain a set of "system" tables. This set of tables is collectively known as the "catalog." These system tables are part of the system. Nobody explicitly issues a CREATE TABLE statement to create these tables. A comprehensive discussion of the system tables is beyond the scope of this book. Our present intent is to introduce just one such table, the SYSSYNONYMS table.

The SYSSYNONYMS table will contain one row for each synonym that the system recognizes. Whenever you issue a CREATE SYNONYM statement, the system automatically inserts a new row into this table. Whenever you issue a DROP SYNONYM statement, the system automatically deletes a row from this table.

In order to determine which synonyms are currently in effect, you merely examine the contents of the SYSSYNONYMS table. The nice thing about the process is that you use the standard SELECT statement to examine this table. In effect, there is nothing new to learn. Like any table, you must know two things, (1) the precise table name, and (2) the precise column names.

DB2 and SQL/DS are different systems. The catalog of system tables for each system is "similar in spirit" but considerably different in detail. This is why we noted that you must know the "precise" table and column names. Both DB2 and SQL/DS have a SYSSYNONYMS table. There are some minor differences which are not problematic in this case. We describe the SYSSYNONYMS table for each system.

DB2:

1. The precise table name is SYSIBM.SYSSYNONYMS.

2. The precise column names are:
    NAME   — Name of synonym
    CREATOR   — Authorization id of creator of synonym
    TBNAME   — Name of table
    TBCREATOR   — Authorization id of creator of table

Sample Query 12.7.1:   What synonyms are currently in effect for user "HGC001"?

```
SELECT NAME, TBNAME
FROM    SYSIBM.SYSSYNONYMS
WHERE   CREATOR = 'HGC001'
```

SQL/DS:

1. The precise table name is SYSTEM.SYSSYNONYMS.

2. The precise column names are:
    ALTNAME   — Name of synonym
    USERID   — Authorization id of creator of synonym
    TNAME   — Name of table
    CREATOR   — Authorization id of creator of table

Sample Query 12.7.2:   What synonyms are currently in effect for user "HGC001"?

```
SELECT ALTNAME, TNAME
FROM    SYSTEM.SYSSYNONYMS
WHERE   USERID = 'HGC001'
```

Comments:

1. Each of the SYSSYNONYMS tables was qualified by the name of system. For DB2, the name of the system is "SYSIBM". Hence, the precise name of its synonyms table is "SYSIBM.SYSSYNONYMS". For SQL/DS, the name of the system is "SYSTEM". Hence, the precise name of its synonyms table is "SYSTEM.SYSSYNONYMS".

2. The SYNONYMS table contains a row for every synonym for every user who has access to the system. For this reason, the sample queries included the following WHERE clause.

    ```
    WHERE CREATOR = 'HGC001'
    ```

    Without this WHERE clause, all synonyms for every user would have been displayed. By including the WHERE clause in the query, only the synonyms for user HGC001 are displayed.

3. The preceding discussion of the SYSSYNONYMS table assumes that you have full access to this table. Sometimes, the database administrator will restrict your access to this table. Usually you are only permitted to select those rows corresponding to your authorization id. (The database administrator uses the view mechanism to achieve this objective. See Chapter 16.) If this is the case, you will not have direct access to SYSSYNONYMS. Instead, you will be told the name of another table (really a view) which contains just the synonyms that you created. For example, you might be told that table SYNHGC001 is the table which contains your synonyms. In this case, to see all your synonyms you would execute the following command.

    ```
    SELECT * FROM SYNHGC001
    ```

4. You cannot directly issue an INSERT, DELETE, or UPDATE command for the SYSSYNONYMS table. (Not even the database administrator can do this.) All changes to this table occur indirectly by execution of the CREATE SYNONYM and DROP SYNONYM commands.

SUMMARY

This chapter introduced the CREATE SYNONYM statement. Its primary purpose is to construct abbreviations for table names. The general syntax for this statement is

```
CREATE SYNONYM synonym FOR table
```

Once created, a synonym can be substituted for the table name in any SQL statement. We noted that synonyms are local to your sign-on id and that they remain in effect until they are explicitly dropped. The general syntax of the DROP SYNONYM statement is

```
DROP SYNONYM synonym
```

Both systems keep information about synonyms in a special system table. In DB2 this table is called SYSIBM.SYSSYNONYMS. In SQL/DS this table is called SYSTEM.SYSSYNONYMS. Users can query this table to determine which synonyms are currently in effect. The CREATE SYNONYM causes the system to insert a row in this table; the DROP SYNONYM causes the system to delete a row.

In Chapter 16 we will discuss a special type of table known as a view. We mention this here for the purpose of stating that a synonym can also be created for a view. Whenever we have mentioned "table" in this chapter, the term "view" could have been used.

Finally, note that synonyms can only be created for table or view names. Although it might be desirable, synonyms cannot be created for column names.

SUMMARY EXERCISES

    12A. Display all the synonyms currently in effect for your authorization id. (Same as Sample Query 12.7.)

    12B. Create any synonym for any table.

    12C. Display all your synonyms. Note the new row.

    12D. Drop the previously created synonym.

    12E. Display all your synonyms. Note the row for the previous synonym is removed.

13

Subqueries

This chapter introduces the technique of nesting a SELECT statement within another SELECT statement. Figure 13.1 shows the basic structure of a SELECT statement which contains another SELECT statement nested within it. The nested SELECT statement is called a "subquery," a "subselect," or an "inner SELECT." We will refer to the first SELECT as the "main query" or the "outer SELECT." Most of the sample queries presented in this chapter can be solved using the join operation. However, the use of subqueries is often considered to provide a simpler solution. There are some circumstances where the use of a subquery becomes necessary. Chapter 15, which describes correlated subqueries, will present examples of such queries.

BACKGROUND

We first examine a deceptively simple query, which cannot be conveniently expressed in a single SELECT statement given the SQL techniques described thus far.

Query 1: Display the course number and name of the course(s) with the highest labfee.

Recall that it is easy to display the highest labfee. This is achieved by executing the following statement:

```
SELECT  MAX(CLABFEE)
FROM    COURSE
```

The system would return 500.00, which enables us to formulate the following statement.

```
SELECT  CNO, CNAME
FROM    COURSE
WHERE   CLABFEE = 500.00
```

While this procedure will work, it requires the execution of two independent SELECT statements. This is less than desirable for the same reasons specified earlier in our discussion of the join operation. (See preliminary discussion of Chapter 11.)

Recall that the following statement will *not* work:

```
SELECT  CNO, CNAME, MAX(CLABFEE)
FROM    COURSE
```

Because the SELECT clause contains a built-in function, MAX(CLABFEE), the other columns, CNO and CNAME, must be referenced in a GROUP BY clause.

The basic problem is that we do not know what the largest CLABFEE value is. Essentially, we want to construct a WHERE clause for an unknown value. This represents a class of queries where a subquery can be used to determine an unknown value.

A second reason to use a subquery is to avoid explicit coding of a join operation for a query which requires examination of multiple tables, but only displays columns from a single table. The following query illustrates this situation.

Query 2: Display the name and title of every staff member who works in the Humanities building.

Sample Query 11.4 presented a solution to this query by joining the DEPARTMENT and STAFF tables. This was

```
SELECT  ENAME, ETITLE
FROM    STAFF, DEPARTMENT
WHERE   STAFF.DEPT = DEPARTMENT.DEPT
AND     DBLD = 'HU'
```

Because the displayed columns, ENAME and ETITLE, are in a single table, the STAFF table, it is possible to code a subquery solution to this problem. Sample Query 13.8 will illustrate this solution. Many users will prefer this solution because it circumvents the logical complexities associated with the join operation.

The sample queries presented in this chapter employ subquery solutions to solve a variety of problems. The first seven examples present subqueries which produce a single value. The remaining example contain subqueries which can produce multiple values. We will see that you must be aware of whether a subquery can produce more than a single value.

```
SELECT _ _ _ _ _ _ _ _
FROM _ _ _ _ _ _ _ _         Main Query
WHERE _ _ _ _ _ _ _ _        (Outer Select)
    (SELECT _ _ _ _ _ _ _
    FROM _ _ _ _ _ _          Subquery
    WHERE _ _ _ _ _ _ )       (Subselect)
```

Figure 13.1 Subquery SELECT statement.

Subquery: WHERE Clause Examines Unknown Value

The first seven sample queries in this chapter have a WHERE clause which compares a column to a single unknown value. This unknown value is resolved by a nested subquery. After the subquery is evaluated, its result is returned to the WHERE clause of the main query which is then evaluated to determine which rows should be selected for display.

Sample Query 13.1:   Display the course number and name of the course(s) with the highest labfee.

```
SELECT  CNO, CNAME
FROM    COURSE
WHERE   CLABFEE =
    (SELECT MAX(CLABFEE)
     FROM COURSE)
```

```
-----------------------------------------
CNO      CNAME
-----------------------------------------
C66      RELATIONAL DATABASE
```

Comments:

1. Logic: The system will execute the subquery first. In this case, it will find the maximum labfee value of 500.00 and substitute this value in the WHERE clause of the main query. The main query then becomes:

    ```
    SELECT  CNO, CNAME
    FROM    COURSE
    WHERE   CLABFEE = 500.00
    ```

The main query is then executed and the result is displayed. Note that the subquery result of 500.00 is not displayed. It is just substituted in the WHERE clause of the main query. If you also wanted to display the maximum labfee value, you would reference CLABFEE in the main query SELECT clause. The entire statement would be:

```
SELECT  CNO, CNAME, CLABFEE
FROM    COURSE
WHERE   CLABFEE =
        (SELECT MAX(CLABFEE)
         FROM COURSE)
```

2. Syntax:
   - The subquery must be enclosed within parentheses.
   - The WHERE clause in the main query has an equal sign. Effectively, it is stating "where the CLABFEE is equal to some value" (not "values"). Because the WHERE clause is written to compare the CLABFEE with a single value, the subquery must be coded so that only a single value is returned by the subquery. In the current example the subquery returns the maximum labfee value, which is a single value (500.00). Note that this would be the case even if multiple COURSE rows contained the same maximum value.
   - Both the main query and the subquery happen to reference the COURSE table. This is not necessary. (See Sample Query 13.7.)
   - As with all previous SQL statements, the format is free form. Indentation is arbitrary.

Exercise:

13A. Display the course number, name, and department of the course(s) with the smallest labfee.

Subquery Contains a WHERE Clause

To further influence the result of the main query, the subquery could contain a WHERE clause to exclude certain rows. A subquery can contain any valid WHERE clause.

Sample Query 13.2:   Display the course number, name, and labfee of the course(s) with the smallest nonzero labfee.

```
SELECT  CNO, CNAME, CLABFEE
FROM    COURSE
WHERE   CLABFEE =
    (SELECT MIN(CLABFEE)
     FROM    COURSE
     WHERE   NOT CLABFEE = 0)
```

```
------------------------------------------------------------
CNO     CNAME                         CLABFEE
------------------------------------------------------------
P22     RATIONALISM                     50.00
C22     DATA STRUCTURES                 50.00
```

Comments:

1. Logic: The WHERE clause in the subquery will exclude zero as a minimum value. Assuming there are no negative labfee values, the subquery will return the smallest positive labfee value to the WHERE clause of the main query. The main query will select rows based on this value. The output will display this value after the course number and name of any courses which have this labfee value.

   This WHERE clause is simple. It has only one condition. In general, the WHERE clause can include any number of conditions connected with Boolean operators.

2. The subquery WHERE clause could have been written as

   ```
   WHERE CLABFEE > 0
   ```

   This would eliminate any concern about possible negative labfee values.

3. Syntax: No special syntax requirements exist. The subquery is a standard SELECT statement enclosed with parentheses.

Exercise:

13B. Assume you know that the highest labfee is 500.00. Write a SELECT statement which will display the course number, name, department, and labfee of the course(s) having the second highest labfee.

The next sample query includes the same WHERE clause in both the main query and the subquery. The logic of the query forces us to code it this way. Once again, we see that although SQL is simple, the logic of a query can be subtle.

Sample Query 13.3: Display the course number and name of the philosophy course(s) with the highest labfee.

```
SELECT  CNO, CNAME
FROM    COURSE
WHERE   CDEPT = 'PHIL'
AND     CLABFEE =
    (SELECT MAX(CLABFEE)
     FROM   COURSE
     WHERE  CDEPT = 'PHIL')
```

```
-------------------------------------
CNO       CNAME
-------------------------------------
P33       EXISTENTIALISM
```

Comments:

1. Logic: The subquery determines the maximum labfee for any philosophy course. This value (200.00) is substituted in the WHERE clause of the main query. Thus, the statement reduces to:

```
SELECT  CNO, CNAME, CLABFEE
FROM    COURSE
WHERE   CDEPT = 'PHIL'
AND     CLABFEE = 200.00
```

Both the main query and the subquery must contain the same condition (WHERE CDEPT = 'PHIL') in order to restrict the displayed courses to those offered by the Philosophy Department. This might appear to be redundant, but it is not. Consider the effect of excluding this WHERE condition from either the main query or the subquery.

```
SELECT  CNO, CNAME, CLABFEE
FROM    COURSE
WHERE   CLABFEE =
        (SELECT MAX(CLABFEE)
         FROM    COURSE
         WHERE  CDEPT = 'PHIL')
```

This statement displays all courses with a 200.00 labfee. In particular, it would display the row for the "T44" theology course. This is not consistent with the objective to display only philosophy courses. The following statement is also incorrect, but for a different reason.

```
SELECT  CNO, CNAME
FROM    COURSE
WHERE   CDEPT = 'PHIL'
AND     CLABFEE =
        (SELECT MAX(CLABFEE)
         FROM    COURSE)
```

This statement results in a "no hit" because the subquery evaluates to 500.00 and the main query determines that no philosophy courses have a labfee equal to this value.

2. Syntax: The subquery is simply another condition which is AND-connected to the main query WHERE clause. Subqueries do not need to be written last. The following statement is valid.

```
SELECT  CNO, CNAME, CLABFEE
FROM    COURSE
WHERE   CLABFEE =
        (SELECT MAX(CLABFEE)
         FROM    COURSE
         WHERE  CDEPT = 'PHIL')
AND     CDEPT = 'PHIL'
```

Exercise:

13C. Display the course number, name, department, and labfee of the six-credit course(s) with the most expensive labfee.

The logic of the preceding sample query required the same WHERE clause to be included in both the main query and subquery. This is not always the case. You need to be very sensitive to the goal of the query and the logic to achieve the goal. Again, this is an issue which transcends the relatively simple syntax rules of SQL (or that of any other computer language). The next two sample queries demonstrate this point. They have different objectives, but they are similar enough so that ambiguity can occur unless the objectives are precisely articulated and understood.

Sample Query 13.4: Display the course number and name of any non-CIS course with the smallest labfee of all courses. (This is the smallest labfee recorded in the COURSE table, including rows for CIS courses.)

```
SELECT  CNO, CNAME
FROM    COURSE
WHERE   NOT CDEPT = 'CIS'
AND     CLABFEE =
        (SELECT MIN(CLABFEE)
        FROM COURSE)
```

```
----------------------------------------
CNO       CNAME
----------------------------------------
T33       HEDONISM
P44       SOLIPSISM
```

Comment:

The sample query examines courses offered by every department, including CIS, to determine the minimal CLABFEE value. However, because of the WHERE clause in the main query, the output will not contain any CIS courses with this minimal labfee. Note the difference between this example and Sample Query 13.5, which has a WHERE clause in both the main query and subquery.

Sample Query 13.5:   Do not consider CIS courses. Display the course number and name of the course(s) with the smallest labfee.

```
SELECT  CNO, CNAME
FROM    COURSE
WHERE   NOT CDEPT = 'CIS'
AND     CLABFEE =
        (SELECT  MIN(CLABFEE)
         FROM    COURSE
         WHERE   NOT CDEPT = 'CIS')
```

```
------------------------------------
CNO      CNAME
------------------------------------
T33      HEDONISM
P44      SOLIPSISM
```

Comment:

This result is the same as the previous query. However, it is important to note that this is just a coincidence. It happened because the current contents of the COURSE table has CIS rows and non-CIS rows with the same minimal CLABFEE value of zero.

Assume that the COURSE table was updated so that courses T33 and P44 have labfees of 5.00. This means that neither the Philosophy nor the Theology Departments have any courses with zero labfees. Under this circumstance, the difference between the two preceding queries would be observable in the displayed results. Sample Query 13.4 would result in a "no hit" situation because none of the non-CIS courses have the minimal labfee of zero. However, Sample Query 13.5 would display the same two rows for courses T33 and P44.

All previous subquery examples showed the WHERE clause of the main query with an "equals" comparison operator. In practice, any of the other comparison operators (<, >, <=, >=, <>, ¬=) can be used. The next sample query uses the "less than" operator in comparing the intermediate result produced by the subquery.

Sample Query 13.6:   Display the course number, name, and labfee of any course with a labfee which is less than the overall average labfee.

```
SELECT CNO, CNAME, CLABFEE
FROM    COURSE
WHERE   CLABFEE <
    (SELECT AVG(CLABFEE)
     FROM    COURSE)
```

CNO	CNAME	CLABFEE
T12	FUNDAMENTALISM	90.00
T33	HEDONISM	0.00
P11	EMPIRICISM	100.00
P22	RATIONALISM	50.00
P44	SOLIPSISM	0.00
C11	INTRO TO CS	100.00
C22	DATA STRUCTURES	50.00
C33	DISCRETE MATHEMATICS	0.00
C44	DIGITAL CIRCUITS	0.00
C55	COMPUTER ARCH.	100.00

Comments:

1. The WHERE clause of the main query contains a "less than" comparison operator. Any valid comparison operator is permitted.

2. The subquery references the AVG built-in function. Like the previous subqueries, this returns a single value which is used as the comparison value in the WHERE clause of the main query. Because the average labfee value is 110.00, the main query reduces to:

```
SELECT  CNO, CNAME, CLABFEE
FROM    COURSE
WHERE   CLABFEE < 110.00
```

Exercise:

13D. Display the course number, name, and labfee of any course with a labfee which is less than the average labfee of courses offered by the Theology Department.

13E. Display all information about any course with a labfee which exceeds the maximum labfee for any theology or philosophy course.

All the preceding examples illustrated subqueries which reference the same table as the main query. Although this is common, it is not a requirement. In the next example, the main query and subquery reference different tables.

To understand the basis of this query, we assume that it may be poor policy to have the labfee of any course greater than or equal to the salary of any staff member. The goal is to determine which courses, if any, have such labfees.

Sample Query 13.7:   Display the course number, name, and labfee of any course which has a labfee greater than or equal to the salary of any staff member.

```
SELECT CNO, CNAME, CLABFEE
FROM    COURSE
WHERE   CLABFEE >=
    (SELECT MIN(ESALARY)
     FROM    STAFF)
```

```
--------------------------------------------------------
CNO      CNAME                    CLABFEE
--------------------------------------------------------
T11      SCHOLASTICISM             150.00
T12      FUNDAMENTALISM             90.00
T44      COMMUNISM                 200.00
P11      EMPIRICISM                100.00
P33      EXISTENTIALISM            200.00
C11      INTRO TO CS               100.00
C55      COMPUTER ARCH.            100.00
C66      RELATIONAL DATABASE       500.00
```

Comments:

1. The logic determines the lowest salary paid to any staff member, and then which courses, if any, have labfees greater than or equal to this amount.

2. The main query references the COURSE table and the subquery references the STAFF table. The subquery returns the minimum salary which, as a legitimate numeric value, can be compared to labfee values in the main query. Because the minimum ESALARY value is 51, the main query reduces to

   ```
   SELECT  CNO, CNAME, CLABFEE
   FROM    COURSE
   WHERE   CLABFEE >= 51
   ```

3. There exists an alternative solution to this problem. See Sample Query 11.13 which presented the "theta" join.

Exercise:

13F. Display the employee name and salary of any staff member whose salary is less than or equal to the maximum course labfee.

13G. Display all information about any CIS course with a labfee which is less than the average salary of staff members assigned to the Theology Department.

Subquery: WHERE Clause Examines Multiple Unknown Values

All previous subquery examples and workshop exercises involved a subquery which returned a single value. The value was substituted in the WHERE clause of the main query. This basic format is:

```
WHERE column comparison-operator single-value
```

Subsequent sample queries will illustrate subqueries which may return multiple values to be referenced by the main query. In place of a single comparison operator, the WHERE clause uses the IN keyword.

```
WHERE column IN set-of-values
```

Allowing the subquery to return multiple values extends the use of the subquery technique to a broader class of problems. It also permits alternative SQL solutions to some problems which could be solved using the join operation.

Sample Query 13.8: Display the name and title of every staff member who works in the Humanities building. (Same as Sample Query 11.4)

```
SELECT ENAME, ETITLE
FROM    STAFF
WHERE   DEPT IN
    (SELECT DEPT
     FROM    DEPARTMENT
     WHERE   DBLD = 'HU')
```

```
-------------------------------------------
ENAME             ETITLE
-------------------------------------------
HANK KISS         JESTER
DICK NIX          CROOK
MATTHEW           EVANGLIST1
MARK              EVANGLIST2
LUKE              EVANGLIST3
JOHN              EVANGLIST4
```

Comments:

1. The logic of this sample query is to have the subquery examine the DEPARTMENT table to determine which departments are located in the Humanities building. Then the main query will examine the STAFF table to determine the name and title of staff members who work in these departments.

2. The subquery will return the department identifiers for the two departments located in the Humanities buliding. These are "THEO" and "PHIL." These values will be substituted into the WHERE clause of the main query as follows:

```
SELECT  ENAME, ETITLE
FROM    STAFF
WHERE   DEPT IN ('THEO', 'PHIL')
```

3. Note that, unlike previous subqueries, multiple values are returned as an intermediate result. For this reason, the main query WHERE clause must use the IN keyword. If the WHERE clause contained an equal sign, an error would result. This is because, after substitution of the subquery values, the clause would be WHERE DEPT = ('THEO', 'PHIL'). This is invalid because the comparison operators can only be applied to a single value.

4. This same problem was solved using the join technique in Sample Query 11.4. The reason the subquery technique can be applied is that all the displayed columns come from a single table (STAFF). This is the only table referenced in the main query.

   Many users find the subquery approach easier to understand than the join technique. This is a matter of personal preference from a logical problem solving point of view. (It should be noted that, from a machine efficiency point of view, current versions of DB2 and SQL/DS favor the join technique.)

Exercise:

13H. Display the department name and the chairperson faculty number for all departments responsible for a six-credit course.

It was noted in our previous discussion of the join operation that sometimes many matches could occur and duplicate rows could be displayed. Sample Query 11.5 was such a case where the same row was displayed four times. You were instructed to use the DISTINCT keyword to avoid this duplication. The following shows a subquery solution to the same sample query. However, note that this solution does not contain DISTINCT, yet dupicate rows are not displayed. Our comments will address this point.

Sample Query 13.9:   Where can I find an evangelist? Display the building and room of any academic department which employs a staff member whose title contains the character string 'EVANGLIST'.

```
SELECT  DBLD,  DROOM
FROM    DEPARTMENT
WHERE   DEPT IN
   (SELECT DEPT
    FROM    STAFF
    WHERE   ETITLE  LIKE  'EVANGLIST%')
```

```
-------------------
DBLD     DROOM
-------------------
HU       200
```

Comments:

1. Why were dulpicate rows not displayed?

    Consider the intermediate result returned by the subquery. If it were executed as an independent query, it would display the following table.

    ```
    THEO
    THEO
    THEO
    THEO
    ```

This table is interpreted by the system as a "set" of four department values. These same values were substituted into the WHERE clause of the main query, the query would be evaluated as

```
SELECT  DBLD, DROOM
FROM    DEPARTMENT
WHERE   DEPT IN ('THEO', 'THEO', 'THEO', 'THEO')
```

Execution of the above statement would display the same single row shown for the subquery solution. The precise explanation involves recognition of the fact that a mathematical set does not contain duplicate elements. SQL would interpret the four occurrences of "THEO" as one value. Hence, the main query effectively becomes:

```
SELECT  DBLD, DROOM
FROM    DEPARTMENT
WHERE   DEPT IN ('THEO')
```

2. The following solution makes the logic explicit by using DISTINCT in the subquery.

```
SELECT  DBLD, DROOM
FROM    DEPARTMENT
WHERE   DEPT IN
        (SELECT DISTINCT DEPT
         FROM   STAFF
         WHERE  ETITLE LIKE 'EVANGLIST%')
```

The use of DISTINCT in a subquery is always superfluous. However, this is not the case with the main query. The next sample query describes a situation where DISTINCT must be present in the main query SELECT clause.

The next sample query uses DISTINCT in the main query. This is necessary if we assume that a faculty member could be the chairperson of more than one academic department.

Sample Query 13.10:   Display the faculty number of any faculty member who serves as chairperson of any department which offers a six-credit course. Do not display duplicate values.

```
SELECT DISTINCT DCHFNO
FROM DEPARTMENT
WHERE DEPT IN
     (SELECT CDEPT
      FROM   COURSE
      WHERE  CRED = 6)
```

```
---------
DCHFNO
---------
10
60
```

Comments:

1. In this example, the subquery returns the CDEPT values of rows in the COURSE table which have a CRED value of 6. Only two rows match this condition. Their CDEPT values are "THEO" and "PHIL." Hence, the main query is evaluated as:

    ```
    SELECT  DISTINCT DCHFNO
    FROM    DEPARTMENT
    WHERE   DEPT IN ('THEO', 'PHIL')
    ```

2. Examination of the current contents of the DEPARTMENT table reveals that DCHFNO values are unique. (At this point, it just happens to be the case that no faculty member is serving as chairperson for more than one department.) Hence, the displayed results would have been the same if you omitted DISTINCT in the main query. It is important to note this is a matter of luck. Because school policy permits a faculty member to chair multiple departments, it is possible for the same DCHFNO to occur in multiple rows of the DEPARTMENT table. It is a poor show to write SQL code which is correct only under special conditions. Therefore, DISTINCT should be included in the main query SELECT clause.

3. This query displayed faculty numbers. What if you wanted to display faculty names? Note that faculty names are not stored in the DEPARTMENT table. This problem can be solved by nesting the current example within another SELECT statement. Try to code this query before examining the next sample query which describes the solution in detail.

Exercise:

13I. Display the course number, section number, and building of any class which is offered in the same building where staff member Dick Nix works.

SECOND LEVEL OF NESTING

The next sample query is an extension of the previous query. This extension requires that we nest the previous SELECT statement, which already contains a subquery, within another SELECT statement. This leads to multiple levels of nesting of SELECT statements. We will see that there is nothing new to learn relative to syntax. However, the logic of the query becomes slightly more complex.

Sample Query 13.11:   Display the faculty number and name of any faculty member who serves as chairperson of any department which offers a six-credit course.

```
SELECT  DISTINCT  FNO, FNAME
FROM     FACULTY
WHERE    FNO  IN
     (SELECT  DCHFNO
      FROM     DEPARTMENT
      WHERE    DEPT  IN
           (SELECT  CDEPT
            FROM     COURSE
            WHERE    CRED = 6))
```

```
----------------------------------------
FNO      FNAME
----------------------------------------
10       JULIE  MARTYN
60       JESSIE MARTYN
```

Comments:

1. The system will execute the innermost subquery first. In this example, it will return the department identifiers of all six-credit courses. The COURSE table has two such courses. One is offered by the Theology Department, and the other is offered by the Philosophy Department. Hence, the query reduces to:

```
SELECT  DISTINCT FNO, FNAME
FROM    FACULTY
WHERE   FNO IN
        (SELECT DCHFNO
         FROM    DEPARTMENT
         WHERE DEPT IN ('THEO', 'PHIL'))
```

This intermediate result still contains a subquery which requires evaluation. This subquery will examine the DEPARTMENT table and return the faculty numbers of chairpersons of the Theology and Philosophy Departments. These values are 10 and 60. The query is now reduced to:

```
SELECT  DISTINCT FNO, FNAME
FROM    FACULTY
WHERE   FNO IN (10, 60)
```

2. The use of DISTINCT in the main query is unnecessary because FNO values are unique within the FACULTY table. From a logical point of view, it is simpler to always use DISTINCT to avoid displaying duplicate rows. Note, however, this does incur the cost of sorting associated with DISTINCT. (Refer to initial discussion of DISTINCT in Chapter 1.)

3. Note that if a single department offered multiple six credit courses, or if any faculty member was chairperson of multiple departments where each department offered at least one six credit course, duplicate values would have been produced by the subqueries. Recall that DISTINCT is always superfluous in a subquery. (See Sample Query 13.9 for discussion.)

4. This query could have been expressed as a three-way operation.

```
SELECT  DISTINCT FNO, FNAME
FROM    FACULTY, DEPARTMENT, COURSE
WHERE   FNO = DCHFNO
AND     DEPT = CDEPT
AND     CRED = 6
```

Using NOT IN With Subqueries

The intermediate result generated by a subquery can be compared using NOT IN. The next example illustrates this fact. The logic is simple enough. However, there is a subtle circumstance which occurs with this example that can lead to an erroneous interpretation of the result. Try to detect this circumstance prior to reading the comments.

Sample Query 13.12:   Display the name, title, and department id of every staff member assigned to a nonexistent department. This is a department with a department id not found in the DEPARTMENT table.

```
SELECT ENAME, ETITLE, DEPT
FROM    STAFF
WHERE   DEPT NOT IN
   (SELECT DEPT
    FROM    DEPARTMENT)
```

```
-------------------------------------------------
ENAME            ETITLE          DEPT
-------------------------------------------------
EUCLID           LAB ASSIST      MATH
ARCHIMEDES       LAB ASSIST      ENG
```

Comments:

1. The subquery produces the set of DEPT values found in the
    DEPARTMENT table. These are "THEO", "PHIL", "CIS", and
    "MGT". Hence, the main query reduces to

    ```
    SELECT  ENAME, ETITLE, DEPT
    FROM    STAFF
    WHERE   DEPT NOT IN ('THEO', 'PHIL', 'CIS', 'MGT')
    ```

2. Note that "DA VINCI" does not occur in the output. This is the
    subtle circumstance which needs to be recognized. This staff
    member has a null DEPT value. It cannot evaluate to "true" on
    any comparison. Hence, it is not selected for display.

    Note that this sample query was articulated to request a dis-
    play of staff members assigned to nonexistent departments.
    (DA VINCI, because he has a null DEPT value, is not assigned
    to any department.) This query is not equivalent to "Display
    the name and number of every staff member not having de-
    partment id found in the set of DEPT values present in the
    DEPARTMENT table." (Chapter 15 will present a solution to
    this problem. See Sample Query 15.5.) The current example
    illustrates why null values should be avoided wherever possi-
    ble.

Exercise:

13J. Display the name and department of any faculty member
     who is not teaching a class this semester.

Subquery Within HAVING Clause

All previous subqueries have been specified within a WHERE clause. The next sample query illustrates the use of a subquery to generate an intermediate result for subsequent comparison within a HAVING clause. Other than the fact that the subquery is located within a HAVING clause, there is really nothing new to learn. In general, a subquery can be used to generate intermediate results for comparison within both WHERE and HAVING clauses. The logic of the query determines which type of clause to use. The syntax of the subquery is the same in both instances.

Sample Query 13.13:   For every department which offers courses, display the department identifier and the average labfee of courses offered by the department if that average is less than the overall average labfee for all courses.

```
SELECT CDEPT, AVG(CLABFEE)
FROM    COURSE
GROUP   BY CDEPT
HAVING AVG(CLABFEE) <
          (SELECT AVG(CLABFEE)
           FROM    COURSE)
```

```
-------------------------------
CDEPT               COL1
-------------------------------
PHIL 87.5000000000000
```

Comments:

1. Because we want to display the average labfee by department, it is necessary to establish groups using the GROUP BY clause. Because we only want to display those groups where the average is less than the overall average, a HAVING clause is required to compare the group averages to the overall average. A subquery is necessary to calculate this overall average. The subquery will determine that the overall average is 110.00. The main query is then evaluated as:

```
SELECT  CDEPT, AVG(CLABFEE)
FROM    COURSE
GROUP   BY CDEPT
HAVING  AVG(CLABFEE) < 110.00
```

2. This query referenced just the COURSE table in both the main query and the subquery. This was because we articulated the query ("for every department which offers courses") to exclude other departments which have a corresponding row in the DEPARTMENT table but do not offer courses. Only the Management Department falls into this category. Note that "MGT" does not appear in our output display. It is possible to append a row corresponding to the Management Department to the current result. This would require use of the union operation which will be described in the next chapter.

The next sample query is more complex than previous examples. It incorporates many of the aforementioned subquery techniques and it includes an ORDER BY clause to sort the final displayed result. Note however that the SQL statement is only longer than previous examples because of the complexity of the query. No new concepts are introduced.

Sample Query 13.14:   For those departments recorded in the DE-PARTMENT table which employ staff members, display the department identifier and the average salary of staff members in the department if that average is less than the largest labfee recorded in the COURSE table. Show the average salary as a decimal value with one place after the decimal point. Sort the displayed result by department identifier.

```
SELECT     STAFF.DEPT, DECIMAL (AVG(DECIMAL(ESALARY)),5,1)
FROM       STAFF,DEPARTMENT
WHERE      STAFF.DEPT = DEPARTMENT.DEPT
GROUP BY   STAFF.DEPT
HAVING     AVG(DECIMAL(ESALARY)) < (SELECT MAX(CLABFEE)
                                          FROM COURSE)
ORDER BY   STAFF.DEPT
```

```
------------------------------
DEPT                COL1
------------------------------
THEO               52.5
```

Comments:

1. The query is processed as follows. A join of the STAFF and DEPARTMENT tables is performed as prescribed by the condition in the WHERE clause. From those rows which satisfy the condition, the DEPT and ESALARY values are collected. From these rows, logical groups are formed based on a common DEPT value. At this point, the intermediate result consists of rows with two columns, DEPT and ESALARY. All rows for the CIS department are grouped together, as are those for the PHIL and THEO departments. The system then acts upon these logical groups to summarize the average salary for the comparison in the HAVING clause. Each group is then represented by a single row containing the DEPT value together with the average salary of all staff members associated with that department.

    The subquery in the HAVING clause is evaluated to return the highest labfee value of any course recorded in the COURSE table (500.00). This value is compared with each average salary value in summarized group records. If the average salary for the group is less than 500.00, the summary record for the group is selected for display. Observe that the salary values (which are stored as integers) are converted to decimal before the AVG function is applied to the column. This ensures the decimal accuracy of the average.

2. Prior to the display of the records, the average of the salary values is again passed through the DECIMAL function. This time, we use additional operands to tailor the precision and scale of the result, thereby truncating to 1 position. The final step in processing is to satisfy the ORDER BY clause and sequence the result by ascending DEPT values.

ANY and ALL

The keywords ANY and ALL can be used with WHERE conditions which reference subqueries. Before discussing these keywords we emphasize two facts.

1. Given a query which can be solved using ANY or ALL, it is always possible to specify an alternative SQL solution which does not contain these keywords.
2. Under certain circumstances, it is easy to misinterpret the logical behavior of statements containing ANY or ALL.

For these reasons, some authorities have argued that ANY and ALL should not be part of the SQL language. However, this is wishful thinking. They are part of SQL. Hence, we discuss them with the preliminary recommendation that you should understand these keywords, but should also restrict your use of such.

We need to review an important point prior to discussing the use of ANY and ALL. When a subquery is executed, it can return one or more values. Sample Queries 13.8 through 13.12 were coded so that the subquery could produce multiple values. These queries used the IN keyword. Sample Queries 13.2 through 13.7 were coded so that the subquery always produced a single value. Therefore, the WHERE condition in the main query used the standard comparison operators (=, <, >, ¬=) when evaluating the subquery result. The following sample queries use the standard comparison operators in conjunction with ANY and ALL to evaluate an intermediate result produced by a subquery which can return multiple values.

The following sample query introduces the ANY keyword. The ANY keyword can be used with any of the standard comparison operators when the subquery can return multiple values. When ANY is used in a comparison, the condition evaluates to "true" if the expression is true for any of the values returned by the subquery.

Sample Query 13.15:   Display the name and title of any staff member employed by an existing academic department.

```
SELECT  ENAME, ETITLE
FROM    STAFF
WHERE   DEPT = ANY (SELECT DEPT
                    FROM DEPARTMENT)
```

```
-----------------------------------------
ENAME            ETITLE
-----------------------------------------
HANK KISS        JESTER
DICK NIX         CROOK
MATTHEW          EVANGLIST1
MARK             EVANGLIST2
LUKE             EVANGLIST3
JOHN             EVANGLIST4
```

Comments:

1. The subquery returns the name of existing departments: "CIS", "PHIL", "THEO" and "MGT". Hence, the query reduces to:

   ```
   SELECT  ENAME, ETITLE
   FROM    STAFF
   WHERE   DEPT = ANY ('CIS','PHIL','THEO','MGT')
   ```

   Only staff members with a DEPT value "equal to any" of the values returned by the subquery appear in the output display.

2. An alternative solution to the sample query is:

   ```
   SELECT  ENAME, ETITLE
   FROM    STAFF
   WHERE   DEPT IN (SELECT DEPT FROM DEPARTMENT)
   ```

   The only differenece is that "IN" has replaced "= ANY" in the WHERE clause. In effect, "IN" and "= ANY" are synonymous.

3. Another solution involves use of the join operation.

   ```
   SELECT  ENAME, ETITLE
   FROM    STAFF, DEPARTMENT
   WHERE   STAFF.DEPT = DEPARTMENT.DEPT
   ```

4. The keyword SOME can be used instead of ANY. Its meaning is the same. However, SOME is rarely used in practice.

All of the comparison operators can be used with ANY. The next sample query illustrates an application of "> ANY".

Sample Query 13.16: Display the course number, name, and labfee of each course which has a labfee exceeding the salary of any staff member.

```
SELECT  CNO, CNAME, CLABFEE
FROM    COURSE
WHERE   CLABFEE > ANY (SELECT ESALARY
                              FROM STAFF)
```

```
-------------------------------------------------------------
CNO      CNAME                    CLABFEE
-------------------------------------------------------------
T11      SCHOLASTICISM             150.00
T12      FUNDAMENTALISM             90.00
T44      COMMUNISM                 200.00
P11      EMPIRICISM                100.00
P33      EXISTENTIALISM            200.00
C11      INTRO TO CS               100.00
C55      COMPUTER ARCH.            100.00
C66      RELATIONAL DATABASE       500.00
```

Comments:

1. Note that the subquery returns every ESALARY value in the STAFF table. If a course has a CLABFEE value greater than any of these ESALARY values, then its number, name, and labfee are present in the output.

2. Note that if a CLABFEE value is greater than any of the ES-ALARY values, then it is greater than the smallest ESALARY value. This observation motivates the following alternative solution:

```
SELECT  CNO, CNAME, CLABFEE
FROM    COURSE
WHERE   CLABFEE > (SELECT MIN(ESALARY)
                          FROM STAFF)
```

3. We stated that all of the comparison operators can be used with ANY. Regardless of the operator, an alternative solution can be specified which is usually more straightforward. This especially applies to "¬= ANY", which can be very misleading. See the discussion about the logical behavior of the ANY and ALL operators which follow Sample Query 13.18)

Exercise:

13K. Display the name and number of dependents for faculty members who have as many dependents as the number of credits offered for any course. Formulate two solutions. The first should use the ANY keyword. The second should not.

The ALL keyword, like ANY, can be used with any of the standard comparison operators when a subquery can return multiple values. When ALL is used, the condition evaluates to "true" if the expression is true for all of the values returned by the subquery.

Sample Query 13.17:   Display the course number, name, and labfee of any course having a labfee less than all the salaries of staff members.

```
SELECT  CNO, CNAME, CLABFEE
FROM    COURSE
WHERE   CLABFEE < ALL (SELECT ESALARY
                       FROM STAFF)
```

```
-----------------------------------------------------
CNO     CNAME                    CLABFEE
-----------------------------------------------------
T33     HEDONISM                    0.00
P22     RATIONALISM                50.00
P44     SOLIPSISM                   0.00
C22     DATA STRUCTURES            50.00
C33     DISCRETE MATHEMATICS        0.00
C44     DIGITAL CIRCUITS            0.00
```

Comments:

1. The subquery returns every ESALARY value in the STAFF table. If a course has a CLABFEE value "less than all" of these ESALARY values, then its number, name, and labfee appear in the output.

2. Note that if a CLABFEE value is less than all the ESALARY values, then it is less than the smallest ESALARY value. This observation motivates the following alternative solution:

```
SELECT  CNO, CNAME, CLABFEE
FROM    COURSE
WHERE   CLABFEE < (SELECT MIN(ESALARY) FROM STAFF)
```

Sample Query 13.18:   Display the name and salary of any staff member whose salary is greater than or equal to all the course labfees.

```
SELECT  ENAME, ESALARY
FROM    STAFF
WHERE   ESALARY >= ALL (SELECT CLABFEE
                        FROM COURSE)
```

```
--------------------------------------------
ENAME                    ESALARY
--------------------------------------------
HANK KISS                   25000
DICK NIX                    25001
DA VINCI                      500
EUCLID                       1000
```

Comments:

1. The subquery returns every CLABFEE value in the COURSE table. If a staff member has a labfee value "greater than or equal to all" of these values, then his or her name and salary appear in the result.

2. Note that if an ESALARY value is greater than or equal to all the CLABFEE values, then it is greater than or equal to the largest CLABFEE value. This observation motivates the following alternative solution:

    ```
    SELECT  ENAME, ESALARY
    FROM    STAFF
    WHERE   ESALARY = (SELECT MAX(CLABFEE)
                       FROM COURSE)
    ```

3. We stated that all of the comparison operators can be used with ALL. Regardless of the operator, an alternative solution can be specified which is usually more direct. This especially applies to "= ALL" which can only evaluate to "true" if the subquery returns just one value which equals the comparison field value.

Logic of ANY and ALL

The following comments pertain to the logical behavior of ANY and ALL when used with certain comparison operators.

1. "= ANY" is equivalent to "IN". (But, do not jump to the erroneous conclusion that "¬= ANY" means the same thing as "NOT IN". See Comment 4 below.)

2. "¬= ANY" has little application. Consider the following examples.
   a. WHERE COLX ¬= ANY (2,4,6)
      This condition is always true.
   b. WHERE COLX ¬= ANY (4)
      This condition is the same as WHERE COLX ¬= 4

3. "= ALL" has little application. Consider the following examples.
   a. WHERE COLX = ALL (2,4,6)
      This condition is always false.
   b. WHERE COLX = ALL (4)
      This condition is the same as WHERE COLX = 4

4. "¬= ALL" means the same thing as "NOT IN". (It is good mental exercise to think this through. It may be helpful to reexamine the previous discussion on NOT IN in Sample Query 3.14.)

These comments reinforce the position that use of ANY and ALL should be restricted. Alternative solutions were presented to each sample query which used these keywords. From a formal point of view both ANY and ALL are superfluous. However, they can be useful for expressing certain queries which transcend the data retrieval goal of SQL. The next sample query demonstrates the point.

The final sample query of this chapter illustrates use of ALL within the context of a problem which requires grouping for the purpose of performing calculations.

Sample Query 13.19: Display the department id and average labfee of the academic department(s) having the highest average course labfee.

```
SELECT  CDEPT, AVG(CLABFEE)
FROM    COURSE
GROUP   BY CDEPT
HAVING  AVG(CLABFEE) >=
    ALL  (SELECT AVG(CLABFEE)
          FROM    COURSE
          GROUP   BY CDEPT)
```

```
CDEPT                          COL1
CIS                            125.00
```

Comments:

1. The intermediate result produced by the subquery is a set of three values (87.50, 110.00, 125.00) corresponding to the average labfees of the PHIL, THEO, and CIS departments. ALL is necessary because the subquery returns multiple values. Thus, the main query is reduced to:

```
SELECT  CDEPT, AVG(CLABFEE)
FROM    COURSE
GROUP   BY CDEPT
HAVING  AVG(CLABFEE) >= ALL (87.50, 110.00, 125.00)
```

2. Note that the objective of the query is to determine the average labfee for each department and then display the maximum. What we want is a "maximum of averages." But SQL does not provide a tidy way to express this. (Recall that SQL does not permit the nesting of the column built-in functions.) The use of ALL was necessary because of the grouping and computational aspects of this problem.

SUMMARY

This chapter has introduced the use of a subquery to generate an intermediate result for comparison purposes within a WHERE or HAVING clause. You can use this technique when you want to compare a field with an unknown value. The subquery serves the purpose of determining the unknown value. The subquery was also illustrated as an alternative to coding a join operation when the desired displayed results all come from one table.

In general, the subquery is simply another SELECT statement with the restriction that it produces a single column result which is compatible with the comparison operation to be performed within the WHERE or HAVING clause. There are a few other restrictions which also apply.

A subquery cannot contain an:

1. **ORDER BY** clause: Sorting applies to the result table. The ORDER BY clause must be the last clause in the entire statement.

2. **UNION** clause: The purpose of this clause will be described in Chapter 14. We will see that UNION is a very useful operation which, unfortunately, cannot be used within a subquery.

This chapter introduced the fundamental subquery techniques which are used most often. Chapter 15 will continue our discussion of subqueries by presenting alternatives to some of the techniques shown in this chapter and introducing new keywords and techniques which can be applied to more challenging problems.

SUMMARY EXERCISES

13L. Display the course number and name for every course that student 800 is registered for.

13M. Display all information about any scheduled class which has a labfee less than $100 and is not offered on a Friday.

13N. Display the student number and date of registration for all students who are registered for at least one course offered by a department located in the science SC building.

13O. Display the name and number of dependents for faculty members who have fewer dependents than the number of credits offered for any course.

14

UNION Operation

This chapter describes a simple but very useful feature of SQL, the union operation. The purpose of the union operation is introduced by means of an example. Assume you were asked to display the names of all faculty and staff members. This simple request could be satisfied by executing two separate SELECT statements.

1. Display all the faculty names.

```
SELECT   FNAME
FROM     FACULTY
```

2. Display all the staff member names.

```
SELECT   ENAME
FROM     STAFF
```

These are two *separate* SELECT commands which are executed independently of each other and generate two *separate* result tables. This approach is not satisfactory if we want all the faculty and staff member names to be merged into a single result table. The union operation must be used to achieve this objective.

UNION KEYWORD

The union operation allows execution of multiple SELECT statements as a single command. The result of each statement is merged into and subsequently displayed as a single result table.

Sample Query 14.1: Display the names of all faculty and staff members (in a single result table).

```
SELECT  FNAME
FROM    FACULTY
UNION
SELECT  ENAME
FROM    STAFF
```

```
--------------------
FNAME
--------------------
AL HARTLEY
ARCHIMEDES
BARB HLAVATY
DA VINCI
DICK NIX
EUCLID
HANK KISS
JESSIE MARTYN
JOE COHN
JOHN
JULIE MARTYN
KATHY PEPE
LISA BOBAK
LUKE
MARK
MATTHEW
```

Comments:

1. Syntax: The keyword UNION is placed between the two
   SELECT statements separated by one or more spaces. As with
   other SQL commands, the format is free form and can be written on any number of lines.

2. Logic: The UNION keyword tells the system to execute each
   SELECT statement and then merge the intermediate results
   into a single result table.

   Question: What if duplicate rows occur in the intermediate
               results?

   Answer: Duplicate rows selected by individual SELECT
               statements are not displayed. This is because the
               UNION keyword corresponds to the union opera-
               tion as defined in classical set theory. This theory
               defines the union of two sets as the set of all val-
               ues taken from both sets. Because a mathematical
               set must contain distinct values, the result of the
               union operation, which is a set, will not contain
               duplicate values.

               For example, given set A = {2,4,6,8} and set B =
               {1,4,5,6}, the union of sets A and B is {1,2,4,5,6,8}.
               Observe that the values common to both sets, 4
               and 6, occur only once in the union result. The
               same principle applies to the formation of a result
               table which is the union of two or more intermedi-
               ate tables generated by independent SELECT
               statements. We emphasize that duplicate rows are
               not displayed, even though the DISTINCT keyword
               is not specified in either SELECT statement.

   Notice that all the FNAME values in the FACULTY table are
   distinct from all ENAME values in the STAFF table. Hence, in
   this example it just so happens that duplicate rows do not
   occur in the intermediate results.

3. We cannot arbitrarily form the union of any two SELECT statements. The intermediate tables produced by the individual SELECT statements must be "union compatible." This means that:

   a. Each table must have the same number of columns.

   b. Corresponding columns must have comparable data types. If a given column contains numeric, character, date or time data, then its corresponding column must respectively contain numeric, character, date, or time data.

   In the current example each SELECT statement produces a table with just one column. The first contains FNAME values which are defined as CHAR(15). The second contains ENAME values defined as CHAR(10).

4. Observe that the corresponding column names in the SELECT statements do not need to be identical. However, only one such name can occur as the column heading for the displayed result. The system will use the first SELECT statement to determine the column headings for the output display. Hence, the output column heading shows FNAME. Because the column values actually represent both faculty and staff names, it is recommended that you use the host system facilities to change the heading to a more representative title (e.g. "EMPLOYEE NAME").

5. It is not possible by mere examination of the output display to determine which rows were selected from which table. Sample Query 14.5 will illustrate a technique to realize this objective.

6. Observe that the result is sorted even though the ORDER BY clause is not specified. This is because the current versions of DB2 and SQL/DS automatically perform an internal sort to facilitate the identification of duplicate values. Again, we state that you should not rely on this sort. Sample Query 14.3 will illustrate use of the ORDER BY clause with the union operation.

The next example illustrates a situation where the union operation causes duplicate rows to be removed from the displayed result.

Sample Query 14.2:   Display every department id referenced in the STAFF and FACULTY tables.

```
SELECT DEPT FROM STAFF
UNION
SELECT FDEPT FROM FACULTY
```

```
------
DEPT
------
CIS
ENG
MATH
PHIL
THEO
-
```

Comments:

1. This example illustrates how the union operation removes duplicate rows from the intermediate results. For example, THEO occurs many times in both the FACULTY and STAFF tables, but it only appears once in the output display. Also, multiple null values are considered duplicates so that only one null value appears in the output.

2. Again, note that an internal sort was done to facilitate the removal of duplicate rows. The null value appears at the high end of the sequence. The next example will show use of the ORDER BY clause which should be used to specify a desired row sequence.

Exercise:

14A. Display the salaries of all staff and faculty in a single result table.

The next example illustrates union compatible SELECT statements which display multiple columns. The SELECT statements contain WHERE clauses and the result is sorted in a specified row sequence.

Sample Query 14.3: Display the name, department id and title (in that order) of all staff members assigned to the Theology Department. Include the name, department id and address (in that order) of all faculty members assigned to that department. Sort the output by name in descending sequence.

```
SELECT  ENAME, DEPT, ETITLE
FROM    STAFF
WHERE   DEPT = 'THEO'
UNION
SELECT  FNAME, FDEPT, FADDR
FROM    FACULTY
WHERE   FDEPT = 'THEO'
ORDER   BY 1 DESC
```

ENAME	DEPT	ETITLE
MATTHEW	THEO	EVANGLIST1
MARK	THEO	EVANGLIST2
LUKE	THEO	EVANGLIST3
LISA BOBAK	THEO	77 LAUGHING LANE
JOHN	THEO	EVANGLIST4
JESSIE MARTYN	THEO	2135 EASTON DRIVE

Comments:

1. The SELECT statements fit the definition of union compatible even though the contents of the third column, which is a mixture of titles and addresses, is probably confusing. The point is that the system has no insight into the fact that the ETITLE and FADDR columns contain semantically different kinds of data.

2. Both WHERE clauses happen to reference columns containing the same type of data (department ids). This is typical, but it is not necessary. In general, each individual SELECT statement may contain any valid WHERE clause.

3. Special rules apply to the ORDER BY clause when used with the union operation.

    a. The ORDER BY clause can only appear once and it must be the last clause of the entire statement.

    b. The ORDER BY clause must reference a column by its relative column number, not by a column name.

Exercise:

14B. Display the department id, number of credits, and the description of all Philosophy courses together with the department id, number of dependents, and the address of all faculty from that same department.

UNION ALL

Assume our mythical college had a policy which prohibited anyone from simultaneously holding both a faculty and a staff appointment. If we know that employee names (i.e., FNAME and ENAME values) are unique, we can conclude that any union operation involving these values would not encounter duplicate rows. Under these circumstances, effort on the part of the system to remove duplicate rows is unnecessary. This situation occurred in Sample Query 14.1. It did not require a sorted result, and there were no duplicate rows to be removed, but the system still performed a sort. In such circumstances the use of UNION ALL is appropriate. The next sample query illustrates UNION ALL, which behaves like UNION with the exception that duplicate rows are not removed from the output display. This means the system will not initiate an internal sort for this purpose.

Sample Query 14.4:   Display every department id referenced in the STAFF and FACULTY tables. Show duplicate department id values.

```
SELECT DEPT FROM STAFF
UNION   ALL
SELECT FDEPT FROM FACULTY
```

```
-----
DEPT
-----
THEO
THEO
THEO
PHIL
PHIL
THEO
MATH
ENG
-
THEO
PHIL
CIS
THEO
PHIL
CIS
CIS
```

Comments:

1. Compare this result with that shown in Sample Query 14.2, which uses UNION instead of UNION ALL. The output for this example displays duplicate rows which are not sorted. UNION ALL simply combines the intermediate result tables into a single table.

2. The output presents some idea of how many employees are assigned to the different departments. Assume that you would like a precise count of this number. It seems reasonable to apply grouping with the COUNT function to the above result table. Unfortunately, this cannot be done. A general restriction on the use of both UNION and UNION ALL is that the column built-in functions cannot be applied to the final result table as a whole. SQL simply has no way to express this process. All arithmetic must be coded within individual SELECT statements. The intermediate results can contain calculated values (see the next sample query), but calculations cannot be applied to the final result table. You must use the host system report generation facilities to achieve this objective.

3. The real advantage of UNION ALL occurs when it is impossible for duplicate values to occur in any of the intermediate result tables. This was the case with Sample Query 14.1 and is the same for the next sample query. It becomes the user's responsibility to deduce this fact. Then you should use UNION ALL instead of UNION. This can lead to a significant savings in computing time.

The last sample query of this chapter uses UNION ALL because it is impossible for the individual SELECT statements to select duplicate rows. The individual SELECT statements of this query display constant data as a means of attaching identification labels to rows displayed in the final result.

Sample Query 14.5:   Assume the second character of a course's CNO value represents the level of the course. Lower-level courses have a "1" or "2". Intermediate-level courses have a "3" or "4". Upper-level courses have a "5" or "6". Calculate the average labfee for each of the three levels of courses. Also, tag a self-identifying label to each row.

```
SELECT  'LOWER', AVG(CLABFEE)
FROM    COURSE
WHERE   CNO LIKE '_1%'
OR      CNO LIKE '_2%'
UNION ALL
SELECT  'INTERMEDIATE', AVG(CLABFEE)
FROM    COURSE
WHERE   CNO LIKE '_3%'
OR      CNO LIKE '_4%'
UNION ALL
SELECT  'UPPER', AVG(CLABFEE)
FROM    COURSE
WHERE   CNO LIKE '_5%'
OR      CNO LIKE '_6%'
```

```
-------------------------------------------------
COL1                            COL2
-------------------------------------------------
LOWER              90.000000000000
INTERMEDIATE       66.666666666666
UPPER             300.000000000000
```

Comments:

1. Observe that the output does not indicate a sort of the final result table. If we had used the UNION keyword, the same rows would have been displayed, but their row sequence would be different.

2. The specification of a constant identifier in each SELECT statement is most helpful in this example. The preceding examples did not include any self-identifying constants, but such constants would have made the output more readable.

3. Unlike the previous sample queries, the individual SELECT statements in this example refer to the same table (COURSE) and utilize a column function (AVG). In effect, the three individual SELECT statements perform a calculation with rows from the COURSE table to produce three summary rows which are subsequently merged into the final result by UNION ALL.

    This example shows the utility of the union operation. Note that it allows for a type of grouping which cannot be done with the GROUP BY clause. The GROUP BY clause will form a group for each individual value found in a specified column. The current example illustrates the formation of groups where each group corresponds to a set of different values.

SUMMARY

This chapter presented the UNION keyword, which allows for the union of different sets of rows selected by individual SELECT statements. The specification of UNION will cause the system to sort all the selected rows as a means of detecting and removing duplicate rows. Because this involves some performance costs, and because there may be circumstances where the removal of duplicate rows is unnecessary or undesirable, SQL provides the UNION ALL feature, which simply merges all the intermediate tables without examining for or removing duplicate rows.

It is possible to use both UNION and UNION ALL in the same command. In this case, you have to consider the order of evaluation. The system will perform the evaluation in a left-to-right sequence. (Visually, this is a "top-to-bottom" sequence.) It simply performs whatever union operation it first encounters. Parentheses can be used to override this default sequence.

We conclude this chapter by listing constraints associated with the UNION and UNION ALL keywords. Some of these have been specified in the previous examples; others are specified for the first time.

1. All intermediate result tables produced by the SELECT statements must be union compatible. This means they have the same number of columns and each corresponding column has a comparable data type. Whenever a given column is union compatible with its corresponding column but the two columns do not have the exact same SQL data type, the data type conversion rules specified in Chapter 5 apply. For example, a column defined as SMALLINT is union compatible with a DECIMAL column. When they are merged by the union operation, the final result is displayed as a DECIMAL column.

2. The ORDER BY clause may be specified only once. If it is specified, it must be placed after the last SELECT statement. Furthermore, it must reference the sort column(s) by relative column number(s).

3. It is not possible to apply any of the column built-in functions to the final result table which is produced by the union operation.

4. A maximum of 15 table names may be specified in all the SE-LECT statements. This is a total of 15 references, not distinct table names. For example, in Sample Query 14.5, the COURSE table is referenced three times. This constitutes three distinct table references.

5. A SELECT statement may contain a subquery. However, the subquery itself may not contain UNION or UNION ALL.

6. Views (to be described in Chapter 16) may not be defined with UNION or UNION ALL.

A final comment: The union operation is a very important and powerful feature of SQL. This is evidenced by the fact that every example presented in this chapter required the union operation and could not have been expressed using just those SQL facilities described earlier in this text.

SUMMARY EXERCISES:

14C. Display the labfee value and number of credits for each CIS course together with a label of "COURSE". Along with these rows include rows which contain the salary and number of dependents for each faculty member from the CIS department. Identify the faculty rows with a tag of "FACULTY".

14D. Display the course name, department id, and the labfee value for any course with a labfee that is at least 200.00. Append a label of "EXPENSIVE" on each row retrieved. Display the columns for those courses with a labfee value of 50.00 or less. Append to these rows the label of "CHEAP". Display all the rows in a single result.

14E. Display all of the salaries of staff and faculty members. Do not remove any duplicate values from the result.

15

Correlated Subqueries

This chapter expands upon the subquery concept by introducing a variation known as a correlated subquery. This is an important and powerful feature which allows you to solve certain data retrieval problems which cannot be solved by previously described techniques. There are significant differences between correlated subqueries and the subqueries introduced in Chapter 13. These differences introduce a new level of complexity which motivate the placement of this topic in a separate chapter.

PRELIMINARY COMMENTS

Before presenting correlated subquery problems and their solutions, it is important to make three preliminary observations about the subquery examples presented in Chapter 13. These observations are made to emphasize the unique features of correlated subqueries.

Observation 1:

Previous examples presented subqueries which were "self-contained." This is an informal term to describe the fact that the subquery constitutes a valid SELECT statement which could be independently executed if it were detached from the main query. For example, consider the following SELECT statement which displays information about any course with a labfee equal to the maximum labfee of all Theology courses.

```
SELECT  CDEPT, CNO, CNAME, CLABFEE
FROM    COURSE
WHERE   CLABFEE =
            (SELECT MAX(CLABFEE)
             FROM   COURSE
             WHERE CDEPT = 'THEO')
```

The subquery, considered as an independent statement, is

```
SELECT  MAX(CLABFEE)
FROM    COURSE
WHERE   CDEPT = 'THEO'
```

This statement could be executed to return a result of 200.00. All previous subquery examples demonstrated this "self-contained" property. We emphasize this point because the correlated subqueries presented in this chapter do not have this property. Trying to execute these correlated subqueries as independent queries will cause errors. This is because the SELECT statement of a correlated subquery will contain a variable (a correlation variable) which references the main query.

Observation 2:

The second observation is that the system will execute a self-contained subquery just once. In the above example, the single execution of the subquery returned a value (200.00). This result is used to reformulate the outer query as

```
SELECT  CDEPT, CNO, CNAME, CLABFEE
FROM    COURSE
WHERE   CLABFEE = 200.00
```

Even though the COURSE table contains 14 rows, the self-contained subquery is executed just once. This behavior differs from a correlated subquery which will usually be executed many times. This means that you will not be able to conceptualize the solution as a one-time execution on the subquery to obtain an intermediate result, followed by a one-time substitution of the result to reformulate the outer query as shown above. For correlated subqueries, each execution of the subquery presumably produces a different result which leads to a different reformulation of the outer query.

Observation 3:

The third observation pertains to syntax. None of the previously described self-contained subqueries contained a correlation variable. Correlation variables are usually used to reference values specified by the outer query. (This is why the subquery is not self-contained.) We will see that correlation variable can be explicitly specified in the FROM clause or, in some cases, implicitly specified by simple reference in the subquery. The following sample queries will illustrate both explicit and implicit specification of correlation variables.

(Correlation variables are referred to as "correlation names" in the IBM reference manuals. Also, other authors have called them "aliases" or "range variables.")

Finally, for the sake of completeness, we comment (without explanation at this point) that correlation variables can be used in SELECT statements which do not contain subqueries.

The first sample query of this chapter shows a correlated subquery containing "CX" as the correlation variable. We introduce this problem and its solution as the basis of a detailed discussion on this topic.

Sample Query 15.1:   For each department which offers courses, display that department's identifier followed by the number, name, and labfee of the department sponsored course having the largest labfee.

```
SELECT  CDEPT, CNO, CNAME, CLABFEE
FROM    COURSE CX
WHERE   CLABFEE =
        (SELECT MAX(CLABFEE)
         FROM    COURSE
         WHERE CDEPT = CX.CDEPT)
```

CDEPT	CNO	CNAME	CLABFEE
CIS	C66	RELATIONAL DATABASE	500.00
PHIL	P33	EXISTENTIALISM	200.00
THEO	T44	COMMUNISM	200.00

Comments:

1. Syntax: The FROM clause in the main query contains

    ```
    FROM COURSE CX
    ```

    The presence of CX after COURSE means that CX is defined as a correlation variable for the COURSE table. There must be one or more spaces between the table name and the corresponding correlated variable name. (Do not use a comma as a separator. If you do, the system will incorrectly interpret CX as the name of another table.) The specification of names for correlation variables follows the same rules as table and column names—begin with a letter, optionally followed by letters, digits, or underscore symbols for a maximum of 18 characters.

Assuming the correlation variable CX has been defined in the outer SELECT statement, it can then be referenced in a subquery. In the current example, we see

```
WHERE CDEPT = CX.CDEPT
```

We will describe the function of CX.CDEPT below. For the moment we ask you to consider just the subquery in isolation and note that it is not self-contained.

```
SELECT  MAX(CLABFEE)
FROM    COURSE
WHERE   CDEPT = CX.CDEPT
```

Independent execution of this statement would result in an error because the system has no knowledge of CX.CDEPT. However, it is valid as a correlated subquery where CX has been specified as a correlation variable in the FROM clause of an outer SELECT statement.

2. Logic: It is absolutely imperative that you understand the logic of this sample query in order to understand the purpose of the correlation variable. It is helpful to distinguish the objective of this example from the aforementioned problem which could be solved using a self-contained subquery.

The previous problem used the subquery to determine that the maximum labfee value for any theology course was 200.00. Then the system compared the CLABFEE value in every row to 200.00. If the CLABFEE value equaled 200.00, it was selected for display. The key point is that every row, regardless of its CDEPT value, had its CLABFEE value compared to 200.00. This value remained constant throughout the execution of the statement.

The current sample query is quite different because the system needs to compare the CLABFEE value in each row to the maximum CLABFEE value *for the department identified by the CDEPT value in the row under consideration*. This CDEPT value will vary from row to row. Hence, the maximum CLABFEE will vary from row to row.

In effect, for each row in the table, the system must:

- Examine the CDEPT value of the row.
- Execute the subquery to determine the maximum CLABFEE value for that department.
- Compare the CLABFEE value of the row under consideration to see if it equals the value returned by the subquery. If it does, the row is selected for display.

This is the essence of a correlated subquery. The execution of the subquery must be correlated with a particular value (CDEPT in this case) which will vary from row to row. Hence, the subquery must be executed for each row in the table. It also means that the system needs a correlation variable to keep track of the particular row being processed. This is the precise purpose of a correlation variable. It serves as a pointer to the row being considered for selection. These concepts will be illustrated in detail below.

Because the COURSE table has 14 rows, the system will execute the subquery 14 times. On each execution, the system will use CX to point to a row. In order to illustrate the overall process, we need to assume that the system encounters the COURSE table rows in some sequence. Assume the first three rows of this sequence are

CNO	CNAME	CDESCP	CRED	CLABFEE	CDEPT
T11	SCHOLASTICISM	FOR THE PIOUS	3	150.00	THEO
P33	EXISTENTIALISM	FOR CIS MAJORS	3	200.00	PHIL
C11	INTRO TO CS	FOR ROOKIES	3	100.00	CIS
.	.	.	.	.	.
.	.	.	.	.	.
.	.	.	.	.	.

We describe the system logic for processing the first three rows.

a.   The system examines the first row shown below.

T11	SCHOLASTICISM	FOR THE PIOUS	3	150.00	THEO

This means the correlation variable CX will initially point to this row. Hence, the CDEPT value of this row (THEO) is substituted for CX.CDEPT in the subquery. Thus, the subquery is evaluated as

```
SELECT  MAX(CLABFEE)
FROM    COURSE
WHERE   CDEPT = 'THEO'
```

Execution of this query returns a value of 200.00. After substitution of this intermediate result, the main query is evaluated as

```
SELECT CDEPT, CNO, CNAME, CLABFEE
FROM    COURSE CX
WHERE   CLABFEE = 200.00
```

This query is effectively asking whether or not the current row under consideration (i.e., the row pointed to by CX—the T11 row) has a CLABFEE value of 200.00. It does not. Hence, this row is not selected and does not appear in the output display.

We emphasize that this behavior is considerably different from other main query SELECT statements which scanned the entire table and selected all rows which matched the selection criteria. This main query SELECT statement, which has a CX in its FROM clause, is only asking if the current row, the one referenced by the correlation variable, has a CLABFEE value of 200.00. The same logic will be described for the next two rows.

b. Next, the system examines the second row shown below.

P33	EXISTENTIALISM	FOR CIS MAJORS	3	200.00	PHIL

The CDEPT value of "PHIL" is substituted for CX.CDEPT in the subquery. Thus, the subquery is evaluated as

```
SELECT  MAX(CLABFEE)
FROM    COURSE
WHERE   CDEPT = 'PHIL'
```

Execution of this query returns a value of 200.00. Then the main query is evaluated as

```
SELECT  CDEPT, CNO, CNAME, CLABFEE
FROM    COURSE CX
WHERE   CLABFEE = 200.00
```

This statement is asking if the current row (P33) has a CLABFEE value of 200.00. It does, so it appears in the output.

c. The system then examines the third row shown below.

C11	INTRO TO CS	FOR ROOKIES	3	100.00	CIS

Its CDEPT value of "CIS " is substituted for CX.CDEPT in the subquery. Thus, the subquery is evaluated as

```
SELECT  MAX(CLABFEE)
FROM    COURSE
WHERE   CDEPT = 'CIS '
```

Execution of this query returns a value of 500.00. Then the main query is evaluated as

```
SELECT  CDEPT, CNO, CNAME, CLABFEE
FROM    COURSE CX
WHERE   CLABFEE = 500.00
```

This statement is asking if the current row (C11) has a CLABFEE value of 500.00. It does not, so it does not appear in the output.

The same process continues for the remaining 11 rows. Each time the subquery determines the maximum departmental labfee value for the department corresponding to the CDEPT value of the row. If the CLABFEE value equals this maximum, then the row is selected for display.

3. Efficiency: The execution of a correlated subquery for each row in a table will obviously use more computer time than the single execution of a self-contained subquery. This is especially true if the table has a large number of rows. However, for some problems, like the current example, there is no alternative way of expressing the query in a single SELECT statement.

4. The current example shows the *explicit declaration* of the CX correlation variable by specifying it in the main query FROM clause. There are circumstances where a correlation variable can be *implicitly* declared. The next sample query will show the implicit declaration of a correlation variable.

The explicit declaration of a correlation variable is necessary in the current example because the main query and subquery both reference the same table. If CX were omitted, the statement would be *incorrectly* written as:

```
SELECT CDEPT, CNO, CNAME, CLABFEE
FROM    COURSE
WHERE   CLABFEE =
        ( SELECT MAX ( CLABFEE )
          FROM    COURSE
          WHERE CDEPT = CDEPT )
```

Note this subquery WHERE clause, 'WHERE CDEPT = CDEPT' is always true and hence meaningless in this context.

Exercise:

15A. Display the name, department id, and salary of those faculty members who have a salary which is greater than the average faculty salary for their department.

The next sample query illustrates a correlated subquery which utilizes, but does not explicitly declare a correlation variable.

Sample Query 15.2:   For each department which offers courses, display the department id, number, name, and labfee of any department-sponsored course having a labfee which exceeds the salary of the highest paid staff member employed by that department.

```
SELECT  CDEPT, CNO, CNAME, CLABFEE
FROM    COURSE
WHERE   CLABFEE >
    (SELECT DECIMAL(MAX(ESALARY))
    FROM    STAFF
    WHERE   DEPT = COURSE.CDEPT)
```

CDEPT	CNO	CNAME	CLABFEE
THEO	T11	SCHOLASTICISM	150.00
THEO	T12	FUNDAMENTALISM	90.00
THEO	T44	COMMUNISM	200.00

Comments:

1. Logic: The logic of this query requires a correlated subquery because we want to compare the labfee for each course with the maximum salary of a staff member employed by the same department which offers the course. The department is identified by the CDEPT value which changes from row to row. Hence, the need for a correlated subquery.

2. Syntax: Consider the subquery as an independent SELECT statement.

```
SELECT DECIMAL(MAX(ESALARY))
FROM    STAFF
WHERE   DEPT = COURSE.CDEPT
```

As an independent statement the WHERE clause is invalid because COURSE.CDEPT does not refer to a column in the STAFF table. However, this SELECT statement is meaningful as a subquery within an outer query which contains a "FROM COURSE" clause. Then, it will interpret the subquery as a correlated subquery with COURSE.CDEPT as an implicitly declared correlation variable.

The explicit definition of a correlation variable (similar to CX in the previous example) is unnecessary because the main query and subquery reference different tables in their FROM clauses. However, it enhances readability and, therefore, it is better to explicitly define correlation variables whenever you need to write a correlated subquery. The current example is rewritten using C as a correlation variable.

```
SELECT  CDEPT, CNO, CNAME, CLABFEE
FROM    COURSE C
WHERE   CLABFEE > (SELECT DECIMAL(MAX(ESALARY))
                   FROM    STAFF
                   WHERE   DEPT = C.CDEPT)
```

It is common practice to define a correlation variable for all tables, including those identified in the FROM clause of the subquery. The following equivalent statement includes S as a correlation variable for STAFF.

```
SELECT  CDEPT, CNO, CNAME, CLABFEE
FROM    COURSE C
WHERE   CLABFEE > (SELECT DECIMAL(MAX(ESALARY))
                   FROM    STAFF S
                   WHERE   S.DEPT = C.CDEPT)
```

4. As a reminder, notice the use of the DECIMAL function to convert the maximum ESALARY value, an integer, to a decimal before comparing it to the CLABFEE value which is a decimal value. This helps avoid any potential problems which can occur when comparing values of different data types.

Exercise:

15B. Display the name and department id for those faculty members who have a number of dependents greater than the average number of credits for courses offered by their department.

EXISTS Keyword

In previous subquery examples the main query WHERE clause was used to perform an explicit comparison with the intermediate result returned by the subquery. Sometimes the logic of the problem implies that an explicit comparison is unnecessary. Instead, a subquery is used only to determine if there are any rows in a table which match some condition. In this case, the main query can use the EXISTS keyword to test whether or not any match on the condition occurred. The remaining examples illustrate the use of EXISTS.

Sample Query 15.3:   Display the name and title of any staff member assigned to an existing department. More precisely, display the ENAME and ETITLE values in those STAFF table rows which have a DEPT value equal to any DEPT value in the DEPARTMENT table.

```
SELECT ENAME, ETITLE
FROM STAFF
WHERE EXISTS
    (SELECT *
     FROM    DEPARTMENT
     WHERE   DEPARTMENT.DEPT = STAFF.DEPT)
```

```
----------------------------------------
ENAME              ETITLE
----------------------------------------
LUKE               EVANGLIST3
MARK               EVANGLIST2
MATTHEW            EVANGLIST1
DICK NIX           CROOK
HANK KISS          JESTER
JOHN               EVANGLIST4
```

Comments:

1. Logic: The subquery is a correlated subquery where STAFF.DEPT is an implicitly defined correlation variable in the subquery. Therefore, the system will execute the subquery for each row in the STAFF table. Assume that the first STAFF table row encountered corresponds to "LUKE" which has a DEPT value of "THEO". Then the subquery (for the "LUKE" row) reduces to

   ```
   SELECT  *
   FROM    DEPARTMENT
   WHERE   DEPARTMENT.DEPT = 'THEO'
   ```

   This statement results in a "hit" because there is at least one row in the DEPARTMENT table with a DEPT value of "THEO." This means that the EXISTS test of the main query results in a "true" condition and the "LUKE" row is selected for display.

   Next, assume that the second STAFF table row corresponds to "EUCLID" which has a DEPT value of "MATH". Then the subquery reduces to:

   ```
   SELECT  *
   FROM    DEPARTMENT
   WHERE   DEPARTMENT.DEPT = 'MATH'
   ```

   This statement results in a "no hit" because there are no rows in the DEPARTMENT table with a DEPT value of "MATH". This means that the main query EXISTS test results in a "false" condition; hence the "EUCLID" row is not selected. Likewise, the row corresponding to "ARCHIMEDES" is not selected because its CDEPT value ("ENG") does not exist in the DEPARTMENT table. The "DA VINCI" row is not selected because its DEPT value is null. (Note that the "DA VINCI" row would not be selected even if a null value did exist in the DEPT column of DEPARTMENT. This is because the "null = null" compare results in "unknown," not "true.")

2. Syntax: The subquery SELECT clause contains an asterisk even though column names could be specified. An asterisk is usually specified in the subquery when the main query performs an EXISTS test because the system does not return values from the subquery; rather it confirms existence based on the test.

3. The current example is presented for tutorial purposes only. The query could have been satisfied by equivalent SELECT statements without using EXISTS. The following statements would produce the same result.

```
SELECT  ENAME, ETITLE
FROM    STAFF, DEPARTMENT
WHERE   STAFF.DEPT = DEPARTMENT.DEPT

SELECT  ENAME, ETITLE
FROM    STAFF
WHERE   DEPT IN
             (SELECT DEPT
              FROM DEPARTMENT)
```

In fact, these solutions may be preferable because they would not incur the costs associated with a correlated subquery. The same will be true for the next three sample queries where alternative solutions without using EXISTS can be found. However, there are problems which can be solved only by using the EXISTS keyword. (See Sample Query 15.8.) For this reason, you should recognize that EXISTS is an important keyword in the SQL language and understand its behavior.

Exercise:

For the following exercise write three SELECT statements which will satisfy the query. The first statement should be a correlated subquery which utilizes the EXISTS keyword. The second statement should be a self-contained subquery. The third statement should represent a join operation.

15C. Display the name and department id of any faculty member assigned to a department which offers a six-credit course.

The next example demonstrates the use of EXISTS with a correlated subquery where the correlation variables are explicitly specified.

Sample Query 15.4: Display the course number, name, and labfee of any course where there exists some staff member (regardless of department assignment) whose salary is less than that labfee.

```
SELECT CNO, CNAME, CLABFEE
FROM COURSE C
WHERE EXISTS
    (SELECT *
    FROM    STAFF S
    WHERE   S.ESALARY < C.CLABFEE)
```

```
-------------------------------------------------------
CNO     CNAME                       CLABFEE
-------------------------------------------------------
C11     INTRO TO CS                 100.00
C55     COMPUTER ARCH               100.00
C66     RELATIONAL DATABASE         500.00
P11     EMPIRICISM                  100.00
P33     EXISTENTIALISM              200.00
T11     SCHOLASTICISM               150.00
T12     FUNDAMENTALISM               90.00
T44     COMMUNISM                   200.00
```

Comment:

For each row in the COURSE table the subquery determines if any row in the STAFF table has an ESALARY value less than the CLABFEE value of that COURSE row. If such a row exists in the STAFF table, then the COURSE row is selected.

Exercise:

15D.   Rewrite the current sample query using (a) a self-contained subquery and (b) a join operation.

NOT EXISTS

A correlated subquery can be formulated using NOT EXISTS which, as you would expect, tests for a "does not exist" condition. It will select precisely those rows which would not be selected by the EXISTS condition. In fact, you will probably find that NOT EXISTS is more useful than EXISTS. This is because it can avoid a potentially problematic situation which can occur when a table contains null values. This sample query illustrates such a situation.

Sample Query 15.5:   Display the name, title, and department id of any staff member who is not assigned to an existing department. More precisely, display the ENAME, ETITLE, and DEPT values of any row in the STAFF table with a DEPT value which does not match any value in the DEPT column of the DEPARTMENT table.

```
SELECT  ENAME, ETITLE, DEPT
FROM    STAFF
WHERE   NOT EXISTS
    (SELECT *
     FROM    DEPARTMENT
     WHERE   DEPARTMENT.DEPT = STAFF.DEPT)
```

```
--------------------------------------------
ENAME           ETITLE          DEPT
--------------------------------------------
EUCLID          LAB ASSIST      MATH
ARCHIMEDES      LAB ASSIST      ENG
DA VINCI        LAB ASSIST      -
```

Comments:

1. The subquery is identical to that of Sample Query 15.3. Here, the main query will select just those rows where a "no hit" occurs in the subquery.

2. Observe that the "DA VINCI" row, which has a null DEPT value, is shown in the output display. When the main query was considering the "DA VINCI" row for selection, the subquery did not select any rows because it is impossible for the STAFF.DEPT value, which is null, to equal any DEPARTMENT.DEPT value, including another null value. This "no hit" situation in the subquery means the "DA VINCI" row (or any other STAFF row with a null DEPT value) will be selected under the NOT EXISTS condition.

We emphasize this aspect of the NOT EXISTS test to emphasize that the following statement is *not equivalent* to the current example.

```
SELECT  ENAME, ETITLE, DEPT
FROM    STAFF
WHERE   DEPT NOT IN
                ( SELECT DEPT
                  FROM    DEPARTMENT )
```

This statement will not select the "DA VINCI" row because it has a null DEPT value.

It is possible to write a SELECT statement which is equivalent to the current example, but you must remember to test explicitly for null values.

```
SELECT  ENAME, ETITLE, DEPT
FROM    STAFF
WHERE   DEPT NOT IN
                ( SELECT DEPT
                  FROM DEPARTMENT )
OR      DEPT IS NULL
```

3. The correlation variable STAFF.DEPT is implicitly specified in the subquery. There is no possible ambiguity because the main query and subquery reference different tables in their FROM clauses.

Exercise:

For the following exercise, specify two SELECT statements which will satisfy the query. The first statement should be a correlated subquery which utilizes the NOT EXISTS keywords. The second statement can use any other technique.

15E. Display the name and department id of any faculty member in a department which does not offer a six-credit course.

The next sample query uses NOT EXISTS with a correlated subquery. Correlation variables are explicitly specified because the main query and subquery both reference the same table.

Sample Query 15.6:   Display the course number, name, and labfee of any course which has a unique labfee. This is a labfee which does not equal the labfee of any other course recorded in the COURSE table.

```
SELECT CNO, CNAME, CLABFEE
FROM COURSE C1
WHERE NOT EXISTS
    (SELECT *
    FROM   COURSE C2
    WHERE  C1.CLABFEE = C2.CLABFEE)
    AND    C1.CNO <> C2.CNO)
```

```
------------------------------------------------------
CNO     CNAME                       CLABFEE
------------------------------------------------------
C66     RELATIONAL DATABASE          500.00
T11     SCHOLASTICISM                150.00
T22     FUNDAMENTALISM                90.00
```

Comments:

1. The correlated variable C1 is necessary. C2 is not necessary, but its use makes the statement more readable.

2. Each row in the COURSE table is considered for selection with C1 serving as the correlation variable for referencing these rows. The corresponding course number and labfee value are substituted for C1.CNO and C1.CLABFEE for each execution of the subquery. If the subquery results in a "no hit," the row under consideration (the one pointed to by C1) is selected.

CORRELATION VARIABLES WITHOUT SUBQUERIES

It is possible to utilize correlation variables in SELECT statements which do not contain a subquery. Sample Queries 11.11 and 11.12 illustrated the joining of a table with itself. The SELECT statement for 11.12 is shown below.

```
SELECT  ST1.DEPT, ST1.ENAME, ST2.ENAME
FROM    STAFF ST1, STAFF ST2
WHERE   ST1.DEPT = ST2.DEPT
AND     ST1.NAME < ST2.NAME
```

In our previous discussion of this example we referred to ST1 and ST2 as "aliases." They effectively gave two names to the same table so that we could write a SELECT statement which joined these tables. In fact, ST1 and ST2 are correlation variables. The system will use ST1 as a pointer to a given row. It will then execute the statement substituting that row's DEPT value for ST1.DEPT and that row's NAME value for ST1.NAME. Likewise, it will do the same for ST2. (The system does not produce a duplicate copy of this table.) If the WHERE condition is true after substituting the corresponding values referenced by ST1 and ST2, the ST1.DEPT, ST1.NAME, and ST2.NAME values are displayed. Both ST1 and ST2 range over the entire STAFF table to compare every possible pair of rows.

This discussion provides insight into an alternative, but less elegant, solution to Sample Query 15.6.

```
SELECT  CNO,CNAME,CLABFEE
FROM    COURSE
WHERE   CNO NOT IN
        (SELECT CA.CNO
         FROM   COURSE CA, COURSE CB
         WHERE  CA.CLABFEE = CB.CLABFEE
         AND    CA.CNO <> CB.CNO)
```

Observe that the subquery is self-contained; it is *not correlated with the main query*. However, the subquery does use correlation variables, CA and CB, to implement the join of the COURSE table with itself.

OUTER JOIN

In Chapter 11 we emphasized that the result of joining two tables will only contain rows where a match occurred on the join condition. The expression "inner join" is a more precise label for this kind of join operation. This distinguishes it from a different kind of join operation, called the "outer join." The result of an outer join operation will contain the same rows as an inner join operation plus a row corresponding to each row from the original tables which did not match on the join condition.

Figure 15.1(a) illustrates an outer equijoin of TABLE1 and TABLE2 using columns C2 and CA as the join columns. The result is shown in table FULLOJ. Note that the first three rows of FULLOJ correspond to the inner equijoin of TABLE1 and TABLE2. The fourth and fifth rows correspond to rows in TABLE1 (the "left" table) which did not match in the join operation. The last row of table FULLOJ corresponds to the row in TABLE2 (the "right" table) which did not match. The "no match" rows from the left table have null values appended to the right. And the "no match" rows from the right table have null values appended to the left.

The FULLOJ outer join result shown in Figure 15.1(a) is a "full outer join" of TABLE1 and TABLE2. If we excluded the "no match" rows of TABLE2 from the result, then the result would be called a "left outer join." LEFTOJ in Figure 15.1(b) shows the left outer join result. Likewise, if we excluded the "no match" rows of TABLE1 from the result, then the result would be called a "right outer join." RIGHTOJ in Figure 15.1(c) shows the right outer join result. In practice you will find greater application for the left and right outer join operations than the full outer join operation.

The currrent versions of DB2 and SQL/DS do not directly support outer join operations. However, it is possible to formulate a statement which can effectively produce any variation of the outer join. The next sample query illustrates this point.

C1   C2

A	10
B	45
C	45
D	20
E	20

TABLE1

CA   CB

10	S
20	U
35	Z

TABLE2

C1   C2   CA   CB

A	10	10	S
D	20	20	U
E	20	20	U
B	45	–	–
C	45	–	–
–	–	35	Z

(a) FULLOJ

C1   C2   CA   CB

A	10	10	S
D	20	20	U
E	20	20	U
B	45	-	-
C	45	-	-

(b) LEFTOJ

C1   C2   CA   CB

A	10	10	S
D	20	20	U
E	20	20	U
-	-	35	Z

(c) RIGHTOJ

Figure 15.1   Outer join operations.

LEFT OUTER JOIN

The next example uses previously described techniques to construct a left outer join of the STAFF and DEPARTMENT tables over the DEPT columns in both tables. In this example, the STAFF table is the "left" table, which means that all of its rows are preserved in the result.

Sample Query 15.7: For every staff member recorded in the STAFF table, record his name, title, salary, and department id along with all information about the department he is assigned to (i.e., the department's id, building, room, and faculty number of the department chairperson). If the staff member is not assigned to an existing department, or if the assignment is unknown (null), display blanks for department information.

```
SELECT  *
FROM    STAFF, DEPARTMENT
WHERE   STAFF.DEPT = DEPARTMENT.DEPT
UNION   ALL
SELECT  ENAME, ETITLE, ESALARY,
        STAFF.DEPT, ' ', ' ', ' ', ' '
FROM    STAFF
WHERE   NOT EXISTS
        (SELECT *
         FROM DEPARTMENT
         WHERE DEPARTMENT.DEPT = STAFF.DEPT)
```

ENAME	ETITLE	ESALARY	DEPT1	DEPT2	DBLD	DROOM	DCHFNO
DICK NIX	CROOK	25001	PHIL	PHIL	HU	100	60
HANK KISS	JESTER	25000	PHIL	PHIL	HU	100	60
JOHN	EVANGLIST4	54	THEO	THEO	HU	200	10
LUKE	EVANGLIST3	53	THEO	THEO	HU	200	10
MARK	EVANGLIST2	52	THEO	THEO	HU	200	10
MATTHEW	EVANGLIST1	51	THEO	THEO	HU	200	10
EUCLID	LAB ASSIST	1000	MATH				
ARCHIMEDES	LAB ASSIST	200	ENG				
DA VINCI	LAB ASSIST	500	-				

Comments:

1. The left outer join is formed by using UNION ALL to merge the rows selected by two independent SELECT statements. The first SELECT statement generates those rows which correspond to the conventional (inner) equijoin of DEPARTMENT and STAFF along the DEPT columns. The second SELECT statement generates those rows which correspond to the "no match" rows from the STAFF table. These rows pertain to those employees who are not assigned to an existing department. This second SELECT uses NOT EXISTS in conjunction with a correlated subquery.

2. The output for this example, unlike Figure 15.1, shows blanks instead of null values appended to the "no match" rows. What if you wanted to display null values instead of blanks? This cannot be done. Although it seems reasonable, the following SELECT clause will *not work*.

```
SELECT ENAME, ETITLE, ESALARY, STAFF.DEPT, NULL, NULL, NULL,
NULL
```

   The NULL keyword cannot be used in the SELECT clause. (However, users of QMF could save the result table and then use an UPDATE command to change the blanks to null values.)

3. We could form a full outer join of the STAFF and DEPARTMENT tables along the DEPT columns by appending the following code to the current example.

```
UNION ALL
SELECT ' ', ' ', 0, ' ', DEPARTMENT.DEPT, DBLD, DROOM, DCHFNO
FROM    DEPARTMENT
WHERE   NOT EXISTS
          (SELECT *
           FROM    STAFF
           WHERE   STAFF.DEPT = DEPARTMENT.DEPT)
```

   Note that zero, or any other numeric value, instead of blanks, must be displayed in the ESALARY column. This is necessary for reasons of union compatibility.

"FOR ALL"

The last sample query in this part of the text illustrates the formulation of a SELECT statement which embodies the notion of "for all the values in a column, there exists . . . ." SQL has no keyword which directly supports "for all." However, it is possible to write an equivalent statement using NOT EXISTS twice. This is effectively a "double negative" which is poor grammar, but logically correct. In fact, it is the only way to express the concept of "for all" within SQL.

The complexity of the following example occurs for two reasons. The first is that SQL is far from a perfect language. In this case, the absence of a "for all" operator means that the query must be reformulated into an equivalent, but far less concise, expression of the problem. The second reason is that five different tables need to be referenced in order to satisfy the query objective. This means that you must have a good understanding of the semantic relationships reflected in the database design. Finally, the authors felt that it would be "good for the soul" to conclude our discussion of the SELECT statement with a problem which is deceptively nasty. This is a problem which is simple to articulate in everyday English, but can be considered a real challenge.

Sample Query 15.8: Are there any students who are taking a course from every department which offers courses? If so, display the name of each student. Or, to state the problem another way:

Display the name of any student who has registered for at least one class in a course offered by each department which offers courses. Or, to put it yet another way by using a double negative articulation of the problem:

Display the name of any student where there does not exist a department (which offers courses), so that there does not exist a class in a course offered by that department where the student has registered for a class offered by that department.

```
SELECT SNAME
FROM    STUDENT S
WHERE   NOT EXISTS
        (SELECT *
        FROM    DEPARTMENT D
        WHERE   D.DEPT IN
            (SELECT CDEPT
            FROM    COURSE)
            AND    NOT EXISTS
            (SELECT *
            FROM    REGISTRATION R,
                    COURSE C,
                    CLASS CL
        WHERE   R.CNO = C.CNO
        AND     R.CNO = CL.CNO
        AND     R.SEC = CL.SEC
        AND     C.CDEPT = D.DEPT
        AND     R.SNO = S.SNO))
```

```
----------------------------------
SNAME
----------------------------------
MOE     DUBAY
ROCKY   BALBOA
```

Comments:

1. Syntax: The example shows a second-level subquery which contains two other third-level subqueries. (Nesting of subqueries was introduced in Sample Query 13.11.) The key difference here is that the second-level subquery and one of the third-level subqueries are correlated subqueries. This is no more than an extension of the idea of a correlated subquery to a lower-level subquery.

2. Logic: In this example, the top-level SELECT statement of the main query references the STUDENT table. This means the system will examine each row in the STUDENT table to determine if any rows are selected by the second-level SELECT statement. If no rows are selected then the corresponding SNAME value is displayed. Assume the system encounters a row corresponding to a student who matches the selection criteria (i.e., the student has registered for at least one course offered by the Theology, Philosophy, and Computer and Information Science Departments). If this student has an SNO value "999", then the second-level SELECT statement, after making the substitution for S.SNO, reduces to:

```
SELECT  *
FROM    DEPARTMENT D
WHERE   D.DEPT IN (SELECT CDEPT FROM COURSE)
AND     NOT EXISTS
        (SELECT *
        FROM    REGISTRATION R, COURSE C, CLASS CL
        WHERE   R.CNO = C.CNO
        AND     R.CNO = CL.CNO
        AND     R.SEC = CL.SEC
        AND     C.CDEPT = D.DEPT
        AND     R.SNO = '999')
```

For the moment, consider this statement as an independent SELECT statement. The first subquery, "SELECT CDEPT FROM COURSE", is a self-contained subquery which selects the department ids of those departments which offer courses. We can replace this subquery with the CDEPT values found in the COURSE table. This statement then becomes

```
SELECT  *
FROM    DEPARTMENT D
WHERE   D.DEPT IN ('CIS', 'PHIL', 'THEO')
AND     NOT EXISTS
        (SELECT *
        FROM    REGISTRATION R, COURSE C, CLASS CL
        WHERE   R.CNO = C.CNO
        AND     R.CNO = CL.CNO
        AND     R.SEC = CL.SEC
        AND     C.CDEPT = D.DEPT
        AND     R.SNO = '999')
```

This statement contains the second correlated subquery, which causes the system to examine each row of the DEPARTMENT table to determine if any rows are selected by the low-level subquery. If none are selected, and the department id is "CIS", "PHIL", or "THEO", the corresponding DEPARTMENT row is selected. Assume the system encounters the CIS Department row. Then the bottom-level subquery reduces to:

```
SELECT *
FROM    REGISTRATION R, COURSE C, CLASS CL
WHERE   R.CNO = C.CNO
AND     R.CNO = CL.CNO
AND     R.SEC = CL.SEC
AND     C.CDEPT = 'CIS'
AND     R.SNO = '999'
```

The statement is a three-way join of the REGISTRATION, COURSE and CLASS tables. (Sample Query 11.8 originally introduced a three-way join.) The objective of this statement is to determine if the student identified by SNO value "999" has registered for any class offered by the CIS Department. One row will be selected for each CIS course the student has registered for.

Returning to the second-level SELECT statement, a "hit" on student 999 registering for a CIS course means that the NOT EXISTS condition evaluates to false, and hence the row for the CIS Department is not selected. For the same reason, the DEPARTMENT rows for the Theology and Philosophy Departments are not selected. Finally, the row for the Management Department is not selected because its id is not in the set ("CIS," "PHIL," "THEO"). This means that none of the four DEPARTMENT rows are selected by the second-level subquery. Returning to the top-level SELECT statement, the NOT EXISTS condition is met because none of the DEPARTMENT rows were selected. Hence, the STUDENT row for student 999 is selected and the SNAME value is displayed.

The same process begins for the next STUDENT row encountered by the system. The SNO value is held constant during the iteration over the four DEPARTMENT rows indicated by the second-level sub-query. The bottom-level correlated subquery then determines if the student registered for a course offered by the department. You are encouraged to work through the example for a student who did not register for a course offered by some department which offers courses. A "no hit" on the bottom-level correlated subquery means the second-level NOT EXISTS condition is true for some department, which in turn means that the top-level NOT EXISTS condition is not met. Hence, the name of this student would not be displayed.

SUMMARY

This chapter introduced the notion of a correlated subquery, a subquery which relates back to, and is dependent upon, the main query. The reference is made through a correlation variable. The concept of existence testing was introduced through the EXISTS keyword. We saw that the "for all" operation could be implemented using NOT EXISTS. Finally, it was demonstrated that the outer join operation could be implemented through the use of correlated subqueries and EXISTS. All told, this chapter revealed some very important aspects of relational database which are supported (albeit not directly) in SQL.

SUMMARY EXERCISES

15F.   Display the course name, department id and labfee for each course which has the largest labfee of all courses in that department.

15G.   Display a list for each department of all classes offered by the department. The list contains department id and department building/room location, followed by course number and name of courses offered by the department, followed by section number and day of any classes on those courses. If a department does not offer any courses, or a course has no class offerings, display spaces in the respective positons.

IV

More About SQL

The previous parts of this text introduced the data definition and data manipulation statements of the SQL language. Part IV introduces another dimension of SQL by presenting statements which facilitate the management of your data. In particular, we focus on those techniques which allow you to share your data with other users of the system. We conclude by presenting the idea of a database transaction as it relates to database integrity and recovery. You will find the SQL statements presented in these chapters to be useful, powerful, and easy to learn.

ORGANIZATION OF CHAPTERS

Chapter 16 presents a comprehensive discussion of the CREATE VIEW statement. This statement permits you to define a view which is essentially a "virtual" table. A view corresponds to the notion of a "local view" which is applicable within most multiuser database systems. This is an important chapter because many companies have a policy which states that users can only retrieve data from views.

Chapter 17 introduces some of the key ideas behind database security. This is not a comprehensive discussion of the topic. Instead, we present a programmer/user (vs. database administrator) perspective by introducing those variations of the GRANT and REVOKE statements which are relevant to this audience.

Chapter 18 introduces the transaction concept by presenting the COMMIT WORK and ROLLBACK WORK statements. This is an important chapter for programmers who will write application programs which update tables. Most users can skip this chapter. However, those users who intend to execute interactive update operations (a questionable practice) should read this chapter because of its relevancy to database integrity and recovery.

16

The View Concept

Most database management systems provide some facility which allows for the definition of a "local view" of the database. "Local view" is a generic expression corresponding to some subset of the database which a particular user or group of users can manipulate. A local view is usually defined by the database administrator and then made available to a user. Because a local view is usually defined for each user, a given data base may have many local views defined on it. Both DB2 and SQL/DS support the local view concept through the CREATE VIEW command. Execution of this command will create a "SQL view" which is similar but not identical to the "local view" concept.

The local view approach serves two purposes.

1. Security: The user has no access to any data which is not part
    of his local view. Also, the user may only be allowed to perform
    certain operations on the local view's data. This prevents acci-
    dental or intentional retrieval or modification of data which is
    not within the defined local view.

2. Simplicity: The user can disregard all data which is not within
    his local view. In fact, the user might not even be aware that
    such data exists. Because a local view is usually much smaller
    than the entire database, the user's view is simplified and a
    possible source of confusion is removed.

Below we describe a "SQL view" and then relate it to the "local view"
concept.

The CREATE VIEW statement is used to define the content of a
SQL view which is sometimes called a virtual table. We say "table"
because the user perceives and manipulates a SQL view in the same
manner as the COURSE table has been processed throughout this
text. We say "virtual" because the rows and columns of a view do not
really exist. The view corresponds to data in a table which was previously established with a CREATE TABLE statement. To introduce
some SQL terminology, we use the phrase "base table" to designate
any table created by a CREATE TABLE command. All the tables
previously referenced in this book (COURSE, STAFF, DEPART-
MENT, etc.) are base tables. The CREATE VIEW command is used
to establish a SQL view which is defined on some base table. A SQL
view can be thought of as a window into some subset of a base table.
Figure 16.1 illustrates this perspective of a SQL view. Later, we will
see that the CREATE VIEW statement provides more power and
flexibility than the window analogy implies.

Once a SQL view is established, you can execute a SELECT statement which references the view. The system will associate the SQL
view with a base table and then extract and display the data from
the base table. This approach means that a view does not contain
replicated data from a base table. It doesn't contain any data at all
because it is not a real table. All processing is done with the data
stored in the base table. Later, we will examine how the system does
this.

This chapter will introduce the details of the CREATE VIEW statement. We will see that a SQL view is perceived as exactly one (virtual) table. To relate a SQL view to the generic notion of a local view, note that a user might have a local view which consists of multiple tables. Some of these tables might be base tables and others might be SQL views. We will also see that the CREATE VIEW statement defines only the content of the virtual table. It does not specify which user can access a view, nor does it specify what operations may be performed against the view. The next chapter will present the GRANT statement which serves these purposes. There we will see that the local view concept is usually implemented by utilization of both the CREATE VIEW and GRANT statements. For the remainder of this chapter the term "view" implies a SQL view.

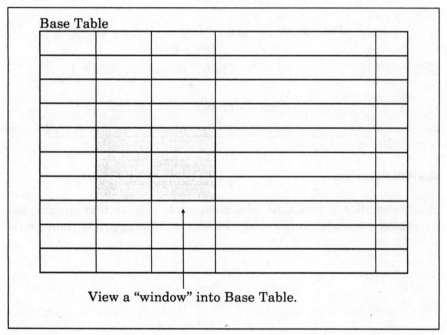

Figure 16.1   View concept.

CREATE VIEW STATEMENT

The first example illustrates the aforementioned window analogy for a view by creating a view which corresponds to a subset of columns and rows from the COURSE table.

Sample Statement 16.1:   Create a view (a virtual table) called CISC which contains just the rows corresponding to courses offered by the CIS Department. The view should contain all of the columns from the COURSE table with the exception of the CDEPT column. The left-to-right column sequence of the view should be CNAME, CNO, CRED, CLABFEE, and CDESCP.

```
CREATE VIEW CISC AS
        SELECT CNAME, CNO,
               CRED, CLABFEE, CDESCP
        FROM   COURSE
        WHERE  CDEPT = 'CIS'
```

System Response:

Like all previous CREATE commands, the system should display a message confirming the successful creation of the view.

Comments:

1. The name of the view, CISC, immediately follows the CREATE VIEW keywords. View names are formulated according to the same rules that apply to table names. A view name, like a table name, has a prefix which the system defines as the authorization id of the user who entered the CREATE VIEW command.

2. The keyword AS follows the view name. The definition of the view follows the AS keyword. Observe that this definition is simply a "good old" SELECT statement. In this example it is:

```
SELECT  CNAME, CNO, CRED, CLABFEE, CDESCP
FROM    COURSE
WHERE   CDEPT = 'CIS'
```

If we were to directly execute this SELECT statement, the result would correspond to the content of the desired view definition. Here the SELECT statement is not executed. Instead, the system uses its catalog to save the text of the SELECT statement as a definition of view. Later we will see how it uses this definition.

3. In this example the view inherited the names of its columns from the COURSE table. Sample Statement 16.4 will demonstrate a version of the CREATE VIEW statement which allows the assignment different column names.

PROCESSING VIEWS

We can usually manipulate views just as we have done with base tables throughout this text. However, there are some important exceptions which will be described as we progress through the examples. In general, you will find that many views can be treated exactly like base tables, so much so that a view is often referred to as a "table" instead of "virtual table."

Sample Query 16.2:   Display the entire CISC table.

```
SELECT  *
FROM    CISC
```

```
----------------------------------------------------------------------
CNAME                        CNO    CRED    CLABFEE  CDESCP
----------------------------------------------------------------------
INTRO TO CS                  C11     3      100.00   FOR ROOKIES
DATA STRUCTURES              C22     3       50.00   VERY USEFUL
DISCRETE MATHEMATICS         C33     3        0.00   ABSOLUTELY NECESSARY
DIGITAL CIRCUITS             C44     3        0.00   AH HA!
COMPUTER ARCH.               C55     3      100.00   VON NEUMANN'S MACH.
RELATIONAL DATABASE          C66     3      500.00   THE ONLY WAY TO GO
```

Comment:

The syntax of the SELECT statement (and all other SQL data manipulation statements) remains unchanged. In this example we see the view name is referenced in the FROM clause.

Exercise:

16A. Create a view called FPAYROLL on the FACULTY table. The view is to contain the FNAME, FSALARY, FHIRE_DATE, and FNUM_DEP columns. Issue a SELECT statement against this view and examine the results.

Sample Query 16.3: For any row in the CISC table with a labfee greater than or equal to $100, display its name followed by the labfee. Sort the result by course name in ascending sequence.

```
SELECT  CNAME, CLABFEE
FROM    CISC
WHERE   CLABFEE >= 100
ORDER   BY CNAME
```

```
-----------------------------------------------------
CNAME                      CLABFEE
-----------------------------------------------------
COMPUTER ARCH.             100.00
INTRO TO CS               100.00
RELATIONAL DATABASE       500.00
```

Comments:

1. Again observe that the view is referenced like a base table. In the current sample a WHERE clause and an ORDER BY clause were used to select specific rows from the view and to display them in a specific row sequence.

2. This query could have been satisfied by executing the following statement which refers to the base table.

```
SELECT  CNAME, CLABFEE
FROM    COURSE
WHERE   CDEPT = 'CIS'
AND     CLABFEE >= 100
ORDER   BY CNAME
```

However, this statement is more complex. It presumes that the user is aware of the existence of and the content of the COURSE table. In many situations the DBA only allows the user to access a view.

SPECIFYING COLUMN NAMES FOR A VIEW

The column names in the CISC view were inherited from the COURSE table. The next example illustrates a method for explicitly naming the columns of a view and then referencing them in a SELECT statement.

Sample Statement 16.4: Create a view called VEXPCOURSE corresponding to rows from the COURSE table where the labfee exceeds $150. The columns of the view correspond to CNO, CNAME, and CLABFEE. Their respective names in the view are CNUMBER, COURSE_NAME, and EXPENSIVE_LABFEE.

```
CREATE VIEW VEXPCOURSE
(CNUMBER, COURSE_NAME, EXPENSIVE_LABFEE)
AS SELECT CNO, CNAME, CLABFEE
    FROM    COURSE
    WHERE   CLABFEE > 150
```

System Response:

Like all previous CREATE commands, the system should display a message confirming the successful creation of the view.

Comments:

1. In the CREATE VIEW statement, the column names of the view are specified after the view name. Note that they are enclosed within parentheses and separated by commas.

2. We chose to begin the view name with the letter "V" to serve as a reminder that this table is really a view. This technique is useful, but it is not necessary.

Sample Query 16.5:   Display the VEXPCOURSE table in course name sequence.

```
SELECT *
FROM    VEXPCOURSE
ORDER   BY COURSE_NAME
```

```
-----------------------------------------------------------------------
CNUMBER COURSE_NAME                                   EXPENSIVE_LABFEE
-----------------------------------------------------------------------
T44            COMMUNISM                                    200.00
P33            EXISTENTIALISM                               200.00
C66            RELATIONAL DATABASE                          500.00
```

Comment:

The SELECT statement must reference the column names as defined in the view. These names appear as column headings in the displayed result. An attempt to reference the column names of the corresponding base table would result in an error.

RULES FOR CREATE VIEW

Figure 16.2 outlines the general format of the CREATE VIEW command. We address the issues of specification of column names and the formulation of a valid SELECT statement.

As Sample 16.1 indicated, the designation of specific column names may be optional. If you do not specify the column names, the view inherits its column names from the base table. Sample 16.4 illustrated a situation where the columns of VEXPCOURSE were assigned names different from the underlying base table. Observe that we could allow the columns of VEXPCOURSE to inherit the column names from the COURSE table. Sometimes the creator of a view is required to specify column names. Sample 16.6 will present a situation where the view contains a column of derived values. In such cases it is necessary to explicitly specify column names, because the values in a column do not directly correspond to any predefined (base table) column and, hence, cannot inherit its name.

"Almost any" SELECT statement is permitted as a view definition. There are two limitations which apply to interactive SQL.

1. The ORDER BY clause cannot be included in the SELECT statement. This is reasonable when you consider that the relational model dictates that a table (base tables and views) should not have any predefined sequence. The ORDER BY clause may be attached to the SELECT statement which retrieves data from the view.

2. The UNION clause cannot be included in the SELECT statement. This restriction is not so reasonable. However, it applies to the current releases of DB2 and SQL/DS.

Aside from these restrictions, any valid SELECT statement can serve as a view definition. In particular, this includes statements which involve built-in functions, expressions, the join operation, and subqueries. Also, the FROM clause may even specify a view, which means that it is possible to define a view on top of a view. See Sample Statement 16.10.

```
CREATE  VIEW viewname (col1,col2,...)
AS      SELECT    _____ ┐
        FROM      _____  ├── "almost" any
        WHERE     _____ ┘     SELECT statement
```

Figure 16.2   CREATE VIEW statement.

This approach of using a SELECT statement to define a view is simple, powerful, and conceptually elegant. In all previous examples the direct execution of a SELECT statement was interpreted by the system as the definition of a subset of the database to be retrieved for display. (This perspective is consistent with the theory of a relational database which defines the database structure as a collection of sets and the query language as a notation which defines a subset to be retrieved.) In the context of CREATE VIEW the SELECT statement constitutes the definition of a subset (i.e., a window) which is a view into a base table.

Update Restrictions on Views:

Views can be updated using the INSERT, UPDATE, and DELETE commands presented in Chapter 9. Such view updates are applied to the underlying base table. However, there are a number of restrictions on view updates which we will summarize at the end of this chapter. For the moment, we merely note that a view which is defined as a "mirror image" of some subset of rows and columns from a single base table can be updated. Therefore, the CISC and VEXPCOURSE views can be referenced in INSERT, DELETE, and UPDATE commands. Modifications will be applied to the corresponding values in the underlying COURSE table.

Many views, like CISC and VEXPCOURSE, are defined so that the above restrictions do not apply. The database administrator could create these views and make them available to users without even telling the users that these tables are views. Such users might not even be familiar with the concept or syntax of the CREATE VIEW command. They simply reference these tables using the SELECT, INSERT, UPDATE, and DELETE statements.

Other views which are not mirror images of some part of a single table cannot be updated. The nex two examples illustrate views which are subject to update restrictions. Users of a view with update restrictions need to be aware of the fact that they are working with a view. For this reason, we recommend using "V" as the first character in the name of the view.

VIEW DEFINED AS A STATISTICAL SUMMARY

The next example shows it also is possible to create a view with columns containing summary data derived from a base table.

Sample Statement 16.6: Create a view called VCSTAT which has one row for each department which offers courses. The columns are the department id followed by the sum and the average labfee values for each department.

```
CREATE VIEW VCSTAT
        (CDEPT, SUM_CLABFEE, AVG_CLABFEE)
  AS    SELECT CDEPT, SUM(CLABFEE), AVG(CLABFEE)
        FROM    COURSE
        GROUP   BY CDEPT
```

System Response:

Like all previous CREATE commands, the system should display a message confirming the successful creation of the view.

Comments:

1. The SELECT clause contains built-in functions which perform calculations for each department group. The derived results effectively become the values of the second and third columns of the view.

2. The example shows the column names of the view explicitly named. This is necessary because view columns which contain derived data do not directly correspond to, and hence cannot inherit the names of, any base table columns.

3. Recall that GROUP BY clause will cause the system to sort by the grouping field. This sorting is incidental to the grouping process. You should explicitly use the ORDER BY clause if you want the result to be sorted. However, we did not include an ORDER BY clause in the definition of VCSTAT because the ORDER BY clause is not permitted in the definition of any view.

4. This view cannot be updated because it contains derived data. To be precise, the system will not permit update operations on any view which is defined with a GROUP BY clause or a built-in function.

Sample Query 16.7:   Display the average labfee for courses offered by the Philosophy and Theology Departments. Sort the result by this average in descending sequence.

```
SELECT  CDEPT, AVG_CLABFEE
FROM    VCSTAT
WHERE   CDEPT = 'PHIL'
OR      CDEPT = 'THEO'
ORDER   BY AVG_CLABFEE DESC
```

```
--------------------------------------------------
CDEPT                         AVG_CLABFEE
--------------------------------------------------
THEO                      110.000000000000
PHIL                       87.500000000000
```

VIEW DEFINED AS JOIN OF TABLES

In Chapter 11 we described the subtle issues associated with the join operation. We noted that the SQL syntax was easy, but the logic of the join could be misunderstood by the user. The database administrator can help unsophisticated SQL users avoid the potential problems of the join operation by creating a view which is a join of some tables. Then the user would perceive the tables as a single table. Such a user could then utilize just those techniques described in Part I of this text. This approach involves extra effort by the database administrator. However, it simplifies the user's task and removes potential sources of error. The next example illustrates the creation of such a view.

Sample Statement 16.8:   Create a view called VCSD, which is the join of the COURSE, STAFF, and DEPARTMENT tables along the columns containing department id values. VCSD should contain all the columns from these base tables with the exception of the department ids, which will be equal to each other and, therefore, should only occur once in the view.

```
CREATE VIEW VCSD AS
SELECT CNO, CNAME, CDESCP,
       CRED, CLABFEE, DEPARTMENT.DEPT,
       DBLD, DROOM, DCHFNO, ENAME,
       ETITLE, ESALARY
FROM   COURSE, STAFF, DEPARTMENT
WHERE  CDEPT = STAFF.DEPT
AND    CDEPT = DEPARTMENT.DEPT
```

System Response:

Like all previous CREATE commands, the system should display a message confirming the successful creation of the view.

Comments:

1. Recall that certain rows from the STAFF table and the DE-
    PARTMENT table will not appear in the join result. The cre-
    ator of this view should be aware of this fact and verify that it
    is acceptable within the context of the application environment.
    This would be the case for the following sample query where
    we make the same semantic assumptions specified in Chapter
    11. Namely, a staff member can tutor any course offered by his
    department; the staff member is also located in the same build-
    ing and room as is specified for his department in the DE-
    PARTMENT table.

2. Because DEPT is a column in both the STAFF and DEPART-
    MENT tables, the SELECT statement must qualify the column
    names. The view inherited the column name DEPT from the
    DEPARTMENT.DEPT column which contains the department
    ids. It does not inherit the qualifier (DEPARTMENT). The
    complete column name in the view becomes VCSD.DEPT. The
    SELECT statement in the view definition could have refer-
    enced STAFF.DEPT instead of DEPARTMENT.DEPT, in which
    case the view column would still inherit the same name
    (VSCD.DEPT).

    The content of the view would be the same if the SELECT
    clause referenced CDEPT, in which case the view would have
    inherited the name of CDEPT (really VCSD.CDEPT). We could
    have explicitly named the view columns using the technique
    shown in Sample 16.4.

3. If we wanted to include all base table columns in the view,
    especially the three identical columns containing the depart-
    ment id values, then we would have to code the department id
    column names so that they are unique. Furthermore, we must
    explicitly name the view columns because inheritence would
    imply that two columns would be named DEPT, which is in-
    valid. For example, the SELECT clause in the CREATE VIEW
    command could be written as

```
CREATE VIEW
VCSD2  (CNO, CNAME, CDESCP, CRED, CLABFEE, CDEPT, DDEPT,
        DBLO, DROOM, DCHFNO, SDEPT, ENAME, ETITLE,
        ESALARY) AS
SELECT CNO, CNAME, CDESCP, CRED, CLABFEE,
        CDEPT, DEPARTMENT.DEPT, DBLD, DROOM,
        DCHFNO, STAFF.DEPT, ENAME, ETITLE, ESALARY
FROM   COURSE, STAFF, DEPARTMENT
WHERE  CDEPT = STAFF.DEPT
AND    CDEPT = DEPARTMENT.DEPT
```

In this view, the three columns containing the department ids are named CDEPT, DDEPT, and SDEPT. Also note that the SELECT statement had to explicitly reference the name of every column in all three tables. A common error is the writing of the SELECT clause with an asterisk (SELECT * FROM. . .). This would cause an error whenever the same column name is used in multiple tables. Such is the case with DEPT in the current example.

4. Restriction on Updating VCSD: No view which is defined as the join of multiple tables can be updated. The system will reject any update command which references a view defined with more than one table specified in the FROM clause. Hence, INSERT, DELETE, and UPDATE commands cannot reference VCSD.

Sample Query 16.9:   For any staff member who can tutor Philosophy courses, display his name, the name of the course he can tutor, and his building and room location. Sort the result by staff member name.

```
SELECT  ENAME,  CNAME,  DBLD,  DROOM
FROM    VCSD
WHERE   DEPT = 'PHIL'
ORDER   BY ENAME
```

ENAME	CNAME	DBLD	DROOM
DICK NIX	EMPIRICISM	HU	100
DICK NIX	RATIONALSM	HU	100
DICK NIX	EXISTENTIALISM	HU	100
DICK NIX	SOLIPSISM	HU	100
HANK KISS	SOLIPSISM	HU	100
HANK KISS	EXISTENTIALISM	HU	100
HANK KISS	RATIONALISM	HU	100
HANK KISS	EMPIRICISM	HU	100

Comment:

This query is comparatively simple. The user extracts all the data from one (virtual) table instead of constructing a complex query using the join operation. The complexity of constructing the VCSD view has been passed onto the database administrator (where it belongs).

Exercise:

16B.   Create a view on the FACULTY table, called VFSAL, which presents the highest and lowest salaries of faculty members by department. The columns in the view will have the names of DEPARTMENT, HIGHEST_SALARY, and LOWEST_SALARY. Issue a SELECT statement against this view and examine the results.

VIEW DEFINED ON ANOTHER VIEW

The SELECT statement which defines a view can itself reference another view. The next example creates a view based on the CISC view which is, in turn, based upon the COURSE base table. (Review Sample Statement 16.1)

Sample Statement 16.10:   Create a view called VCHEAPCISC, which, contains rows for CIS courses with a cheap labfee. These are CIS courses with a labfee less than $100. The view should contain just the CNAME and CLABFEE columns and inherit those column names.

```
CREATE VIEW VCHEAPCISC AS
SELECT CNAME, CLABFEE
FROM   CISC
WHERE  CLABFEE < 100
```

System Response:

Like all previous CREATE commands, the system should display a message confirming the successful creation of the view.

Comments:

1. All the data required for the VCHEAPCISC view is found in the CISC view. It may be the case that the user does not have access to the COURSE table, but does have access to CISC. Hence, the FROM clause in the SELECT statement references CISC.

2. Restrictions: Obviously, the previous restrictions on view definition apply. (No ORDER BY or UNION clauses are allowed.)

3. Can we define another view on the VCHEAPCISC view? (Can we base a view on a view on a view, etc.?) Yes. There is no arbitrary limit on the number of views dependent on other views.

Sample Query 16.11: Display the entire VCHEAPCISC table.

```
SELECT  *
FROM    VCHEAPCISC
```

```
-------------------------------------------
CNAME                       CLABFEE
-------------------------------------------
DATA STRUCTURES               50.00
DISCRETE MATHEMATICS            .00
DIGITAL CIRCUITS                .00
```

Commnents:

1. Observe that only CIS department courses appear in the result. This is because the underlying view, CISC, allows access to only CIS courses.

2. The labfee values are all less than $100, as prescribed in the definition of VCHEAPCISC.

Exercise:

16C. Create a view on the view FPAYROLL which presents the average faculty salary and average number of dependents. Call the view FAVERAGES and use the column names of FAVG_SAL and FAVG_NUM_DEP. Issue a SELECT statement against this view and examine the results.

DROP VIEW Statement

This chapter illustrated the creation of five views (CISC, VEXPCOURSE, VCSTAT, VCSD, and VCHEAPCISC). The DROP VIEW statement is very simple and can be used to remove the view from the database. The next example demonstrates its use.

Sample Statement 16.12:   Drop the VCSTAT table from the database. More precisely, drop the VCSTAT view.

DROP VIEW VCSTAT

System Response:

The system will display a message confirming that VCSTAT has been dropped.

Exercise:

16D.   Drop the view VFSAL which was created in Exercise 16B. Issue a SELECT statement against this view and notice the system response.

The next example drops a view which has another view based on it. When this occurs, all views dependent on the dropped view are also automatically dropped.

Sample Statement 16.13: Drop the CISC table from the database. More precisely, drop the CISC view and any other views dependent on it.

```
DROP VIEW CISC
```

Comment:

This command drops CISC and VCHEAPCISC, the only view dependent on CISC.

Finally, recall that the DROP TABLE statement also drops any indexes which are dependent on the table. The DROP TABLE command will also drop all views which are dependent on the table. Hence, dropping the COURSE table would automatically drop all the views created by the sample statements illustrated in this chapter.

Exercise:

16E) Drop the view FPAYROLL. Issue a SELECT statement against the view FAVERAGES, which was based on the FPAYROLL view.

SUMMARY

We conclude this chapter by noting that the CREATE VIEW statement is quite simple because it utilizes the SELECT statement as a vehicle for defining a view. The only potential problems pertain to the restrictions for defining and updating views. Before we summarize these restrictions, it is helpful to understand how the system handles views. A brief explanation of this process provides insight into the rationale for some of the restrictions.

How Does the System Handle Views?

Recall that the system stores the view definition (the text of the SELECT statement) in the system catalog. When a query is executed against the view, the system consults the catalog and extracts (1) the name of the base table and (2) the view predicates specified in the WHERE clause of the view definition. The system merges the predicates of the query with those of the view definition to form a new query. The view name is replaced with the name of the underlying base table and the predicates are AND-connected. This reformulated query is executed by the system.

Consider the CISC view defined in Sample Statement 16.1. It specifies a base table (COURSE) and a predicate (CDEPT = 'CIS'). Assume a user enters the query shown in Sample Query 16.3 rewritten below.

```
SELECT  CNAME, CLABFEE
FROM    CISC
WHERE   CLABFEE  = 100
ORDER   BY CNAME
```

The system reformulates this query following the process described above. The reformulated query is shown below.

```
SELECT  CNAME, CLABFEE
FROM    COURSE
WHERE   CLABFEE  = 100
AND     CDEPT = 'CIS'
ORDER   BY CNAME
```

This reformulated query is submitted for execution. Observe that it does satisfy the objective of Sample Query 16.3. This approach to defining and processing views means that a query against a view is always applied against the underlying base table. This is why the system does not have to store a duplicate copy of the data to represent a view.

DB2 is more powerful than SQL/DS. It can execute the SELECT statement of the view definition and places the result in a temporary table. The query which you present against the view is then executed against this intermediate result.

Consider the view VCSTAT which, as we saw, used a column function. The view reflected the average labfee values for all departments which offer courses. If we were interested in finding the largest of the averages, we could execute the following query:

```
SELECT  MAX(AVG_CLABFEE)
FROM    VCSTAT
```

The system would resolve this request in the manner just described. This statement would be rejected by SQL/DS.

Summary of View Restrictions:

1. The CREATE VIEW statement cannot contain ORDER BY or UNION.

2. A view is called a "read only" view, which means INSERT, UPDATE, and DELETE statements cannot be applied to the view, if its view definition contains any of the following.

   a. A column built-in function (ex. SUM, MAX, etc.)
   b. DISTINCT
   c. GROUP BY
   d. HAVING
   e. Multiple tables referenced in the FROM clause.

Most of the time, it just doesn't make sense to update a view which is defined using the above SQL features. Then the update restrictions are not really a problem. However, it is still possible to create a view which does include the above features and where an update operation does seem reasonable. In this case, the restrictions become a minor problem. The solution is simply to update the base table.

3. When a view contains a column of values derived from a column built-in function, a query cannot reference the derived column in a WHERE or HAVING clause.

SUMMARY EXERCISES:

16F. Create a view called VTHEO_STAFF based on the STAFF table. It is to reflect the ENAME, ESALARY and ETITLE information for all staff members assigned to the THEO department.

16G. Create a view which presents the average salary of all staff members assigned to each department. The view will be called VAVG_STAFF and will have the column names of DEPT and AVERAGE_SALARY.

16H. Create a view based on the VTHEO_STAFF view which presents the total of the salaries for all staff members in the THEO department.

16I. Create a view which reflects the join of the FACULTY, COURSE, and CLASS tables. The view is to present the name of the faculty member teaching the class and the name of the course for all courses for which there are class offerings. Use the column names of INSTRUCTOR and COURSE_NAME. The view will be called VINSTR.

16J. Drop the VTHEO_STAFF view.

17

Database Security

Database security is a broad topic which can be examined from the systems administrator, database administrator, programmer, or casual user point of view. Both DB2 and SQL/DS have comprehensive authorization subsystems which allow for the protection of any database object from illegitmate access or manipulation. The general scheme involves identification of (1) who the user is, (2) what object is referenced, and (3) what processes can be executed against the specified object. This chapter will examine the authorization scheme from the programmer/user point of view. From this perspective, the authorization schemes of DB2 and SQL/DS are practically identical. Both products support the GRANT and REVOKE statements which are used to grant and subsequently revoke database privileges.

OVERVIEW OF SECURITY

DB2 and SQL/DS allow for different levels of security and different methods of implementation. We have already touched upon one method of preventing unauthorized access to data, namely, through views. In addition to external security systems such as RACF the datasets containing the tables and indexes may be password protected. A complete discussion of all available methods is beyond the scope of this text. The aspect of security which is most relevant to SQL is the one we shall present. This is the method by which access privileges are assigned to individual users, and the system allows or prevents actions based on these privileges.

The following examples assume that the database administrator has granted you permission to create tables. This process of how the database administrator grants you this privilege is not covered here. We assume that you execute the CREATE TABLE statement to create the COURSE table. The system then recognizes you as the creator of this table. As creator of the COURSE table, you automatically have all privileges (to be described below) on this table. Also, with the exception of the database administrator, no other user has any privileges on the COURSE table—until you grant them such privileges. In general, no user has access to any object unless he created the object or has been explicitly granted privileges by the creator of the object.

The GRANT Statement

The general syntax of the GRANT statement is described below. Note that the execution of a single command allows for the simultaneous granting of many privileges to many users.

```
GRANT privilege-1, privilege-2,...
ON    object
TO    authid-1, authid-2, ...
[WITH GRANT OPTION}
```

We describe each of the above parameters within the context of table privileges.

Object: The object may be a base table or a view. (In DB2 it is possible to specify multiple objects.) Database administrators may reference other objects. However, this text only examines base tables and views.

Privileges: We list only those privileges which pertain to base tables or views.

- SELECT
- INSERT
- UPDATE (columns)
- DELETE
- INDEX
- ALTER

The granting of a particular privilege means that the user who is granted the privilege can execute the corresponding statement against the specified object. In particular, note that it is possible to grant permission to another user so that the other user can alter (append a new column) or create an index on your base table. The SELECT, INSERT, UPDATE, and DELETE privileges can be granted on a base table or a view. The INDEX and ALTER privileges can only be granted on a base table. The SELECT, INSERT, and DELETE privileges pertain to entire rows of a base table or view. The UPDATE privilege can be restricted to specific columns.

You can also grant all the above privileges by specifying ALL as a privilege in the statement (GRANT ALL ON . . .).

Authorization Identifier: Your authorization identifier is typically the same sign-on identifier which you used to access the host system. For users of interactive SQL, this will be the TSO sign-on id for DB2 or the CMS sign-on id for SQL/DS. There is a special authorization identifier, PUBLIC, which can be specified when you wish to grant a privilege to all users.

WITH GRANT OPTION: When granting privileges the recipient does not automatically obtain the ability to pass those privileges to other users. If you want to allow another user to be able to do so, you must include the WITH GRANT OPTION clause at the end of your GRANT statement.

Sample Statement 17.1: You would like to give MOE permission to display your COURSE table. You do not want him to be able to perform any other process involving this table. More precisely, you would like to grant SELECT privileges on COURSE to MOE.

```
GRANT SELECT
ON     COURSE
TO     MOE
```

System Response: The system displays a message which confirms the granting of the privilege.

Comments:

1. The general syntax of the GRANT statement is rather straight-forward as described on the previous page.

2. MOE (really the person with the authorization identifier of "MOE") can now issue any valid SELECT statement referencing your COURSE table. He can display all columns of all rows.

3. MOE cannot issue a GRANT statement to pass this privilege to some other user. This is because you did not grant MOE his privilege with the GRANT option. (See the next example.)

Sample Statement 17.2: Allow LARRY and CURLEY to display just those rows from the COURSE table corresponding to courses offered by the CIS Department. Also allow them to modify the course description and labfee amount in these rows. Assume you have already created the CISC view which contains just those CIS rows which LARRY and CURLEY can display and modify. Finally, allow them permission to pass their privileges onto other users.

```
GRANT  SELECT, UPDATE(CDESCP,CLABFEE)
ON     CISC
TO     LARRY, CURLEY
WITH   GRANT OPTION
```

Comments:

1. This example illustrates the general approach to database security for application data. A responsible individual (project leader, professional programmer, sophisticated user) has responsibility for a base table. This individual may have created the base table and inserted the data, or may have been granted all privileges from the database administrator. Then this person grants access to the table to users so that they can do the least damage. This is done by:

   a. Creating a view which limits their access to just certain rows and/or columns of the table
   b. Granting some, usually not all, privileges on this view

   This scheme provides a very simple but powerful and flexible approach to database security.

2. LARRY and CURLEY can issue any SELECT statement against CISC. They can issue an UPDATE statement only if it references the CDESCP or CLABFEE columns.

3. LARRY and CURLEY can grant their privileges to other users. They may also choose to grant these privileges using the grant option. If they do so, recipients can then pass on the same privileges to other users.

The REVOKE Statement

Any granted privilege can subsequently be revoked by executing the REVOKE statement. The syntax is similar to the GRANT statement, but it has the opposite effect. The general syntax is:

```
REVOKE privilege-1, privilege-2,...
ON     object
FROM   authid-1, authid-2,...
```

The following example demonstrates this statement.

Sample Statement 17.3:   CURLEY has abused his update privilege on CISC. Revoke his UPDATE privileges, but allow him to retain his SELECT privilege.

```
REVOKE  UPDATE
ON      CISC
FROM    CURLEY
```

Comments:

1. After execution of this statement the system will reject any UPDATE statement issued by CURLEY which references CISC. Note that CURLEY had privileges on two columns. By not specifying the particular column names after the UPDATE keyword, the system will revoke all UPDATE privileges.

2. Assume CURLEY had previously granted UPDATE privileges to other users, who may in turn have granted them to even more users, etc. In this case, the REVOKE statement will automatically apply to all these users. The effect of the revocation ripples down to all users who obtained an UPDATE privilege on CISC from CURLEY.

3. Note that the UPDATE privileges were not retracted from LARRY. Could LARRY grant the UPDATE privilege to CURLEY after you issued the REVOKE statement? Yes, and it would work. This is because the original privileges were granted with the grant option.

Assume LARRY and CURLEY are transferred to another department. They still have access to the system, but you wish to revoke
all their privileges on CISC.

Sample Statement 17.4: Revoke all privileges LARRY and CURLEY
have on CISC.

```
REVOKE  ALL
ON      CISC
FROM    LARRY, CURLEY
```

Comments:

1. The ALL keyword implies that all privileges on CISC are revoked from LARRY and CURLEY, even though they have different privileges.

2. Any other users who received any privilege on CISC, either
   directly or indirectly from LARRY or CURLEY, will have these
   privileges revoked.

REFERENCING ANOTHER USER'S TABLE

Assume you have been granted privileges on a table or view created by another user. Under these circumstances you must reference the table/view by its complete name. This means that you must include the authorization identifier ("creator name") as a prefix to the table name. Otherwise, the system will assume your authorization identifier as a prefix. This will result in an error because you did not create the table/view.

Sample Query 17.5: In Sample Statement 17.1 you granted SELECT privileges on COURSE to MOE. Assume that your authorization identifier is U48989. What statement must MOE execute in order to display your COURSE table?

```
SELECT *
FROM    U48989.COURSE
```

CNO	CNAME	CDESCP	CRED	CLABFEE	CDEPT
C11	INTRO TO CS	FOR ROOKIES	3	100.00	CIS
C22	DATA STRUCTURES	VERY USEFUL	3	50.00	CIS
C33	DISCRETE MATHEMATICS	ABSOLUTELY NECESSARY	3	.00	CIS
C44	DIGITAL CIRCUITS	AH HA!	3	.00	CIS
C55	COMPUTER ARCH.	VON NEUMANN'S MACH.	3	100.00	CIS
C66	RELATIONAL DATABASE	THE ONLY WAY TO GO	3	500.00	CIS
P11	EMPIRICISM	SEE IT-BELIEVE IT	3	100.00	PHIL
P22	RATIONALISM	FOR CIS MAJORS	3	50.00	PHIL
P33	EXISTENTIALISM	FOR CIS MAJORS	3	200.00	PHIL
P44	SOLIPSISM	ME MYSELF AND I	6	.00	PHIL
T11	SCHOLASTICISM	FOR THE PIOUS	3	150.00	THEO
T12	FUNDAMENTALISM	FOR THE CAREFREE	3	90.00	THEO
T33	HEDONISM	FOR THE SANE	3	.00	THEO
T44	COMMUNISM	FOR THE GREEDY	6	200.00	THEO

Comments:

1. The U48989 prefix is required. If it were omitted, the system would attempt to display a table called MOE.COURSE, which either does not exist or is the name of some other table created by MOE which he coincidentally named COURSE.

2. Many users will not have permission to create tables. Therefore, every table they reference will have the authorization id prefix of some other user.

3. In this text we have occasionally referenced system catalog tables. Whenever we did, the table name always had a prefix. The prefix is SYSIBM for DB2 catalog tables and SYSTEM for SQL/DS catalog tables. This is because the system is the creator of these tables. If the database administrator grants you SELECT privileges on these tables, then you must reference them using the appropriate authorization id prefix.

4. Typing the prefix for every reference to a table is a minor inconvenience. You can reduce this effort by using synonyms. (See Chapter 12.) For example, MOE could execute the following command:

```
CREATE SYNONYM MC FOR U48989.COURSE
```

Then the above query could be entered as

```
SELECT  *
FROM    MC
```

This is a common technique which is used very often in practice.

Note that if MOE was granted privileges on the COURSE table with the grant option, that he could pass these privileges on to other users. However, he would have to reference the U48989.COURSE table and could not grant privileges on his synonym. Remember that synonyms are local to the individual who creates them.

SUMMARY

In this chapter we introduced the notion of database security through the SQL GRANT and REVOKE statements. The scope of our discussion was limited to tables and views.

The GRANT statement is used to allow other users to access a table. With the statement, you specify what privileges (i.e., how the users will be allowed to access the table) are to be given to other users. In general, if a user has not been specifically granted authorization to perform an operation, that user cannot perform that operation. A privilege may be granted to a user along with the ability of that user to pass on the privilege to other users by specifying the WITH GRANT OPTION. The REVOKE statement is used to retract a user's granted privilege. The REVOKE statement has a cascading effect.

18

Transaction Processing

Most databases reflect a dynamic environment rather than a static one. Changes to data within DB2 and SQL/DS systems are accomplished through the INSERT, UPDATE, and DELETE statements originally introduced in Chapter 9. For most production information systems these statements are usually, but not always, placed within application programs. However, there are occasions when these statements will be executed within an interactive environment. When this is necessary, the user should follow procedures which ensure database integrity. An important consideration within this context is the specification of database transactions. This chapter introduces the concept of a transaction and in so doing presents two new SQL statements, COMMIT WORK and ROLLBACK WORK.

PRELIMINARY EXAMPLE

The first example does not introduce any new SQL reserved words, but it does illustrate the objectives of transaction processing. For this example, assume the COURSE table contains a row for a course with a CNO value of "XXX". Also assume that there are classes on this course described in the CLASS table and there are student registrations for these classes described in the REGISTRATION table.

Sample Statements 18.1   Course "XXX" has been dropped from the curriculum and, therefore, must be removed from the COURSE table. All class offerings for this course must be removed from the CLASS table. And, registration information for those classes must be removed from the REGISTRATION table.

```
DELETE
FROM   REGISTRATION
WHERE  CNO = 'XXX'


DELETE
FROM   CLASS
WHERE  CNO = 'XXX'


DELETE
FROM   COURSE
WHERE  CNO = 'XXX'
```

Comments:

1. Recall that CLASS and REGISTRATION are both descendents of COURSE. Assume the referential constraints on the CLASS and REGISTRATION tables have been defined as "delete restrict." This constraint causes the sysytem to prohibit a delete of the "XXX" row from the COURSE table without first deleting the dependent rows in CLASS. Likewise, the "XXX" rows in CLASS cannot be deleted without first deleting the dependent rows in REGISTRATION.

2. The example shows three independent DELETE statements. However, from the user's viewpoint, these changes constitute a single *logical unit of work*: Delete all rows which reference the course with the CNO value of "XXX". From the SQL viewpoint, this unit of work requires the execution of multiple DELETE statements because multiple tables need to be changed due to the particular referential constraints (delete restrict) that exists on these tables. A logical unit of work is called a *transaction*. The next example will illustrate how to bundle the set of DELETE statements to form a single transaction.

Why is it necessary to define the three DELETE statements as a single transaction just because the user sees this as a single logical unit of work? Assuming that each DELETE statement is correct, why not simply execute each statement? In other words, why bundle? The answer to this question lies in recognition of events which are beyond the control of the SQL user.

Computer systems "go down." This can happen in the middle of a terminal session when you are executing any of the three DELETE statements. What is the status of the database if the computer goes down some time just before, during or after you have issued the second DELETE statement? If this happens, you cannot be sure if the updates to the CLASS table actually occurred. (In fact, you cannot even be sure that the changes for the first DELETE statement were written to the disk before the problem occurred.) You could verify the status by displaying the tables. However, this usually is not practical, especially if the tables are large.

What we want is an all-or-nothing situation. Either all the rows in all tables containing a CNO value of "XXX" have been deleted or none of them have. If all rows which reference "XXX" are deleted, we have realized our objective. If none are deleted, we have to start all over again. This requires some extra effort, but it is the necessary cost of database integrity. This all-or-nothing situation is exactly what a transaction provides.

DEFINING TRANSACTIONS

In the previous example we observed that the three separate DELETE statements are logically related. It would be unacceptable if only the first one or two statements executed successfully and not the third. How is the system able to ensure that if only some of the statements execute successfully that their effect will be cancelled? The answer is the system will only consider the initial changes as "tentative" until the completion of the logcal unit of work (the transaction) occurs. Should a problem be encountered prior to the completion of all operations in the logical unit of work, the tentative changes will be undone. Obviously, the system must be informed of which SQL statements constitute a logical unit of work. In other words, we must define the boundaries of each transaction. This is achieved by specifying *synchronization points*.

Synchronization points, often called sync points, define the scope of a database transaction. A sync point is automatically estabished at the beginning of each terminal session or application program. Thereafter, the user or programmer can specify other sync points, which establish the end of a previous transaction and the beginning of a new transaction using the SQL keywords COMMIT or ROLLBACK. Under normal circumstances, a transaction is concluded by executing

- A COMMIT statement which informs the system that all changes made within the transaction are acceptable and that they should be applied to the database, or by executing
- A ROLLBACK statement which informs the system that an unacceptable situation has been encountered and that any changes made since the start of the transaction are to be voided.

If the computer system goes down in the middle of a transaction (before you can issue either a COMMIT or ROLLBACK statement), any changes to the database specified within that transaction are automatically undone. This is because both DB2 and SQL/DS have recovery subsystems which will automatically issue a ROLLBACK command for all transactions which were pending when the problem occurred. Of course, this means that you have to reissue those update statements which were undone.

The COMMIT and ROLLBACK statements will be illustrated in Sample Statements 18.2 and 18.3. Before presenting examples, we must make a few comments regarding the interactive execution of these statements.

TRANSACTIONS IN AN INTERACTIVE ENVIRONMENT

As mentioned earlier, transaction processing is most often handled within application programs rather than performed in an interactive environment. When dealing in an interactive environment the host system (SPUFI, ISQL or QMF) will handle the commit and rollback functions for you. *The mechanics of the commit/rollback procedure are different for each host system.* Each is briefly outlined below.

SPUFI (for users of DB2) has an option which the user can set to enable or disable the automatic commit feature. This feature is known as AUTOCOMMIT. When this feature is enabled (set to ON) the successful completion of all SQL statements will result in any changes to the database being committed. Should any of the SQL statements result in an error, all changes will be undone, i.e., a ROLLBACK statement is executed. When the AUTOCOMMIT feature is disabled (set to OFF), all changes made to the database are made tentatively subject to the review of the user. After reviewing the changes, the user can tell SPUFI to either apply the changes as permanent or to undo them.

ISQL (for users of SQL/DS) can issue a "SET AUTOCOMIT ON" command or a "SET AUTOCOMMIT OFF" command to respectively enable or disable the autocommit feature. (Note that the SET command is not a SQL statement, but a special command unique to ISQL.) If the autocommit feature is disabled, the user must explicitly execute the SQL COMMIT and ROLLBACK statements according to their particular objectives.

QMF (for users of DB2 and SQL/DS) has a similar feature in the CONFIRM option which is specified in the user profile. This option can be enabled and disabled during a terminal session. When this option is enabled, any query which causes a change to the database will be suspended until the user confirms or rejects the change in response to a system prompt. When the feature is set to OFF, any changes made to the database are automatically committed without the user being prompted.

The general concept of enabling or disabling an autocommit feature applies to all three host systems. The next two examples assume that the autocommit feature is disabled and the user explicitly requests the execution of a COMMIT or ROLLBACK statement. The examples mirror the positioning of these statements within an application program. In an ISQL environment, the user would issue the statements as shown. In SPUFI or QMF, the user would respond to system generated prompts to specify the same actions.

COMMIT WORK Statement

The function of the COMMIT WORK statement is to terminate a transaction and cause tentative changes to be applied to the database and thus made permanent. The previous example is extended to define a transaction using the COMMIT WORK statement.

Sample Statement 18.2:   Course "XXX" has been dropped from the curriculum. Remove all references to this course from the COURSE, CLASS, and REGISTRATION tables. Bundle the changes into a single transaction to be committed after successful execution of all DELETE statements.

```
{previous sync point}


DELETE

FROM   REGISTRATION

WHERE  CNO = 'XXX'


DELETE

FROM   CLASS

WHERE  CNO = 'XXX'


DELETE

FROM   COURSE

WHERE  CNO = 'XXX'


COMMIT WORK
```

Comments:

1. The COMMIT statement caused the delete operations to become permanent. All three tables were updated to reflect the removal of the rows with a CNO value of "XXX".

2. The example shows COMMIT WORK. Both COMMIT and COMMIT WORK are accepted by DB2. However, COMMIT WORK must be specified by users of SQL/DS.

ROLLBACK WORK Statement

The following example illustrates the use of the ROLLBACK WORK statement to undo changes made to the COURSE table.

Sample Statements 18.2:   Assume you were told that all classes for course number "C11" were canceled and, therefore, you should delete all rows which reference this course in the CLASS and REGISTRATION tables. After you enter the DELETE statements (but before you commit them), you decide to undo them because you feel that this action should be confirmed by the CIS Departmenet Chairperson.

```
{previous sync point}


DELETE
FROM REGISTRATION
WHERE CNO = 'C11'

DELETE
FROM CLASS
WHERE CNO = 'C11'


ROLLBACK WORK
```

Comments:

1. After execution of the ROLLBACK WORK statement, the rows referencing course C11 remain in the tables. This can be verified by executing a SELECT statement to confirm their presence.

2. The example shows ROLLBACK WORK. Both ROLLBACK and ROLLBACK WORK are accepted by DB2. However, COMMIT WORK must be specified by users of SQL/DS.

DATABASE RECOVERY

The ROLLBACK WORK statement allows you to undo any uncommitted changes to the database. But what if you discover update errors after they have been committed? You could execute further update statements to make corrections. But this is potentially dangerous, especially if the changes are complex. This could lead to a loss of database integrity. It is safer to undo the committed changes. The undoing of committed changes requires the intervention of the DBA who would execute special system utility programs to restore the database to a previous state. Because of the complexity of the recovery systems for both DB2 and SQL/DS, an examination of the recovery procedure is beyond the scope of this text. However, because the recovery subsystem is based upon the transaction concept, it is important that users define their logical units of work and establish transactions via proper utilization of the COMMIT and ROLLBACK statements.

SUMMARY

This chapter introduced two SQL statements, COMMIT WORK and ROLLBACK WORK, which allow the definition of a logical unit of work called a transaction. The effects of these two statements is to mark the end of one transaction and the beginning of another, thus establishing what is called a sync point. The COMMIT WORK statement causes all pending database changes (those which occurred after the last sync point) to be committed. The ROLLBACK WORK statement causes the pending changes to be undone. The effect is just as if the update statements had never been executed.

SUMMARY EXERCISES:

18A.   (SPUFI users) Disable the AUTOCOMMIT feature by setting AUTOCOMMIT to "NO" on the SPUFI panel. Create a query which will delete all of the CIS rows from the COURSE table and execute the query. Examine the output and carefully review the diagnostic messages in the output file. Notice that one message indicates the changes have not been committed because AUTOCOMMIT was set to "NO".

After completing your review of the output attempt to return to the SPUFI panel. Notice that there is a new panel displayed before you are allowed to return. This panel questions you regarding the disposition of the tentative delete operation which you just performed. Respond to this panel with the ROLLBACK request. Now, execute another query, which retrieves all of the rows in the COURSE table. The CIS department courses should still be present.

(ISQL users) Execute the "SET AUTOCOMMIT OFF" statement. Then delete all CIS courses from the COURSE table. Display this table to verify their (tentative) removal. Now issue the ROLLBACK WORK statement. Again, display the COURSE table and observe that the tenative changes have been undone—the CIS rows are back in the table. Finally, execute the "SET AUTOCOMMIT ON" command.

(QMF users) Enter a DELETE statement to delete all CIS courses from the COURSE table. On the command line of the query panel enter the command "RUN QUERY (CONFIRM=YES" and observe what happens. The system will respond with a confirmation panel requiring you to confirm the delete operation or reject it. You should also see the number of rows which will be deleted if the operation is committed. Respond with a negative reply to cancel the operation. Execute a query to retrieve all rows from the COURSE table and verify that the CIS department courses are still present.

Interfacing with DB2 Using SPUFI

In this section we present a brief introduction to accessing DB2 tables through SPUFI.

After logging on to TSO and invoking DB2I in the manner prescribed by your installation you will see the **DB2I Primary Option Menu**, as presented in Figure A.1. Select option 1 to enter the SPUFI feature. With SPUFI you can enter and process SQL statements against DB2 tables.

From the SPUFI panel (Figure A.2) you identify the name of the data set where you will edit SQL statements to be passed to DB2. This data set should be defined prior to entering SPUFI. The procedure is the same as creating any other TSO data set. (We assume that you are either familiar with the process or are able to gain assistance from an experienced individual, and therefore do not discuss it here.) Also from this panel you identify the output data set which will contain the result of the query. This data set does not have to predefined and will be allocated by SPUFI if it does not exist.

The details of the processing options (5 through 9) can be found in the IBM reference publications. We shall briefly discuss them here.

The CHANGE DEFAULTS option allows you to alter the SPUFI parameters which the output data set characteristics, the maximum number of lines of data returned from DB2 and placed in the output data set, and format characteristics of the output. Supplying a "YES" value to the EDIT INPUT option indicates that you wish to examine,

```
                     DB2I PRIMARY OPTION MENU
=== 1
Select one of the following DB2 functions and press ENTER.

1    SPUFI (Process SQL statements)

2    DCLGEN (Generate SQL and source language declarations)

3    PROGRAM PREPARATION (Prepare a DB2 application program to run)

4    PRECOMPILE (Invoke DB2 precompiler)

5    BIND/REBIND/FREE (BIND, REBIND, or FREE application plans)

6    RUN (RUN an SQL program)

7    DB2 COMMANDS (Issue DB2 commands)

8    UTILITIES (Invoke DB2 utilities)

D    DB2I DEFAULTS (Set global parameters)

X    EXIT (Leave DB2I)


PRESS: END to exit HELP for more information
```

Figure A.1   DB2I Primary Menu.

```
                              SPUFI
===
Enter the input data set name:    (Can be sequential or partitioned)
1 DATA SET NAME ...         ===   SQL.CNTL(TEMP)
2 VOLUME SERIAL ...         ===   (Enter if not cataloged)
3 DATA SET PASSWORD         ===   (Enter if password protected)
Enter the output data set name:   (Must be a sequential data set)
4 DATA SET NAME ...         ===   DB2.DATA
Specify processing options:
5 CHANGE DEFAULTS           ===   NO (Y/N - Display SPUFI defaults panel?)
6 EDIT INPUT ......         ===   YES (Y/N - Enter SQL statements?)
7 EXECUTE .........         ===   YES (Y/N - Execute SQL statements?)
8 AUTOCOMMIT ......         ===   YES (Y/N - Commit after successful run?)
9 BROWSE OUTPUT ...         ===   YES (Y/N - Browse output data set?)


PRESS: ENTER to process END to exit HELP for more information
```

Figure A.2   SPUFI Menu.

and possibly alter, the contents of the input data set. This allows the oportunity to enter new SQL statements. This step invokes the ISPF editor. (If you know what statements are in the data set you may execute them directly by entering "NO" for this option.) The EXECUTE option indicates whether you wish to pass the SQL statements contained in the input data set to DB2 for processing. For a discussion of the details of AUTOCOMMIT, refer to Chapter 18. Placing a "YES" value in the BROWSE option will allow you to view the result of the SQL statement processing when it has completed. This step also invokes the services of ISPF.

When you have completed the entries on the screen, press the ENTER key to continue. With the above options specified, the next screen shows the input file for editing. (See Figure A.3.)

After being satisified that the SQL statement is what we want to execute, we terminate the edit process. Note that throughout the text we made mention of both SPUFI and QMF as vehicles for interfacing with DB2. There is one important difference in the SQL statements presented to these two facilities. Notice that the statement above was terminated with a semicolon (;). This is necessary only in SPUFI. In fact, it is only necessary if you wish to execute more than one statement from the same data set. It serves to delimit the different statements. With QMF, you are only able to execute a single statement at a time through the query facility. Therefore, the semicolon is not needed.

The output data set (Figure A.4) contains the SQL statements which were passed from the input data set followed by the data retrieved from DB2. Following the data is a collection of diagnostic

```
EDIT ── USERID.SQL.CNTL(TEMP) - 01.00 ─────── COLUMNS 001 072
COMMAND === SCROLL === PAGE
****** ************************* TOP OF DATA *************************
000001 SELECT *
000002 FROM COURSE;
****** ************************* BOTTOM OF DATA *********************
```

Figure A.3   SPUFI Input Data Set.

messages indicating the degree of success for each statement. In Chapter 8 we made reference to confirmation messages from the system that the CREATE statement was either successful or unsuccessful. This would be indicated by diagnostic messages like the ones shown here.

SPUFI does not provide a method for formatting the output as a report. To accomplish this you need the QMF product or to develop application programs.

Basically, this is all there is to using the SPUFI facility. After terminating the browse function you are returned to the SPUFI screen (Figure A.2) and given the option of processing additional statements or exiting.

```
BROWSE -- USERID.DB2.DATA --------------------- LINE 000000 COL 001 080
COMMAND === >                                    SCROLL ===> PAGE
****** ************************* TOP OF DATA ******************************
      ---------+---------+---------+---------+---------+---------+---------+---------+
      SELECT *
      FROM COURSE;
      ---------+---------+---------+---------+---------+---------+---------+---------+
      CNO  CNAME                CDESCP                  CRED   CLABFEE   CDEPT
      ---------+---------+---------+---------+---------+---------+---------+
      C11  INTRO TO CS          FOR ROOKIES               3    100.00   CIS
      C22  DATA STRUCTURES      VERY USEFUL               3     50.00   CIS
      C33  DISCRETE MATHEMATICS ABSOLUTELY NECESSARY      3       .00   CIS
      C44  DIGITAL CIRCUITS     AH HA!                    3       .00   CIS
      C55  COMPUTER ARCH.       VON NEWMANN'S MACH.       3    100.00   CIS
      C66  RELATIONAL DATABASE  THE ONLY WAY TO GO        3    500.00   CIS
      P11  EMPIRICISM           SEE IT-BELIEVE IT         3    100.00   PHIL
      P22  RATIONALISM          FOR CIS MAJORS            3     50.00   PHIL
      P33  EXISTENTIALISM       FOR CIS MAJORS            3    200.00   PHIL
      P44  SOLIPSISM            ME MYSELF AND I           6       .00   PHIL
      T11  SCHOLASTICISM        FOR THE PIOUS             3    150.00   THEO
      T22  FUNDAMENTALISM       FOR THE CAREFREE          3     90.00   THEO
      T33  HEDONISM             FOR THE SANE              3       .00   THEO
      T44  COMMUNISM            FOR THE GREEDY            6    200.00   THEO

      NUMBER OF ROWS DISPLAYED IS 14
      STATEMENT EXECUTION WAS SUCCESSFUL, SQLCODE IS 100
      ---------+---------+---------+---------+---------+---------+---------+---------+
      ---------+---------+---------+---------+---------+---------+---------+---------+
      COMMIT PERFORMED, SQLCODE IS 0
      STATEMENT EXECUTION WAS SUCCESSFUL, SQLCODE IS 0
      SQL STATEMENTS ASSUMED TO BE BETWEEN COLUMNS 1 AND 72
      NUMBER OF SQL STATEMENTS PROCESSED IS 1
      NUMBER OF INPUT RECORDS READ IS 2
      NUMBER OF OUTPUT RECORDS WRITTEN IS 31
      ***************************** BOTTOM OF DATA *************************
```

Figure A.4   SPUFI Output Data Set.

B

Interfacing with DB2 and SQL/DS Using QMF

In this section we present a brief introdution to accessing DB2 and SQL/DS tables through QMF.

After logging on to TSO (for DB2) and CMS (for SQL/DS) you enter the QMF facililty in the manner prescribed by the installation. The first panel displayed should be the QMF Home Panel which welcomes you to the QMF facility. In fact, this panel is the first panel you see upon entering QMF and the last panel viewed before exiting the product. Enter the command: *DISPLAY QUERY* to enter the SQL QUERY panel (Figure B.1). It is from this panel that queries are edited and subsequently executed.

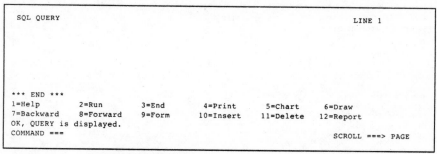

```
SQL QUERY                                                    LINE 1




*** END ***
1=Help        2=Run        3=End       4=Print     5=Chart     6=Draw
7=Backward    8=Forward    9=Form      10=Insert   11=Delete   12=Report
OK, QUERY is displayed.
COMMAND ===                                              SCROLL ===> PAGE
```

Figure B.1   The SQL QUERY Panel.

439

From the SQL QUERY panel, an SQL statement can be entered in the free form manner described in the text. Simply position the cursor on the screen and start typing. Once the query has been entered, it may be executed by issuing the command: *RUN QUERY* from the command line (Figure B.2). The system responds with a panel showing a relative cost estimate. This is a number which reflects the amount of work the system must do to completely satisfy the request. When the query has completed the result is shown in the RE-PORT panel (Figure B.3).

After reviewing the report it may be desirable to reformat the display. This can be accomplished through the formatting facilities provided by QMF through the FORM panels. A complete discussion of the formatting capabilities is beyond the scope of this book. Some of the capabilities include the renaming of columns in the report (to provide more meaningful headings), changing the spacing between columns, defining a page heading and page footing, and defining control break processing.

After completing the review of the report, you may send the report to a printer to obtain a permanent copy by issuing the command: *PRINT REPORT*. To run another query you may issue the *RESET QUERY* command which displays the SQL QUERY panel as in Figure B.1. To exit the QMF product simply enter the command: *EXIT* on the command line and you will be returned to the QMF HOME panel. Press the PF3 key and you will terminate the QMF session.

```
SQL QUERY              MODIFIED                    LINE 1
SELECT * FROM COURSE




*** END ***
1=Help        2=Run        3=End      4=Print     5=Chart     6=Draw
7=Backward    8=Forward    9=Form     10=Insert   11=Delete   12=Report
OK, cursor positioned.
COMMAND ===> Run Query                            SCROLL ===> PAGE
```

Figure B.2   Entering SQL Statements in the SQL QUERY Panel.

```
REPORT                                            LINE 1

CNO        CNAME                 CDESCP                      CRED     CLABFEE     CDEPT
---        ----                  --------------------        ----     -------     -----
C11        INTRO TO CS           FOR ROOKIES                   3      100.00      CIS
C22        DATA STRUCTURES       VERY USEFUL                   3       50.00      CIS
C33        DISCRETE MATHEMATICS  ABSOLUTELY NECESSARY          3        0.00      CIS
C44        DIGITAL CIRCUITS      AH HA!                        3        0.00      CIS
C55        COMPUTER ARCH.        VON NEWMANN'S MACH.           3      100.00      CIS
C66        RELATIONAL DATABASE   THE ONLY WAY TO GO            3      500.00      CIS
P11        EMPIRICISM            SEE IT-BELIEVE IT             3      100.00      PHIL
P22        RATIONALISM           FOR CIS MAJORS                3       50.00      PHIL
P33        EXISTENTIALISM        FOR CIS MAJORS                3      200.00      PHIL
P44        SOLIPSISM             ME MYSELF AND I               6        0.00      PHIL
T11        SCHOLASTICISM         FOR THE PIOUS                 3      150.00      THEO
T12        FUNDAMENTALISM        FOR THE CAREFREE              3       90.00      THEO
T33        HEDONISM              FOR THE SANE                  3        0.00      THEO
T44        COMMUNISM             FOR THE GREEDY                6      200.00      THEO

1=Help            2=          3=End        4=Print      5=Chart              6=Query
7=Backward        8=Forward   9=Form      10=Left      11=Right            12=
OK, RIGHT performed. Please proceed.
COMMAND ===>                                          SCROLL ===> PAGE
```

Figure B.3   REPORT Panel.

C

Interfacing with SQL/DS using ISQL

Users of the SQL/DS database product will follow the regular sign-on procedures for their host operating system environments (VM/SP or DOS/VSE). Thereafter, to issue interactive SQL statements via the ISQL facility of SQL/DS the following command must be executed.

```
ISQLdatabase-name
```

This command requests that the user be allowed to sign onto ISQL for the purpose of working with a particular SQL/DS database identified by the "database-name" argument. The system should respond by displaying the Sign-on screen shown in Figure C.1. The user simply enters the appropriate userid/password data and presses the Enter Key. Assuming this sign-on data is valid, the system usually executes a profile routine and displays a screen similar to that shown in Figure C.2. The screen indicates the actions taken in response to statements placed in the profile routine. (The content of this screen will vary from system to system. For this reason we do not show any details in Figure C.2. We assume the profile routine is established by the DBA and is compatible with the user's objectives.) Next, the user enters his/her first SQL statement as shown in Figure C.3. After pressing the Enter key, the system executes this statement and displays the result as shown in Figure C.4.

```
      WELCOME TO THE INTERACTIVE SQL FACILITY OF SQL/DATA SYSTEM

                IIIIIIII    SSSSSSSS     QQQQQQQQQ  LL
                  II        SS           QQ     QQ  LL
                  II        SSSSSSSS      QQ     QQ  LL
                  II              SS      QQ QQ  QQ  LL
                IIIIIIII    SSSSSSSS      QQQQQQQQQ  LLLLLLLL
                                                QQ

             INTERACTIVE  STRUCTURED  QUERY  LANGUAGE


          ENTER USERID AND PASSWORD, THEN PRESS ENTER

              USERID ==> _         PASSWORD ==>


   AFTER SIGN-ON USE EXIT COMMAND TO EXIT ISQL; USE HELP COMMAND FOR HELP.
```

Figure C.1   ISQL Sign-On Screen.

The panel shown in **Figure C.4** also contains the "ENTER A DISPLAY COMMAND" message. This message invites the user to enter a special ISQL command to reformat the selected data. The are many special ISQL commands which are unique to the ISQL facility. These offer the user some basic report formatting capabilities. However, it is important to note that these commands are not part of SQL. For this reason we assume the user would like to execute another SQL statement instead of reformatting the previously retrieved

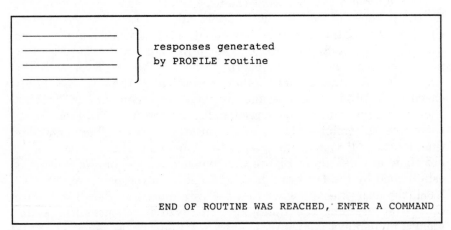

Figure C.2   ISQL Display Screen.

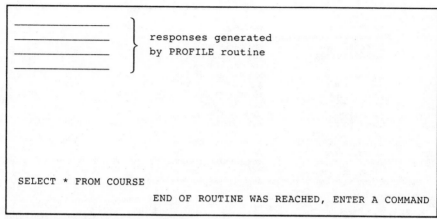

```
 _____  ⎫
 _____  ⎬   responses generated
 _____  ⎪   by PROFILE routine
             ⎭



 SELECT * FROM COURSE
                 END OF ROUTINE WAS REACHED, ENTER A COMMAND
```

Figure C.3   ISQL Display Screen.

data. Figure C.5 shows the entry of another SELECT statement to achieve this objective. Again, after pressing the Enter key, the system executes the statement and displays the result as shown in Figure C.6. The user can continue with this process of entering valid SQL statements and examining the displayed results. Upon completion, the EXIT command is used to terminate the ISQL session and return to the host operating system.

```
CNO      CNAME                  CDESCP                  CRED     CLABFEE    CDEPT
---      --------------------   ------------------     -------   --------   -----
T11      SCHOLASTICISM          FOR THE PIOUS             3       150.00     THEO
T12      FUNDAMENTALISM         FOR THE CAREFREE          3        90.00     THEO
T33      HEDONISM               FOR THE SANE              3         0.00     THEO
T44      COMMUNISM              FOR THE GREEDY            6       200.00     THEO
P11      EMPIRICISM             SEE IT-BELIEVE IT         3       100.00     PHIL
P22      RATIONALISM            FOR CIS MAJORS            3        50.00     PHIL
P33      EXISTENTIALISM         FOR CIS MAJORS            3       200.00     PHIL
P44      SOLIPSISM              ME MYSELF AND I           6         0.00     PHIL
C11      INTRO TO CS            FOR ROOKIES               3       100.00     CIS
C22      DATA STRUCTURES        VERY USEFUL               3        50.00     CIS
C33      DISCRETE MATHEMATICS   ABSOLUTELY NECESSARY      3         0.00     CIS
C44      DIGITAL CIRCUITS       AH HA!                    3         0.00     CIS
C55      COMPUTER ARCH.         VON NEUMANN'S MACH.       3       100.00     CIS
C66      RELATIONAL DATABASE    THE ONLY WAY TO GO        3       500.00     CIS
* END OF RESULT ***** 14 ROWS DISPLAYED ***********************************************


                                            ENTER A DISPLAY COMMAND
```

Figure C.4   ISQL Display Screen.

```
CNO     CNAME                   CDESCP                   CRED    CLABFEE    CDEPT
---     --------------------    ------------------       -------  --------   -----
T11     SCHOLASTICISM           FOR THE PIOUS                3     150.00    THEO
T12     FUNDAMENTALISM          FOR THE CAREFREE             3      90.00    THEO
T33     HEDONISM                FOR THE SANE                 3       0.00    THEO
T44     COMMUNISM               FOR THE GREEDY               6     200.00    THEO
P11     EMPIRICISM              SEE IT-BELIEVE IT            3     100.00    PHIL
P22     RATIONALISM             FOR CIS MAJORS               3      50.00    PHIL
P33     EXISTENTIALISM          FOR CIS MAJORS               3     200.00    PHIL
P44     SOLIPSISM               ME MYSELF AND I              6       0.00    PHIL
C11     INTRO TO CS             FOR ROOKIES                  3     100.00    CIS
C22     DATA STRUCTURES         VERY USEFUL                  3      50.00    CIS
C33     DISCRETE MATHEMATICS    ABSOLUTELY NECESSARY         3       0.00    CIS
C44     DIGITAL CIRCUITS        AH HA!                       3       0.00    CIS
C55     COMPUTER ARCH.          VON NEUMANN'S MACH.          3     100.00    CIS
C66     RELATIONAL DATABASE     THE ONLY WAY TO GO           3     500.00    CIS
* END OF RESULT ***** 14 ROWS DISPLAYED *********************************************


SELECT * FROM DEPARTMENT
                                                      ENTER A DISPLAY COMMAND
```

Figure C.5   ISQL Display Screen.

```
DEPT     DBLD     DROOM    DCHFNO
----     ----     -----    ------
THEO     HU       200      10
MGT      SC       100      -
CIS      SC       300      80
PHIL     HU       100      60
* END OF RESULT ***** 4 ROWS DISPLAYED *************************

                                                      ENTER A DISPLAY COMMAND
```

Figure C.6   ISQL Display Screen.

D

Answers to Exercises

CHAPTER 1

A. SELECT * FROM COURSE WHERE CLABFEE < 150

B. SELECT * FROM COURSE WHERE CRED > 3

C. SELECT * FROM COURSE WHERE CDEPT = 'THEO'

D. SELECT * FROM COURSE WHERE CNAME = 'RELATIONAL DATABASE'

E. SELECT * FROM COURSE WHERE CNO = 'P44'

F. SELECT * FROM COURSE WHERE CNO < 'C01'

G. SELECT * FROM COURSE WHERE CNAME >='RATIONALISM'

H. SELECT CNAME, CDESCP FROM COURSE

I. SELECT CDEPT, CNO, CLABFEE, CRED FROM COURSE

J. SELECT CNO, CLABFEE FROM COURSE WHERE CLABFEE > 100

K. SELECT CNAME FROM COURSE WHERE CDEPT = 'CIS'

L. SELECT CLABFEE FROM COURSE

M. SELECT DISTINCT CLABFEE FROM COURSE

N. SELECT CRED, CLABFEE FROM COURSE WHERE CDEPT = 'CIS'

O. SELECT DISTINCT CRED, CLABFEE FROM COURSE WHERE CDEPT = 'CIS'

P. SELECT * FROM STAFF

Q. SELECT * FROM STAFF WHERE ESALARY < 1000

R. SELECT * FROM STAFF WHERE DEPT = 'THEO'

S. SELECT ENAME, ETITLE FROM STAFF

T. SELECT DISTINCT DEPT FROM STAFF WHERE ESALARY < 900

CHAPTER 2

A. SELECT * FROM COURSE ORDER BY CDEPT

B. SELECT CNAME, CLABFEE FROM COURSE WHERE CDEPT = 'PHIL'
    ORDER BY CNAME DESC

C. SELECT CLABFEE, CNO, CRED FROM COURSE ORDER BY CLABFEE,
    CNO

D. SELECT * FROM COURSE ORDER BY 3 DESC

E. SELECT CDEPT, CLABFEE, CNAME FROM COURSE WHERE CRED = 3
    ORDER BY CDEPT, CLABFEE DESC, CNAME

F. SELECT * FROM STAFF ORDER BY ENAME

G. SELECT ENAME, ESALARY FROM STAFF WHERE ESALARY < 1000
    ORDER BY ESALARY DESC

H. SELECT * FROM STAFF WHERE DEPT = 'THEO' ORDER BY ETITLE

I. SELECT DEPT, ENAME, ESALARY FROM STAFF ORDER BY DEPT,
    ESALARY

J. SELECT DEPT, ETITLE, ESALARY FROM STAFF ORDER BY DEPT,
    ESALARY DESC

CHAPTER 3

A. SELECT * FROM COURSE WHERE CRED = 3 AND CDEPT = 'PHIL'

B. SELECT * FROM COURSE WHERE CLABFEE >= 100 AND CLABFEE
    <=500

C. SELECT * FROM COURSE WHERE CRED = 3 AND CDEPT = 'THEO'
    AND CLABFEE >= 100 AND CLABFEE <=400

D. SELECT * FROM COURSE WHERE CDEPT = 'PHIL' OR CDEPT =
    'THEO'

E.   SELECT * FROM COURSE WHERE CDEPT = 'THEO' OR CRED = 6

F.   SELECT * FROM COURSE WHERE CLABFEE = 0.00
     OR CLABFEE = 90.00 OR CLABFEE = 150.00

G.   SELECT CNO, CNAME, CLABFEE FROM COURSE WHERE NOT
     CLABFEE = 100
     or
     SELECT CNO, CNAME, CLABFEE FROM COURSE WHERE CLABFEE
     <>100

H.   SELECT CNO, CLABFEE FROM COURSE WHERE NOT CLABFEE = 100
     AND NOT CLABFEE = 200

I.   SELECT * FROM COURSE WHERE (CRED = 6 AND CDEPT =
     'PHIL') OR CLABFEE > 200

J.   SELECT * FROM COURSE WHERE CRED = 3
     AND (CLABFEE < 100 OR CLABFEE > 300)

K.   SELECT * FROM COURSE WHERE NOT CLABFEE > 100 OR (CDEPT
     = 'THEO' AND CRED = 6)

L.   SELECT * FROM COURSE WHERE NOT (CRED = 3 AND CDEPT =
     'PHIL')

M.   SELECT * FROM COURSE WHERE CLABFEE IN (12.12, 50.00,
     75.00, 90.00, 100.00, 500.00)

N.   SELECT * FROM COURSE WHERE CLABFEE NOT IN (12.12,
     50.00, 75.00, 90.00, 100.00, 500.00)
     O. SELECT CNO, CLABFEE FROM COURSE WHERE CLABFEE
     BETWEEN 50.00 AND 400.00

P.   SELECT CNO, CLABFEE FROM COURSE WHERE CLABFEE NOT
     BETWEEN 50.00 AND 400.00

Q.   SELECT CNAME, CDESCP FROM COURSE WHERE CNAME BETWEEN
     'FOR ' AND 'FORZ'

R.   SELECT CDEPT, CNO, CDESCP FROM COURSE
     WHERE CDEPT IN ('CIS', 'THEO')
     AND   CLABFEE NOT BETWEEN 100 AND 400
     ORDER BY CDEPT, CNO

S.   SELECT * FROM STAFF WHERE DEPT = 'PHIL' OR DEPT = 'THEO'

T.   SELECT * FROM STAFF WHERE DEPT = 'THEO' AND ESALARY > 52

U. SELECT ENAME FROM STAFF WHERE ESALARY >= 52 AND ESALARY
    <= 1000
    or
    SELECT ENAME FROM STAFF WHERE ESALARY BETWEEN 52 AND
    1000

V. SELECT ENAME, ETITLE FROM STAFF
    WHERE DEPT = 'THEO'
    AND   (ESALARY = 51 OR ESALARY = 54)

W. SELECT ENAME, ESALARY FROM STAFF WHERE ESALARY IN (51,
    53, 100, 200, 25000)

X. SELECT ENAME, ESALARY FROM STAFF
    WHERE ESALARY NOT BETWEEN 100 AND 1000
    ORDER BY ENAME
    or
    SELECT ENAME, ESALARY FROM STAFF
    WHERE ESALARY < 100 OR ESALARY > 1000
    ORDER BY ENAME

Y. SELECT DISTINCT DEPT FROM STAFF WHERE ESALARY > 5000

CHAPTER 4

A. SELECT * FROM COURSE WHERE CDESCP LIKE 'FOR THE%'

B. SELECT CNAME, CDESCP FROM COURSE WHERE CDESCP LIKE '%E'

C. SELECT CNAME, CDESCP FROM COURSE WHERE CDESCP LIKE '%.%'
    OR CDESCP LIKE '%-%'
    OR CDESCP LIKE '%!%'

D. SELECT CDEPT FROM COURSE WHERE CDEPT LIKE '%IL'
    OR CDEPT LIKE '%IL '
    OR CDEPT LIKE 'IL '

E. SELECT CNAME, CDEPT FROM COURSE WHERE CDEPT LIKE '_ _ _
    '

F. SELECT CNAME, CDESCP FROM COURSE WHERE CDESCP LIKE
    '_ _ _ _THE_ _A%'

G. SELECT CNAME, CDESCP FROM COURSE WHERE CNAME NOT LIKE
    '%E' AND CNAME NOT LIKE '%S'

H. SELECT * FROM STAFF WHERE ENAME LIKE 'MA%'

I. SELECT * FROM STAFF WHERE ETITLE LIKE '%1'
    OR ETITLE LIKE '%2'
    OR ETITLE LIKE '%3'

J. SELECT ENAME, ETITLE FROM STAFF WHERE ENAME LIKE '%S%'
    AND ETITLE LIKE '%S%'

K. SELECT DISTINCT DEPT FROM STAFF WHERE DEPT LIKE '_ _E%'

L. SELECT ENAME FROM STAFF WHERE ENAME LIKE '_ _ _ _I%'
    ORDER BY ENAME

M. SELECT DISTINCT DEPT FROM STAFF
    WHERE DEPT LIKE '%G '
    OR DEPT LIKE '%G '
    OR DEPT LIKE 'G   '

CHAPTER 5

A. SELECT CNO, CRED, CRED * 2 FROM COURSE WHERE CDEPT =
    'PHIL'

B. SELECT CNO, CRED * 10.50 FROM COURSE WHERE CDEPT =
    'THEO'

C. SELECT CNO, CLABFEE, CLABFEE / 2.0 FROM COURSE WHERE
    CLABFEE > 0.00

D. SELECT CNO, (CLABFEE * 1.50) + 35 FROM COURSE WHERE
    CLABFEE < 200

E. SELECT CNO, CNAME, (50 * CRED) - CLABFEE FROM COURSE
    WHERE CLABFEE < (50 * CRED) ORDER BY 3 DESC

F. SELECT ENAME, ESALARY + 100 FROM STAFF

G. SELECT ENAME, ESALARY, ESALARY * 1.15 FROM STAFF

H. SELECT ENAME, ESALARY - 100 FROM STAFF WHERE ESALARY -
    100 < 25000

I. SELECT ENAME, ESALARY + 1000 FROM STAFF WHERE ESALARY <
    25000 ORDER BY 2 DESC

CHAPTER 6

A. SELECT AVG(CLABFEE), MAX(CLABFEE), MIN(CLABFEE) FROM
    COURSE WHERE CDEPT = 'CIS' AND CLABFEE <> 0

B. SELECT MIN(CNAME) FROM COURSE

C. SELECT COUNT(*), SUM(CLABFEE) FROM COURSE WHERE CDEPT =
    'PHIL'

D. SELECT AVG(CRED * 50.0) FROM COURSE WHERE CDEPT = 'THEO'

E. SELECT CDEPT, SUM(CRED) FROM COURSE GROUP BY CDEPT

F. SELECT CDEPT, SUM(CLABFEE) FROM COURSE WHERE CRED <> 6
    GROUP BY CDEPT

G. SELECT CDEPT, MAX(CLABFEE) FROM COURSE GROUP BY CDEPT
    HAVING MAX(CLABFEE) > 300

H. SELECT CDEPT, SUM(CRED) FROM COURSE GROUP BY CDEPT
    HAVING SUM(CRED) > 15

I. SELECT CDEPT, SUM(CLABFEE) FROM COURSE
    WHERE CRED = 3
    GROUP BY CDEPT
    HAVING SUM(CLABFEE) < 150

J. SELECT CDEPT, MAX(CLABFEE) FROM COURSE
    WHERE CLABFEE <= 400
    GROUP BY CDEPT
    HAVING MAX(CLABFEE) > 175

K. SELECT CDEPT, AVG(DECIMAL(CRED)) FROM COURSE GROUP BY
    CDEPT

L. SELECT LENGTH(CNAME) FROM COURSE WHERE CDEPT = 'THEO'

M. SELECT SUBSTR(CDESCP,1,5) FROM COURSE WHERE CDEPT =
    'PHIL'

N. SELECT SUBSTR(CNAME,LENGTH(CNAME),1) FROM COURSE WHERE
    CLABFEE > 200

O. SELECT SUBSTR(CNAME,LENGTH(CNAME)-2,3) FROM COURSE
    WHERE LENGTH(CNAME) >= 3

P.   SELECT SUBSTR(DIGITS(CLABFEE),4,2) FROM COURSE WHERE
    CDEPT = 'CIS'

Q. SELECT CNO || CNAME FROM COURSE

R. SELECT SUBSTR(CNO,2,2) || SUBSTR(CNO,1,1) FROM COURSE

S. SELECT CNO || SUBSTR (DIGITS(CRED),5,1) FROM COURSE
    WHERE CDEPT = 'CIS'

T. SELECT SUM(ESALARY), AVG(ESALARY), MAX(ESALARY),
    MIN(ESALARY) FROM STAFF

U. SELECT COUNT(*) FROM STAFF WHERE DEPT = 'THEO'

V. SELECT COUNT(DISTINCT ETITLE) FROM STAFF

W. SELECT SUM(ESALARY) + 5000 FROM STAFF

X. SELECT AVG (ESALARY - 20) FROM STAFF WHERE DEPT = 'THEO'

Y. SELECT DEPT, AVG(ESALARY) FROM STAFF GROUP BY DEPT

Z. SELECT DEPT, SUM(ESALARY) FROM STAFF WHERE ESALARY >
    600 GROUP BY DEPT ORDER BY DEPT

CHAPTER 7

A. SELECT CHAR(REG_DATE,EUR) FROM REGISTRATION WHERE SNO =
    '800' AND CNO = 'C11'

B. SELECT CHAR(REG_DATE,JIS), CHAR(REG_TIME,JIS) FROM
    REGISTRATION WHERE CNO='T11'

C. SELECT SNO, REG_DATE FROM REGISTRATION WHERE CNO =
    'C11' AND MONTH(REG_DATE) = '12' ORDER BY REG_DATE

D. SELECT CNAME, CDESCP, CURRENT TIMESTAMP FROM COURSE
    WHERE CNO = 'C11'

CHAPTER 8

A. CREATE TABLE STUDENT
    (SNO   CHAR(3) NOT NULL,
     SNAME   VARCHAR(30),
     SADDR   VARCHAR(15),
     SPHNO   CHAR(12),
     SBDATE   CHAR(6),
     SIQ   SMALLINT,
     SADVFNO CHAR(3),
     SMAJ   CHAR(4),
     PRIMARY KEY (SNO),

```
      FOREIGN KEY (SADVFNO) REFERENCES FACULTY,
      FOREIGN KEY (SMAJ) REFERENCES DEPARTMENT)
```

B. CREATE TABLE REGISTRATION
```
    (CNO      CHAR(3) NOT NULL,
     SEC      CHAR(2) NOT NULL,
     SNO      CHAR(3) NOT NULL,
     REG_DATE DATE,
     REG_TIME TIME,
     PRIMARY KEY (CNO, SEC, SNO),
     FOREIGN KEY (CNO, SEC) REFERENCES CLASS,
     FOREIGN KEY (SNO) REFERENCES STUDENT )
```

C. CREATE UNIQUE INDEX XSNO ON STUDENT (SNO) CLUSTER

    CREATE INDEX XSMAJ ON STUDENT (SMAJ)

D. CREATE TABLE CISCOURSE
```
    (CISCNO      CHAR(3) NOT NULL,
     CISCNAME    VARCHAR(22) NOT NULL WITH DEFAULT
     CISCRED     SMALLINT,
     CISCLABFEE  DECIMAL(5,2),
     PRIMARY KEY (CISCNO) )
```

    CREATE UNIQUE INDEX XCISCNO ON CISCOURSE (CISCNO)

E. CREATE TABLE FACULTY
```
    (FNO         CHAR(3) NOT NULL,
     FNAME       CHAR(15),
     FADDR       VARCHAR(20),
     FHIRE_DATE  DATE,
     FNUM_DEP    SMALLINT,
     FSALARY     DECIMAL(7,2),
     FDEPT       CHAR(4),
     PRIMARY KEY (FNO),
     FOREIGN KEY (FDEPT) REFERENCES DEPARTMENT )
```

    CREATE UNIQUE INDEX XFNO ON FACULTY (FNO) CLUSTER

    CREATE INDEX XFDEPT ON FACULTY (FDEPT)

CHAPTER 9

A. INSERT INTO STAFF (ENAME, ETITLE, ESALARY, DEPT)
    VALUES ('ALAN', 'LAB ASSIST', 3000, 'CIS')

B. INSERT INTO STAFF (DEPT, ENAME)
    VALUES ('CIS', 'GEORGE')

C. UPDATE STAFF SET ESALARY = 4000 WHERE DEPT = 'CIS'

D. DELETE FROM STAFF WHERE DEPT = 'CIS'

E. CREATE TABLE EXPENSIVE
    (EXPCNO   CHAR(3),
     EXPCNAME   VARCHAR(22),
     EXPCLABFEE   DECIMAL(5,2),
     EXPDEPT   CHAR(4))

    INSERT INTO EXPENSIVE
    SELECT CNO, CNAME, CLABFEE, CDEPT FROM COURSE WHERE
    CLABFEE > 100

F. UPDATE EXPENSIVE
    SET EXPCLABFEE = EXPCLABFEE - 50
    WHERE EXPCLABFEE > 400

G. DELETE FROM EXPENSIVE WHERE EXPDEPT = 'THEO'

H. INSERT INTO EXPENSIVE (EXPCNO, EXPDEPT) VALUES ('X99',
    'XXX')

I. UPDATE EXPENSIVE SET EXPCNAME = 'JUNK'

J. DELETE FROM EXPENSIVE

K. DROP TABLE EXPENSIVE

CHAPTER 10

A. SELECT AVG(FNUM_DEP), SUM(FNUM_DEP), COUNT(*),
    SUM(FNUM_DEP)/COUNT(*) FROM FACULTY

B. SELECT SUM(FSALARY + (250 * FNUM_DEP)) FROM FACULTY
    or
    SELECT SUM(FSALARY) + (250 * SUM(FNUM_DEP)) FROM FACULTY

C. SELECT * FROM NULLTAB WHERE COLA <> COLB

D. SELECT FNAME, FNO, FNUM_DEP FROM FACULTY ORDER BY
    FNUM_DEP

E. SELECT AVG(FSALARY) FROM FACULTY GROUP BY FNUM_DEP

F. SELECT FNAME, FNUM_DEP, FDEPT FROM FACULTY WHERE
    FNUM_DEP IS NULL

G. SELECT ENAME, DEPT FROM STAFF WHERE DEPT IS NULL

H. SELECT DEPT, COUNT(*) FROM STAFF GROUP BY DEPT

CHAPTER 11

A. SELECT * FROM COURSE, DEPARTMENT WHERE CDEPT = DEPT

B. SELECT CNO, CNAME, CDESCP, CRED, CLABFEE, CDEPT, DBLD,
    DROOM, DCHFNO FROM COURSE, DEPARTMENT WHERE CDEPT = DEPT

C. SELECT CNAME, CLABFEE, DCHFNO FROM COURSE, DEPARTMENT
    WHERE CDEPT = DEPT AND CLABFEE > 100.00

D. SELECT CNO, CNAME FROM COURSE, DEPARTMENT WHERE CDEPT =
    DEPT AND DCHFNO = '60' ORDER BY CNO DESC

E. SELECT ENAME, ESALARY FROM STAFF, DEPARTMENT WHERE
    STAFF.DEPT = DEPARTMENT.DEPT AND DBLD = 'SC'

F. SELECT DISTINCT DBLD, DROOM FROM DEPARTMENT, STAFF
    WHERE DEPARTMENT.DEPT = STAFF.DEPT AND ESALARY > 200

G. SELECT MIN(CLABFEE), MAX(CLABFEE) FROM COURSE,
    DEPARTMENT WHERE CDEPT = DEPT AND DBLD = 'SC'

H. SELECT COUNT(*) FROM STAFF, DEPARTMENT WHERE STAFF.DEPT
    = DEPARTMENT.DEPT

I. SELECT ENAME, ESALARY, CLABFEE, CLABFEE - ESALARY FROM
    STAFF, COURSE WHERE DEPT = CDEPT AND (CLABFEE -
    ESALARY) >= 52

J. SELECT DEPARTMENT.DEPT, SUM(ESALARY), AVG(ESALARY) FROM
    STAFF, DEPARTMENT WHERE DEPARTMENT.DEPT = STAFF.DEPT
    GROUP BY DEPARTMENT.DEPT

K. SELECT CNAME, COUNT(*) FROM STAFF, COURSE WHERE DEPT =
    CDEPT GROUP BY CNAME

L. SELECT DEPARTMENT.DEPT FROM DEPARTMENT, STAFF WHERE
    DEPARTMENT.DEPT = STAFF.DEPT GROUP BY DEPARTMENT.DEPT
    HAVING COUNT(*) >= 3

M. SELECT DEPARTMENT.DEPT, COUNT(*) FROM DEPARTMENT, STAFF
WHERE DEPARTMENT.DEPT = STAFF.DEPT GROUP BY
DEPARTMENT.DEPT

N. SELECT DCHFNO FROM DEPARTMENT, COURSE WHERE DEPT =
CDEPT AND CRED = 6

O. SELECT CNO, CNAME, SEC FROM COURSE, CLASS WHERE
COURSE.CNO = CLASS.CNO AND CDAY = 'MO'

P. SELECT CNO, CNAME FROM REGISTRATION, COURSE WHERE
REGISTRATION.CNO = COURSE.CNO AND SNO = '800'

Q. SELECT CLASS.CNO, SEC, CINSTRFNO, CDAY, CTIME, CBLD,
CROOM FROM CLASS, COURSE WHERE CLASS.CNO = COURSE.CNO
AND CLABFEE < 100.00 AND CDAY <> 'FR'

R. SELECT SNO, REG_DATE FROM REGISTRATION, COURSE WHERE
REGISTRATION.CNO = COURSE.CNO AND CDEPT = 'THEO'

S. SELECT COUNT(*) FROM COURSE, REGISTRATION WHERE
REGISTRATION.CNO = COURSE.CNO AND CNAME =
'EXISTENTIALISM'

T. SELECT COUNT(*) FROM REGISTRATION, COURSE WHERE
REGISTRATION.CNO = COURSE.CNO AND CDEPT = 'PHIL'

U. SELECT DISTINCT FNO, FNAME FROM FACULTY, CLASS WHERE
FNO = CINSTRFNO AND CDAY IN ('MO', 'FR')

V. SELECT FNAME FROM FACULTY, DEPARTMENT, COURSE WHERE FNO
= DCHFNO AND DEPT = CDEPT AND CRED = 6

Wa. SELECT CLASS.CNO, CLASS.SEC, CNAME, FNO, SNO FROM
REGISTRATION, COURSE, CLASS WHERE COURSE.CNO =
CLASS.CNO AND CLASS.CNO = REGISTRATION.CNO AND
REGISTRATION.SEC = CLASS.SEC AND REGISTRATION.SEC = '01'

Wb. SELECT COURSE.CNO, CLASS.SEC, CNAME, FNO, SNO, SNAME
FROM REGISTRATION, COURSE, CLASS, STUDENT WHERE
COURSE.CNO = CLASS.CNO AND CLASS.CNO = REGISTRATION.CNO
AND REGISTRATION.SEC = CLASS.SEC AND REGISTRATION.SEC =
'01' AND REGISTRATION.SNO = STUDENT.SNO

Wc. SELECT COURSE.CNO, CLASS.SEC, CNAME, FNAME, SNO, SNAME
FROM REGISTRATION, COURSE, CLASS, STUDENT, FACULTY
WHERE COURSE.CNO = CLASS.CNO AND CLASS.CNO =
REGISTRATION.CNO AND REGISTRATION.SEC = CLASS.SEC AND
REGISTRATION.SEC = '01' AND REGISTRATION.SNO =
STUDENT.SNO AND CINSTRFNO = FNO

X. --- "paper and pencil exercise" ---

Y. SELECT * FROM COURSE, FACULTY

Z. SELECT D1.DEPT, D2.DEPT FROM DEPARTMENT D1, DEPARTMENT
   D2 WHERE D1.DBLD = D2.DBLD AND D1.DEPT < D2.DEPT

Za. SELECT S1.ENAME, S1.ESALARY, S2.ENAME, S2.ESALARY,
    S1.ESALARY - S2.ESALARY FROM STAFF S1, STAFF S2 WHERE
    (S1.ESALARY - S2.ESALARY) > 1000

Zb. SELECT S1.ENAME, S1.ESALARY, S2.ENAME, S2.ESALARY,
    S1.ESALARY - S2.ESALARY FROM STAFF S1, STAFF S2 WHERE
    (S1.ESALARY - S2.ESALARY) > 1000 AND S1.DEPT = S2.DEPT

Zc. SELECT S1.ENAME, S1.ESALARY, S2.ENAME, S2.ESALARY,
    S1.ESALARY - S2.ESALARY FROM STAFF S1, STAFF S2,
    DEPARTMENT WHERE S1.DEPT = S2.DEPT AND DEPARTMENT.DEPT
    = S1.DEPT AND (S1.ESALARY - S2.ESALARY) > 1000 AND DBLD
    = 'HU'

CHAPTER 13

A. SELECT CNO, CNAME, CDEPT FROM COURSE WHERE CLABFEE =
   (SELECT MIN(CLABFEE) FROM COURSE)

B. SELECT CNO, CNAME, CDEPT, CLABFEE FROM COURSE WHERE
   CLABFEE = (SELECT MAX(CLABFEE) FROM COURSE WHERE
   CLABFEE <> 500.00)

C. SELECT CNO, CNAME, CDEPT, CLABFEE FROM COURSE WHERE
   CRED = 6 AND CLABFEE = (SELECT MAX(CLABFEE) FROM COURSE)

D. SELECT CNO, CNAME, CLABFEE FROM COURSE WHERE CLABFEE <
   (SELECT AVG(CLABFEE) FROM COURSE WHERE CDEPT = 'THEO')

E. SELECT * FROM COURSE WHERE CLABFEE > (SELECT
   MAX(CLABFEE) FROM COURSE WHERE CDEPT IN ('THEO',
   'PHIL'))

F. SELECT ENAME, ESALARY FROM STAFF WHERE ESALARY <=
   (SELECT MAX(CLABFEE) FROM COURSE)

G. SELECT * FROM COURSE WHERE CDEPT = 'CIS' AND CLABFEE <
   (SELECT AVG(ESALARY) FROM STAFF WHERE DEPT = 'THEO')

H. SELECT DEPT, DCHFNO FROM DEPARTMENT WHERE DEPT IN
   (SELECT CDEPT FROM COURSE WHERE CRED = 6)

I. SELECT CNO, SEC, CBLD FROM CLASS WHERE CBLD = (SELECT
    DBLD FROM DEPARTMENT, STAFF WHERE DEPARTMENT.DEPT =
    STAFF.DEPT AND ENAME = 'DICK NIX')
    --- or ---
    SELECT CNO, SEC, CBLD FROM CLASS WHERE CBLD = (SELECT
    DBLD FROM DEPARTMENT WHERE DEPT = (SELECT DEPT FROM
    STAFF WHERE ENAME = 'DICK NIX'))

J. SELECT FNAME, FDEPT FROM FACULTY WHERE FNO NOT IN
    (SELECT CINSTRFNO FROM CLASS)

K. SELECT FNAME, FNUM_DEP FROM FACULTY WHERE FNUM_DEP =
    ANY (SELECT CRED FROM COURSE)
    --- or ---
    SELECT FNAME, FNUM_DEP FROM FACULTY WHERE FNUM_DEP IN
    (SELECT CRED FROM COURSE)

L. SELECT CNO, CNAME FROM COURSE WHERE CNO IN (SELECT CNO
    FROM REGISTRATION WHERE SNO = '800')

M. SELECT * FROM CLASS WHERE CNO IN (SELECT CNO FROM
    COURSE WHERE CLABFEE 100.00) AND CDAY <> 'FR'

N. SELECT SNO, REG_DATE FROM REGISTRATION WHERE CNO IN
    (SELECT CNO FROM COURSE WHERE CDEPT IN (SELECT DEPT
    FROM DEPARTMENT WHERE DBLD = 'SC'))

O. SELECT FNAME, FNUM_DEP FROM FACULTY WHERE FNUM_DEP
    (SELECT MIN(CRED) FROM COURSE)

CHAPTER 14

A. SELECT ESALARY FROM STAFF UNION SELECT FSALARY FROM
    FACULTY

B. SELECT CDEPT, CRED, CDESCP FROM COURSE WHERE CDEPT =
    'PHIL'
    UNION
    SELECT FDEPT, FNUM_DEP, FADDR FROM FACULTY WHERE FDEPT
    = 'PHIL'

C. SELECT CLABFEE, CRED, 'COURSE' FROM COURSE WHERE CDEPT
    = 'CIS'
    UNION
    SELECT FSALARY, FNUM_DEP, 'FACULTY' FROM FACULTY WHERE
    FDEPT = 'CIS'

D. SELECT CNAME, CDEPT, CLABFEE, 'EXPENSIVE' FROM COURSE
    WHERE CLABFEE >= 200.00
    UNION
    SELECT CNAME, CDEPT, CLABFEE, 'CHEAP' FROM COURSE
    WHERE CLABFEE <= 50.00

E. SELECT ESALARY FROM STAFF UNION ALL SELECT FSALARY FROM
    FACULTY

CHAPTER 15

A. SELECT FNAME, FDEPT, FSALARY FROM FACULTY FX WHERE
    FSALARY >   (SELECT AVG(FSALARY) FROM FACULTY WHERE
    FDEPT = FX.FDEPT)

B. SELECT FNAME, FDEPT FROM FACULTY FX WHERE FNUM_DEP >
    (SELECT AVG(CRED) FROM COURSE WHERE CDEPT = FX.FDEPT)

C. SELECT FNAME, FDEPT FROM FACULTY WHERE EXISTS
    (SELECT * FROM COURSE WHERE CDEPT = FACULTY.FDEPT AND
    CRED = 6)

Da. SELECT CNO, CNAME, CLABFEE FROM COURSE WHERE CLABFEE >
    (SELECT MIN(ESALARY) FROM STAFF)

Db. SELECT DISTINCT CNO, CNAME, CLABFEE FROM COURSE, STAFF
    WHERE CLABFEE > ESALARY

E. SELECT FNAME, FDEPT FROM FACULTY WHERE NOT EXISTS
    (SELECT * FROM COURSE WHERE FACULTY.FDEPT = CDEPT AND
    CRED = 6)

F. SELECT CNAME, CDEPT, CLABFEE FROM COURSE CX WHERE
    CLABFEE =   (SELECT MAX(CLABFEE) FROM COURSE WHERE
    CDEPT = CX.CDEPT)

G. SELECT DEPT, DBLD, DROOM, COURSE.CNO, CNAME, SEC, CDAY
    FROM DEPARTMENT, COURSE, CLASS
    WHERE DEPT = CDEPT AND COURSE.CNO = CLASS.CNO
    UNION ALL
    SELECT DEPT, DBLD, DROOM, COURSE.CNO, CNAME, ' ', ' '
    FROM DEPARTMENT, COURSE
    WHERE DEPT = CDEPT AND NOT EXISTS
        (SELECT * FROM CLASS WHERE CNO = COURSE.CNO)
    UNION ALL
    SELECT DEPT, DBLD, DROOM, ' ', ' ', ' ', ' '
    FROM DEPARTMENT

```
WHERE NOT EXISTS
    (SELECT * FROM COURSE WHERE CDEPT =
DEPARTMENT.DEPT)
```

CHAPTER 16

A. CREATE VIEW FPAYROLL AS SELECT FNAME, FSALARY,
   FHIRE_DATE, FNUM_DEP FROM FACULTY

B. CREATE VIEW VFSAL (DEPARTMENT, HIGHEST_SALARY,
   LOWEST_SALARY) AS SELECT FDEPT, MAX(FSALARY),
   MIN(FSALARY) FROM FACULTY GROUP BY FDEPT

C. CREATE VIEW FAVERAGES (FAVG_SAL, FAVG_NUM_DEP) AS
   SELECT AVG(FSALARY), AVG(FNUM_DEP) FROM FPAYROLL

D. DROP VIEW VFSAL

E. DROP VIEW FPAYROLL

F. CREATE VIEW VTHEO_STAFF AS SELECT ENAME, ESALARY,
   ETITLE FROM STAFF WHERE DEPT = 'THEO'

G. CREATE VIEW VAVG_STAFF (DEPT, AVERAGE_SALARY) AS SELECT
   DEPT, AVG(ESALARY) FROM STAFF GROUP BY DEPT

H. CREATE VIEW MYVIEW (TOTAL) AS SELECT SUM(ESALARY) FROM
   VTHEO_SALARY

I. CREATE VIEW VINSTR (INSTRUCTOR, COURSE_NAME) AS SELECT
   FNAME, CNAME FROM FACULTY, COURSE, CLASS WHERE
   COURSE.CNO = CLASS.CNO AND FNO = CINSTRFNO

J. DROP VIEW VTHEO_STAFF

Sample Educational Database

The design shown in Figure E.1 represents the basic content and structure of the sample tables used throughout this text. This figure used the IBM notation for referential integrity where the arrow points from the parent table to the dependent table. (This differs from the tutorial notation used in Chapter 8.) Only the primary key and foreign key columns are shown in Figure E.1. The primary key columns are underlined. Sample data are shown in Figure E.2.

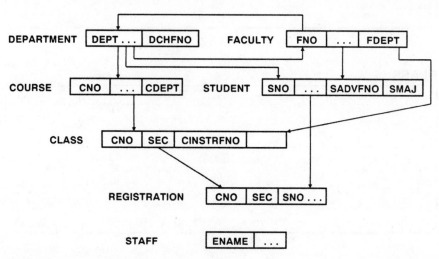

Figure E.1   Educational Database Design.

DEPARTMENT

DEPT	DBLD	DROOM	DCHFNO
THEO	HU	200	10
CIS	SC	300	80
MGT	SC	100	-
PHIL	HU	100	60

STAFF

ENAME	ETITLE	ESALARY	DEPT
LUKE	EVANGLIST3	53	THEO
MARK	EVANGLIST2	52	THEO
MATTHEW	EVANGLIST1	51	THEO
DICK NIX	CROOK	25001	PHIL
HANK KISS	JESTER	25000	PHIL
JOHN	EVANGLIST4	54	THEO
EUCLID	LAB ASSIST	1000	MATH
ARCHIMEDES	LAB ASSIST	200	ENG
DA VINCI	LAB ASSIST.	500	-

COURSE

CNO	CNAME	CDESCP	CRED	CLAGFEE	CDEPT
C11	INTRO TO CS	FOR ROOKIES	3	100.00	CIS
C22	DATA STRUCTURES	VERY USEFUL	3	50.00	CIS
C33	DISCRETE MATHEMATICS	ABSOLUTELY NECESSARY	3	.00	CIS
C44	DIGITAL CIRCUITS	AH HA!	3	.00	CIS
C55	COMPUTER ARCH.	VON NEUMANN'S MACH.	3	100.00	CIS
C66	RELATIONAL DATABASE	THE ONLY WAY TO GO	3	500.00	CIS
P11	EMPIRICISM	SEE IT-BELIEVE IT	3	100.00	PHIL
P22	RATIONALISM	FOR CIS MAJORS	3	50.00	PHIL
P33	EXISTENTIALISM	FOR CIS MAJORS	3	200.00	PHIL
P44	SOLIPSISM	ME MYSELF AND I	6	.00	PHIL
T11	SCHOLASTICISM	FOR THE PIOUS	3	150.00	THEO
T12	FUNDAMENTALISM	FOR THE CAREFREE	3	90.00	THEO
T33	HEDONISM	FOR THE SANE	3	.00	THEO
T44	COMMUNISM	FOR THE GREEDY	6	200.00	THEO

CLASS

CNO	SEC	CINSTRFNO	CDAY	CTIME	CBLD	CROOM
C11	01	08	MO	08:00-09:00A.M.	SC	305
C11	02	08	TU	08:00-09:00A.M.	SC	306
C33	01	80	WE	09:00-10:30A.M.	SC	305
C55	01	85	TH	11:00-12:00A.M.	HU	306
P11	01	06	TH	09:00-10:00A.M.	HU	102
P33	01	06	FR	11:00-12:00A.M.	HU	201
T11	01	10	MO	10:00-11:00A.M.	HU	101
T11	02	65	MO	10:00-11:00A.M.	HU	102
T33	01	65	WE	11:00-12:00A.M.	HU	101

Figure E.2a   Sample Database.

REGISTRATION

```
------------------------------------------------------
 CNO     SEC     SNO     REG_DATE        REG_TIME
------------------------------------------------------
 C11     01      325     1988-01-04      09.41.30
 C11     01      800     1987-12-15      11.49.30
 C11     02      100     1987-12-17      09.32.00
 C11     02      150     1987-12-17      09.32.30
 P33     01      100     1987-12-23      11.30.00
 P33     01      800     1987-12-23      11.23.00
 T11     01      100     1987-12-23      11.21.00
 T11     01      150     1987-12-15      11.35.30
 T11     01      800     1987-12-15      14.00.00
------------------------------------------------------
```

FACULTY

```
---------------------------------------------------------------------------------------
                                                    FNUM_DEP
 FNO    FNAME           FADDR             FHIRE_DATE            FSALARY      FDEPT
---------------------------------------------------------------------------------------
 06     KATHY PEPE      7 STONERIDGE RD   1979-01-15      2     35000.00     PHIL
 10     JESSIE MARTYN   2135 EAST DR      1969-09-01      1     45000.00     THEO
 08     JOE COHN        BOX 1138          1979-07-09      2     35000.00     CIS
 85     AL HARTLEY      SILVER STREET     1979-09-05      7     45000.00     CIS
 60     JULIE MARTYN    2135 EAST DR      1969-09-01      1     45000.00     PHIL
 65     LISA BOBAK      77 LAUGHING LN    1981-09-06      -     36000.00     THEO
 80     BARB HLAVATY    489 SOUTH ROAD    1982-01-16      3     35000.00     CIS
---------------------------------------------------------------------------------------
```

STUDENT

```
-------------------------------------------------------------------------------------
 SNO    SNAME          SADDR         SPHNO           SBDATE    SIQ  SADVFNO  SMAJ
-------------------------------------------------------------------------------------
 325    CURLEY DUBAY   CONNECTICUT   203-123-4567    780517    122  10       THEO
 150    LARRY DUBAY    CONNECTICUT   203-123-4567    780517    121  80       CIS
 100    MOE DUBAY      CONNECTICUT   203-123-4567    780517    120  10       THEO
 800    ROCKY BALBOA   PENNSYLVANIA  112-112-1122    461004     99  60       PHIL
-------------------------------------------------------------------------------------
```

Figure E.2b   Sample Database.

Index